The Other Woman

THE OTHER WOMAN

FEMINISM AND FEMININITY IN THE WORK OF MARGUERITE DURAS

Trista Selous

Yale University Press
New Haven & London 1988

LIBRARY OF CONGRESS
Library of Congress Cataloging-in-Publication Data

Selous, Trista, 1957–
The other woman, feminism and femininity in the work of Marguerite Duras, by Trista Selous.
p.   cm.
Bibliography: p.
Includes index.
ISBN 0-300-04287-6
1. Duras, Marguerite – Characters – Women. 2. Women in literature.
3. Feminism in literature. 4. Sex role in literature. I. Title.
PQ2607.U8245Z86   1988
843'.912-dc19
                                                        88 5744
                                                        CIP

Set in Linotron Plantin by Best-set Typesetter Ltd, Hong Kong
and printed and bound in Great Britain at the University Printing House, Oxford by David Stanford, Printer to the University.

CONTENTS

Introduction   1

PART I
1 The Problem of Femininity   11

Writing the Feminine   11
The Freudian View   19
Redressing the Balance   28

2 The Lacanians   34

Lacan and Femininity   34
'The Ruin of Representation'   47
'Woman-speak'   53

3 Femaleness, Femininity and Feminism   60

The Female and the Feminine   61
Psychoanalysis and Politics   76

PART II
4 The Blanks   87

The Lost Moment   127
The Withering away of Character   128
Symbolism   130
'Seamless' Discourse   130

5 What Does the Reader Want?   138

The Author's Desire   139
The Text as Fetish   146
The Return of the Familiar   149

6 Was will das Weib?   153
   The Woman Figures   153
   The Power of the Woman   184

7 Was das Weib will   203
   Sexual Desire   203
   Motherhood   217
   The Missing Father   230

8 Order, Chaos and Subversive Details   233
   Bibliography   253
   Index   257

Ma passion pour les oeuvres de Marguerite Duras est née de ce que j'y ai entendu à la fois 'résonner' et 'parler' le féminin.

(My passion for the work of Marguerite Duras arose because within it I heard the feminine both 'resound' and 'speak')

– Marcelle Marini

INTRODUCTION

When I first encountered the work of Marguerite Duras and read *Moderato cantabile*, I found myself responding to the text in awkwardly incompatible ways: I was fascinated by this tale of silent passion, simply told in a style both cool and intense, but at the same time something in me resisted the enchantment I was being asked to feel. Pursuing the pleasure of fascination through Duras's work, I found this rather uncomfortable incompatibility of my responses did not resolve itself. It crystallised around the portrayal of women in Duras's texts, and I realised that the conflict which it reflected between different understandings of what it means to be a woman was not just personal to me, but was also apparent in two different currents of feminist thought. This book grew out of my wish to bring the two sides into confrontation and, eventually, to some kind of resolution.

Duras's main concern is with relations of desire: principally between the sexes, but also between mothers and their children. Her women figures occupy central positions in her texts; they are often represented as having great power, sometimes a power of life and death over others, and I found them compelling. But, particularly in work from *Moderato cantabile* onwards, I felt uncomfortable with the form their power took. For it arose most frequently out of their position as object of (men's) desire; it was the power of Woman, the *femme fatale*, which often brings with it a certain passivity and dependence, the power of the catalyst, rather than of the agent, where the woman herself seems somehow to disappear as an independent entity. Many feminists, myself included, have regarded such power as in itself ultimately illusory, on the grounds that any woman who wants to maintain herself as an instance of Woman must ensure that she fits masculine fantasies of what that entails rather than her own, and is subject to the fluctuations not only of men's desire, but also of its other sides, their hostility and aggression. There is something slightly depressing about the role of the object of desire.

Nevertheless, many women, feminist or not and also including myself, find some such representations of women compelling. And feminists have also seen the power they exert as a positive thing, less in terms of a real power over men, than as something which exceeds the heterosexual context altogether and which women can identify with, draw strength from and enjoy about each other. This view seemed particularly pertinent in the case of Duras, whose charismatic women figures are the poduct of a woman's imagination, and certainly, the general consensus of feminist-influenced critical work on Duras puts her in the vanguard of women developing new, 'feminine' cultural forms. So I decided to investigate these ideas on femininity, to see how they have been applied to Duras's work, and how they make sense of the relation of woman to Woman.

'WOMEN'S CULTURE' AND 'GYNOCRITICS'

One of the basic tenets of the feminism which has been developed over the last fifteen years is that the masculinist culture in which we live recognises women only in certain roles: as objects of men's sexual desire – 'sex objects' – or as mothers; whilst our work or activity in other areas remains largely invisible. In order to redress the balance, feminists have stressed the importance of documenting the history and experiences of women as they exceed those two positions, and of rediscovering and reappraising the work of, for example, women writers or painters who have long remained in obscurity, whilst also publicising and encouraging the work of women in the present. Women have become the object of study for other women (and men) in Women's Studies courses or in women's groups. All these manifestations have as part of their aim to extend the area in which women's activity is recognised, not only to give more women the confidence to move into fields traditionally reserved for/by men, but also to show that there have always been women who were painters, political organisers, writers, etc., even if fewer than men. To prove, in other words, that whatever the dominant view, women are and always have been more than simply either mothers or sexual partners for men, whether potential or actual.

One effect of this activity has been the generation of the idea of 'female' or 'women's culture', which may be applied to the way that women relate to each other in the absence of men, or to the creative aspects of work traditionally performed by women, particularly domestic work. Such an idea is also implicit in the search for, or definition of, specifically, 'feminine' qualities in work produced by women in fields dominated by men, such as literature or art.

In the field of literary criticism, the feminist exploration of women's work has led to various studies of women writers, both in the form of analyses of the work of individual authors and in more general discussions of women writers as a category. Elaine Showalter calls such work 'gynocritics'.

> Gynocritics begins at the point where we free ourselves from the linear absolutes of male literary history, stop trying to fit women between the lines of the male tradition and focus instead on the newly visible world of female culture. This is comparable to the ethnographer's effort to render the experience of the 'muted' female half of a society. . . [1]

This quotation reveals two crucial aspects of the gynocritical approach: the first that the determining factor in the critic's choice of text to work on is that its author is a woman, and thus the text is then seen as part of 'female culture'; the second the view that this 'female culture' has been silenced or 'muted'. Gynocritics investigates women's work in an attempt to draw out the features of the 'female culture' of which it is seen as forming a part. It emphasises the relation of the text to its female author, or specifically to work by other women, rather than to other works of, for example, similar genre, style, or historical period, considerations which do not ostensibly take the sex of the author into account. Gynocritics is in this sense author-centred criticism.

Closely related to gynocritics and springing from the same basic assumption of a 'female culture' is the search for a specificity in the way that women write, as opposed to the subject matter or form they choose. This viewpoint tends, explicitly or implicitly, to carry with it an idea of 'feminine psychology', which is assumed to be specific to female human beings. This is a view which is current in our culture in general, manifesting itself in both positive and negative forms, for example, in 'feminine intuition' (erratic, but useful), or the complementary idea that women are 'illogical'.

Those writers who have claimed that Duras's work is subversive on the level of sexual politics, and who see it as a step towards the lifting of the oppression of women, subscribe either implicitly or explicitly to the view that women's oppression consists in the muting, silencing, or crushing of our true nature and our true language, in the denial of our specificity and difference in a world dominated by

---

1 Elaine Showalter, 'Towards a Feminist Poetics', in *Women Writing and Writing about Women*, Mary Jacobus (ed), London, Croom Helm, 1979, p. 28.

men, to whose alien ways we are forced to conform. This view represents one facet of feminism and is in evidence in the work of many writers concerned with women's oppression, and not just those writing on Duras. It is not one which I share, for reasons which I go into in the course of my discussion. However, the idea that 'feminine psychology' produces a specifically 'feminine' use of language is one that has been given greater credence more recently by the work of French psychoanalyst Jacques Lacan, in his elaborations on the work of Sigmund Freud, and by certain French writers who have used Lacan's theoretical framework to explore women's psyches, such as Hélèn Cixous, Luce Irigaray, or Michèle Montrelay. The latter three writers and others have argued that 'feminine' language is rooted in female anatomy, a necessary consequence of the presence of a vagina and the absence of a penis, but that this type of language has been suppressed by the masculine form in the male-dominated culture in which we live. There seems to be a general consensus amongst feminist literary critics who espouse this position to any degree that Duras, at least from the publication of *Moderato cantabile* onwards, escapes the constraints of the masculine and uses language in a more 'feminine' way, although it is not always clear quite what this means.

THE PROBLEMS OF LACANIAN STYLE

The view that Duras's writing makes manifest 'the feminine' in a way which is innovative and politically radical has become orthodox over the last decade or so. It is a view which is almost wholly based on ideas expounded in the writings of Lacanian theorists, many of which are not available in English, or have only recently become so, and all of which are very difficult to read. The Lacanians use a style which is frequently opaque, even to those who are used to it. This style, with its particular terminology, its puns and wordplay, was originally developed by Lacan, ostensibly to undermine the smooth flow of theoretical discourse with invasions of unconscious meanings, and to disturb any illusion that the utterer 'owns', or is in control of the meanings of the uttered; although in fact, I think the effect is to make Lacan seem still more firmly in control. Lacan never defines his terms in such a way as to make them easily comprehensible, nor does he explain his theories step by step; he puts them into practice as he expounds them.

Following Lacan, other writers using his theories have used a similar style for similar reasons, made more complicated by their use of Lacanian terminology which, following Lacan, they do not define in 'simple' terms. Those who write – and read – in English face additional problems of the translation of terminology, which in some cases – such as that of *jouissance* – has been abandoned altogether, and this only compounds the difficulties and makes a critical appraisal of the theories more difficult.

Given the importance of Lacanian theories for the critical context of Duras's work, they must be taken into account by anyone looking at her writing in terms of its relation to feminism or its portrayal of women. Furthermore, I have found these theories invaluable to my understanding of the construction of gender. I also think that the issues they raise of the distinction between or conflation of 'femininity' and 'femaleness' and the idea that there is, or could be, a specifically 'feminine' language have major implications for any feminist politics. I therefore explore these theorists' writings in some detail.

Understanding the Lacanians requires a great deal of effort and emotional investment, which can lead to a suspension of critical disbelief. The ideas of Irigaray, or Montrelay, for example, which are not easy to grasp in the original texts, have often been incorporated into critical work on Duras as if their accounts of femininity were problem-free, once the reader had got used to their style and concepts. Furthermore, their ideas are sometimes used in a rather vague way and those who do not, for linguistic or other reasons, have access to the source-texts have had to take both the theories and their application on trust, or not at all.

This situation is unsatisfactory, in that it restricts debate on these influential ideas about 'feminine language' and femininity to the very few, whilst the uninitiated are left with the feeling that they are missing something without really knowing why. One of my aims in this book is to try to make clearer to those unfamiliar with these theories why they might be worth looking into, whilst also raising problems with them which I have not seen addressed elsewhere.

In order to do this, I have tried as far as possible to avoid a 'Lacanian' style, opting instead for what I hope is greater clarity and for a definition of terms, at least as I understand and use them. In my discussions I try first to explain what I think the different theorists are saying, followed by any questions or criticisms I may have. In this way I hope the reader will be able to see how I arrive at my positions, without necessarily being forced to agree with them. This approach leads me to a certain dissociation of content from form, which goes rather against the Lacanian grain, although I am not the first to attempt it. But I think such an approach is justified, since Lacanian theory constructs accounts of psychic functioning with their own internal rules, logic and concepts, which can be extrapolated from the body of writing, without necessarily denying their validity. In practice, many writers, including Duras's critics, have interpreted the *content* of Lacanian writings, and rearticulated it in their own work in different formulations. My aim is to try to establish exactly what claims are being made in relation to femininity, and why, so that they can be evaluated; and, as my questions come from both within and outside the Lacanian framework, they require that I maintain a certain detachment.

'THE FEMININE'

In Part I of this book, I start my investigations by looking at the development of ideas of 'the feminine' within psychoanalysis, and at their application to Duras's work by writers using a Lacanian, or neo-Lacanian model. Much of Duras's work lends itself to analysis in the light of Lacanian psychoanalysis and it has been used as an illustration of the theoretical positions of writers who use a Lacanian approach, including Lacan himself.

Duras makes no claim to being a theorist, quite the reverse in fact. Indeed, she pours scorn on Man (as opposed to Woman), a theoretical imbecile',[2] who, as she sees it, destroyed the spontaneity of the movement of May 1968 in France. However, she gives credit to Lacan for his analysis of *Le Ravissement de Lol V. Stein:* 'And who was it who brought Lol V. Stein out of her coffin? After all, it was a man, it was Lacan'[3], and she supports the view that the way she writes is particular to women: 'I speak only of what *bubbles up* when I write. And that's a woman's thing.'[4]

The symbiotic relationship between Duras's work and that of Lacanian theorists, whilst highlighting their compatability, tends to obscure their differences and conflicts. For example, the gynocritical and psychoanalytical approach of the feminist critic Marcelle Marini takes Duras's work as an complement to and illustration of Irigaray's theoretical account of the existence of a 'feminine' language. Such an approach emphasises the femaleness of Duras – and of Irigaray – and implicitly constructs that femaleness as the ultimate guarantor of the truth of the critic's position regarding the 'femininity' of the writing. I take issue with this approach, as I think the Lacanian framework, on which Irigaray's theory of a specific and anatomically based 'feminine' language is based, potentially

2 Marguerite Duras, 'Notes in the Margin', in *Les Parleuses*, Paris, Minuit, 1974, p. 225.
3 ibid, p. 161.
4 Interview with Duras, 'Ce que parler ne veut pas dire', in *Les Nouvelles Littéraires*, Paris, 15/4/74.

undermines not only her theory but any equation of 'femininity' with 'femaleness'.

My own view is that the idea of a 'feminine' psychic makeup and relation to language which are anatomically determined and present in all women is a highly dubious one on theoretical grounds. I also think that such an idea can contribute to the oppression of women. For me, feminism is about breaking out from the confines of the 'eternal feminine' and recognising individuality and difference amongst women as amongst men. Ultimately I see the approach to Duras's texts which hails them as manifestations of 'the feminine' as not only theoretically dubious, but also politically counter-productive.

Nevertheless, I do not want simply to dismiss the idea that women may frequently write or express themselves differently from men; coming as we do from different positions within societies and cultures, I think it not unlikely that we might tend to use language differently. But I see the positions of feminine and masculine subject – the place from which the writer (or reader, hearer, spectator, etc.) understands symbolic systems – as ideologically constructed gender positions as opposed to anatomically determined sexual characteristics.

Of course, the construction of gender is based on the anatomical division of the sexes, and since any subject is obliged, in however temporary or incomplete a manner, to identify her/himself in a gendered position, I think it likely, but far from inevitable, that the subject will tend to adopt the gender identity which conforms with her/his anatomically defined sex. But because gender is an ideological construction, the implications of gender positions may vary greatly depending on the cultural context of the subject. For example, even in the narrow cultural confines of the British Isles, different people will have different understandings of what being a woman entails, as will a single individual at different moments. Still, there are dominant ideological constructions of gender in this, as in any, culture, which will no doubt be built into most, if not all, individual subject positions. One example, of this would be the understanding that the physical appearance of women should be 'softer' and 'prettier' than that of men, or that most women are 'by nature' gentler and less aggressive than most men. Overall, I think the masculine position is constructed as the standard human position, the man the standard unit of humanity, whilst the feminine is marked as different or other.

Given the inevitability of adopting a gendered subject position, I would argue that any subject, at any moment, has a gendered relation to meaning although I do not think that relation necessarily has to conform to the anatomical sex of the individual, and furthermore, the workings of the unconscious in producing meanings make any position unstable. For example, a woman laughing at a joke whose butt is, say, women drivers, could be said to be adopting, on a superficial level at least, a masculine position for understanding the foibles of Woman, the illogical Other. Unconsciously other meanings might be produced relating to an identification of the woman who laughs as a woman (driver), but these might remain repressed. The construction of gendered subject positions is a complex business, which I shall discuss in more detail later on. Suffice it to say now that my view is that the possible meanings of gender are constantly being both reproduced and modified and that texts, such as those written by Duras, have, like other representations, a part to play in that proceess. For this reason my interest in Duras's work from a feminist point of view leads me to a more intertextual and reader-centred approach than those I have mentioned so far since I think it is in their references to, and subversions or reinforcements of existing representations of gender, and in the positions they construct for the potential reader, that the political significance of Duras's, or anybody else's, work lies. I am concerned here less with the analysis of one woman's work in order to discover what it says about that woman and her ideas, interesting though they may be in themselves, and more about the meanings generated by her work and the possibilities they open up or close off in relation to shifts in the cultural construction of gender.

INTERTEXTUALITY AND READER-CENTRED CRITICISM

Part II is concerned with how Duras's texts generate meanings – and the meanings they generate. The gynocritical approach to Duras's work has ignored any ideas of intertextuality as a factor in the generation of meaning in a text, and avoided looking at the place of Duras's writing in the context of other texts, or of other representations in general, be they written, spoken, or visible, produced by women, men, or both together. It has also ignored, in its concentration on the relation of the text to its author, the relation of text to reader. This raises theoretical problems, because author-centred criticism constructs both the text and the language it is written in as the property of the author, without taking into account the 'impersonal' nature of language and literary forms, both of which pre-exist the individual author, even if the latter's own combination of linguistic elements into a particular form is unique. Lacanian theory lays particular stress on the pre-existent and 'other' nature of language in relation to the subject who utters or understands and this fits ill with the kind of gynocritical work which has been done on Duras's texts up to now.

I therefore undertake my own investigation of Duras's texts in the light of my reading of Lacanian theory. Firstly I analyse the way in which her writing generates certain effects, in particular the effect of 'blanks'. Various interpretations have been placed on these; I see them as points where the reader is invited to infer meanings in a particular way, guided by the text, and I investigate the inferences the reader is invited to make. I then look more closely at Duras's portrayal of women figures. I see her later writings as 'skeletal' novels, where the figures are little more than symbolic points in the structure, and whilst the sparseness of the texts and apparent transparency of the language are unique to Duras and innovative in relation to other novel forms, I see the symbolic relations they set up, and particularly those between the sexes, as basically conventional. I also find a progression towards increasing fetishization in the portrayal of Duras's central women figures. I do not speculate on the motivations behind this of a putative Duras for my interest lies instead with the power that fetishized images of women can have for other women and the implications of such images in terms of sexual politics. In the latter context, I see such representations as reaffirming the most traditionally Freudian and phallocentric meanings of what it is to be a woman.

Throughout my discussion I assume that Duras's readers, like all others, are gendered subjects. So in referring to a reader (or other person) of unspecified gender I use the forms s/he, her/him and her/his. I also assume that Duras's texts (like others) construct a gendered 'narratee' (*narrataire*), or reading subject, who is distinct from the reader who is reading and in whose place the reader is invited, but not of course obliged, to identify her/himself. It is at the interface of these two positions, that of 'narratee' and that of reader, that I see the meanings of the texts as being generated.

My overall purpose is to investigate the claims made for Duras's work and the theoretical framework used by those writers who regard it as manifesting 'feminine' and or feminist writing. The book divided naturally in two because, whilst I wanted to discuss the Lacanian theories of femininity and language, they were unsatisfactory for the purposes of my own analysis, which had to be done along different lines. In the conclusion I try to draw the two parts of the book together, and to reconcile my own conflicting attitudes to Duras's work, looking at the similarities between Lacanian theory and Duras's fiction and the kind of political positions I see arising out of them. I feel I should stress as the outset that although Duras herself has suggested that her way of writing is in some way 'a woman's thing', she has not, as far as I know, ever described either it or herself as feminist. It is other women who have wanted to claim her work for feminism. My analysis leads me to disagree with them on several counts.

Most of my discussion is based on Duras's novels, beginning with *La Vie tranquille*, published in 1944, and moving through over forty years to the ostensibly autobiographical *L'Amant*, published in 1984. Duras has been very prolific over (so far) forty-three years and besides her novels and autobiography, has written plays, texts she calls *récits* ('narratives'), and made films. I do not go into great detail on the plays, films or short narratives, partly because many of them are not well-known or easily available, particularly in English translation and partly because it is principally in relation to her novels, and certainly in terms of her writing, that the 'femininity' of Duras's work has been discussed. Films and theatre have specific ways of producing meanings which interact with, but are different from the written, which is the one that concerns me here. However, I do refer to some of these other works from time to time when it seems relevant to my argument to do so. Most of the quotations I use from French authors are given in my own English translations. Where I specifically want to discuss the French text, as I do in some of my analyses of Duras's novels, I have given both versions. Finally, before moving on to my discussion proper, I should like to thank Professor Annette Lavers for her encouragement, advice and support, without which this book would not have been written.

PART I

CHAPTER I
The Problem of Femininity

WRITING THE FEMININE

In her early writing, up to and including *Les Petits Chevaux de Tar-quinia*, the novel form Duras uses is that of psychological realism, portraying characters who each have their own 'psychologies' which motivate their actions. The stories unfold chronologically, with any flashbacks constructed as memories and the reader is told what happened and why. It is a form which the critic Marcelle Marini, in *Territoires du féminin avec Marguerite Duras* describes as 'novelized autobiography'.[1] In these novels details are supplied to 'fill out' the characters and to make it easier to understand or interpret the meaning(s) inherent in the sequence of events described. Each of these novels tells a story which poses a question and then answers it within the text. Will Sara in *Les Petits Chevaux de Tarquinia* take 'the man' as her lover, or will she remain faithful to Jacques? Will Suzanne in *Un barrage contre le Pacifique* leave the plain with a man? Will she escape her miserable situation? Will Anna find the sailor from Gibraltar, and if so, what will happen between her and the narrator? The curious reader is not required to put much effort into finding answers for these questions, since they are largely to be found spelt out within the text. S/he only has to read to the end.

However, in her later work, beginning with *Moderato cantabile* (1958), although perhaps heralded by *Le Square* (1955), Duras alters her technique and abandons the style of the realist psychological novel, although not, as I hope to show later, casting off either realism or psychology. It is in these later writings that she has developed the particular and distinctive style which has fascinated her readers and earned her work such critical acclaim. It is a style which has

1 Marcelle Marini, *Territoires du féminin avec Marguerite Duras*, Paris, Minuit, 1977, p 51.

been described by Sylvie Venet in an article on Duras as being 'on the edges of madness'.[2] Marini sees it as a profoundly disruptive style: 'She attacks the organisation of discourse; suppressing links, breaking up its linear unfolding with repetitions, making way for suspensions, spacing, breaks and multiple distorsions; prioritizing the word over the sentence.'[3] It is this disruptiveness that commentators have found in Duras's writing which has led to its being described as 'feminine' by certain critics, who are usually writing from a feminist perspective. Venet refers to the 'dislocation of syntax' and 'numerous elliptical phrases' to be found in Duras's work, and in that of many other contemporary women writers. She says that such writing cannot be read according to pre-established codes. 'The ambiguity of the text is so forceful, the network of relations between the different signifiers is so full of overlaps and interweavings, that the text does not readily lend itself to systematic, logical and ordered analysis.'[4] It is by breaking down the accepted and traditional codes that, according to Venet, Marini and many others, Duras achieves an effect of silence in her texts. This silence, they say, allows her (and her reader) to avoid unthinking acceptance of conventional ways of seeing and of the traditional meanings that are built into the language she uses. For, according to these critics, the existence of such meanings in a text curtails the author's and reader's freedom to create new meanings.

> For Marguerite Duras, writing means first of all creating silence and emptiness. Doing away with ready-made patterns of language, the fixed moulds of a story in which she can only take borrowed rôles. Silencing the cacophony of voices which come from all around to take her over, perpetually talking away inside her, and often in her place; the vast, anonymous voice which inhabits her and which she inhabits. Ridding herself of these forms that surge over her, invading her, the better to contain her.[5]

In this way, says Marini, Duras evades the tyranny of the semantic conventions of the language she uses. She creates silence as a tactical move. 'First she locks herself away in silence, as in a fortress, in order to escape the conventions of language that others want to impose upon her with violence.'[6]

Marini, then, sees the production or reproduction of linguistic

---

2   Sylvie Venet, '*Femme dans l'écriture: Marguerite Duras*', in *La Chouette* no 6, French Department, Birkbeck College, University of London, September 1981, p 4
3   Marini, op cit, p 51.
4   Venet, op cit, p 5.
5   Marini, op cit, p 53.
6   ibid, p 22.

meaning as an act of violence, against Duras in the first instance, and by extension, against women in general. From this I infer that she sees language, or perhaps more accurately, meanings, as being imposed, by those who must be assumed to have invented the language to suit their own ends or experience, on others whose experience is quite different. She does not explain her use of the words 'with violence', but it is evident that she sees the acquisition and use of linguistic conventions as, for some, a process of alienation from the 'truth' of what they are. The victims of this process are, she says, women.

So Marini poses the problem thus: the truth of women's experience, of what it means to be a woman, has been distorted by men's language. The representations of women which are articulated in this language therefore bear little relation to the reality because they were devised by men for men. Women have been forced to identify with/as the mythical women presented as real by male-dominated language. Marini therefore sees Duras's project of 'stemming this unending flood of words inside her, which traces the mythical feminine figures in which she becomes alienated' as an escape from linguistic oppression.[7] Venet takes a similar line. She sees Duras's work as breaking down the 'established codes', and she thinks this is 'linked to the desire to see socio-cultural values explode and to dissociate herself from a discourse which is and has always been the possession of men'.[8]

This idea that different groups in society encode their experiences in terms of different meanings and definitions, and that the meanings of the dominant group prevail to the detriment of the less powerful, is one that has existed on the fringes of linguistics and political theory for some time. It forms the basis of much of the 'gynocritical' work I referred to in the Introduction and, in the general context of sexual politics, was popularised by Dale Spender, in her book *Man Made Language*. Spender claims that women are the 'muted' half of society. According to her view, women's meanings have been excluded from language, or have never been invented at all. Women are then 'alienated' into speaking, writing and understanding themselves in terms of somebody else's definition. She states her viewpoint thus:

> Males, as the dominant group, have produced language, thought and reality. Historically it has been the structures, the categories and the meanings which have been invented by males – though not of course by *all* males – and they have then been validated by

7   ibid p 53.
8   Venet, op cit, p 5.

reference to other males. In this process women have played little or no part. It has been male subjectivity which has been the source of those meanings, including the meaning that their own subjectivity is objectivity.[9]

This formulation of Spender's has no doubt found a sympathetic reader in many a woman – including me – tired of finding herself dismissed and ignored by men in any number of contexts, from social gatherings to history books. I do not think I have ever known a woman who has not expressed an analogous view at some time in her life. However, as a theoretical position, it raises various problems. Maria Black and Rosalind Coward have analysed these in some detail in an article, *Linguistic, Social and Sexual Relations – a Review of Dale Spender's Man Made Language*, and I shall borrow their analysis here.

The fact that women use the 'man-made' language, and even participate in the propagation of meanings which run counter to their own, makes Spender's position somewhat contradictory. Black and Coward sum it up thus: 'Language constructs the positions of men and women, but men pre-exist language and use it to perpetuate their interests.'[10] The problem with this position lies in the idea that men and women each have separate 'interests' and understandings which pre-exist, or are independent of linguistic meanings. As Spender puts it, 'the language has been made by men and... they have used it for their own purposes'.[11] This must ultimately lead one to the view that men force women, by fair means or foul, into using a masculinist language against their will. Many feminists would take this view, and I assume it underlies Marini's phrase, 'the conventions of language that others want to impose upon her by violence'. As I have said above, the form which this violence takes goes unelaborated and Marini does not suggest actual physical violence (although many feminists might argue that it is the constant threat of physical violence against women, and in many cases its actual use, that keeps men in a dominant position). However, she implies that, whatever form this violence takes, it is intentional ('*want* to impose on her'). So, following this line, it is men who have either invented or siezed the means of signification (or perhaps, in this context, of representation) and, making it serve their nefarious purposes, have succeeded in bringing about the alienation of

9 Dale Spender, *Man Made Language*, London, Routledge & Kegan Paul, 1980, p 143.
10 Maria Black and Rosalind Coward, *Linguistic, Social and Sexual Relations – a Review of Dale Spender's Man Made Language*, in *Screen Education* no 39, London, Society for Education in Film and Television, Summer 1981, p 70.
11 Spender, op cit, p 52.

women on a grand scale, whilst ensuring that their own truths remain intact.

This raises the question of how do they do it? Such a position seems to imply that we women are mere pawns in the hands of men, who themselves are thus constructed in the role of geniuses, albeit evil ones, capable at some point in time of conceiving an ideological weapon of extraordinary efficacy and of implementing it against their mainly unwitting, or at least comparatively powerless (and therefore surely in some sense inferior) victims. I am sure that neither Marini, Spender, nor any other women who take this line would contend that men knowingly manipulate their utterances and the whole apparatus of linguistic signification all the time, in order to deny women's self-expression or self-determination. There is no evidence to show that men as a sex possess the superior intelligence necessary to manipulate women in this way, although no doubt many of them do so, or try to do so, at times, with varying degrees of success. So, if linguistic supression and/or repression of 'women's meanings' there be, it must be seen as working on an unconscious or pre-conscious level.

The implication of this latter view is that language shapes thinking, rather than the other way round, and this takes the whole argument both away from the idea of 'men's interests', which they knowingly pursue, and back to a rudimentary notion of a pre-existing language as in some way 'constructing' its user, be the latter man or woman. If this is the case, then it seems to me that it does not make sense to say that language is 'man-made', any more than it is 'woman-made'. Language is made and used by all, and if, as I think is true, it is one of the areas in which women's oppression is perpetuated, it is inadequate to say that this is purely because men have consciously – or even unconsciously – willed it so. Women have also partipated in the development of language, even if some of us feel that it does us a disservice.

Furthermore, the idea of 'group meanings' can lead to rash generalisations, as Black and Coward indicate: 'This understanding of language is problematic, assuming as it does that 'meanings' derive from clear-cut groups, generated by their different social experiences. The division between these groups is simply assumed; all empirical date of speech acts and utterances is then forced to fit these divisions.'[12] Black and Coward cite Spender's discussion of the representation of childbirth. She holds that it is usually portrayed as 'something beautiful, that leaves women consumed and

12   Black and Coward, op cit, p 70.

replete with joy',[13] and goes on to say that many women actually find childbirth an agonisingly painful experience, but that the possibility that women might experience it in this way has been culturally supressed. However, as Black and Coward point out: 'There are women prepared to testify to the simultaneous pain and pleasure of childbirth. Indeed feminists have themselves been at the forefront of attempts to restore dignity to the ways in which childbirth has been seen.'[14] and then, how could Spender forget the words of that arch-patriarch and prime influence on Western culture, God the Father: 'In pain you shall bring forth children'.[15]

The argument between Spender, on the one hand, and Black and Coward, with whom I would agree, on the other, is one between a universalising idea of supressed 'women's meanings' and an attempt to theorise and account for the co-existence of different understandings and attitudes, which may be found present among members of the same identified group, or even in the same individual member of a given group. The criticisms that Black and Coward make of Spender's position can also be levelled at Marini, Venet, and other writers who claim that women's meanings have been excluded from the language. Marini places herself squarely in the camp of the universalisers; to women she says: 'It is our saga that (Duras) retraces, unveiling and passing on to us the story of the murder of ourselves as human beings.'[16] This is addressed to all of us, female human beings, women. Of course, theories based on meanings, attitudes, or experiences regarded as common to all members of a given group find themselves confronting the problem of those group members who do not fit. It is interesting in this context, to compare Michèle Montrelay's reaction to *Le Ravissement de Lol V. Stein:* 'One does not read this novel as one reads other books. One is no longer in control of one's reading. Either you can't take it and give up on the book, or you give way to the Ravishing, which swallows you up, which anihilates you.' Montrelay clearly admires *Le Ravissement de Lol V. Stein*, but she admires it for this process of destruction it produces in her. 'What have I just glimpsed, heard? I no longer know, I grow stupid. This novel makes you relinquish thought. It carries you away into the kind of poverty in which love and memory merge.'[17]

Marini responds rather as Black and Coward might have predicted: she sees this reaction as an abdication of the feminine position on Montrelay's part, saying that, although 'her article bears the

13 Spender, op cit, p 54.
14 Black and Coward, op cit, p 71.
15 The Holy Bible, Revised Standard Version, Genesis, Chapter III, v 16.
16 Marini, op cit, p 49.
17 Michèle Montrelay, *L'Ombre et le Nom*, Paris, Minuit, 1977, p 9.

marks of a struggle', Montrelay has accepted the male-dominated, or masculinist, view of the world. This is, however, understandable, according to Marini, for the Lacanian school of psychoanalysis, from within which Montrelay writes, paints such a terrible picture of femininity as something which 'threatens *every* subject'[18] that, '[Montrelay] should not be reproached for having made her choice in the state of disarray produced by these threats, alternating with commands, to which obedience brings love and (a certain) recognition. Which of us has not done this on some occasion, out of weariness?'[19] Unfortunately, I have not come across a response from Montrelay to this understanding of her position, which seems rather patronising.

To fuel her argument regarding Duras's work, Marini draws heavily on and makes constant reference to that of Luce Irigaray. Irigaray also identifies women as a distinct and homogeneous group, whose language has been in some sense supressed by men. In her book *Ce sexe qui n'en est pas un*, she tells women: *'But your nature was, curiously, always defined by men alone,* your eternal pedagogues: in the social, religious or sexual sciences. Your moral or immoral teachers. They are the ones who have taught you about your needs and desires, without your having begun to say anything about them.'[20]

Irigaray uses the term 'woman-speak' (*parler-femme*)[21] for the way of using language which would correspond to women's nature and sexuality, as she sees it, were it not for the constraints imposed upon women by men. Her position is, however, radically different from that of someone like Spender for she works from within psychoanalysis and her theory owes much to that of the French psychoanalyst Jacques Lacan, although she deviates substantially from some of his positions. She is concerned less with 'women's meanings' that might have been suppressed by masculinist society, and more with what she sees as the different relation women have from men to the process of signification itself. For Irigaray, men's meanings are simple, unified things, whereas women's meanings are complex and plural. For her the suppression of 'woman-speak' is more than a predominance of some meanings over others, or Spender's 'sexist semantic rule'. Instead it is the denial by men of any manifestation of the existence of women's specific relation to language as a whole.

The feminist claims that are made for Duras's writing rely heavily

---

18 Marini, op cit, p 68
19 ibid, 71, n 14.
20 Luce Irigaray, *Ce sexe qui n'en est pas un*, Paris, Minuit, 1977 pp 201–2
21 ibid, p 141.

on not only Irigaray's, but also on other Lacanian theories of femininity. However, the concepts of 'the feminine' they use are usually very vague and ill-defined, a kind of merging of the Spenderesque and the Irigarayan which makes for a great deal of confusion, since it is not always clear exactly which theories are being used and how. As an example of the kind of problems I am referring to, I want to cite part of a conversation between Duras and a writer with a similar approach to that of Marini, Xavière Gauthier.

X.G. ...In *L'Amour* – we're beginning at the end – at one point you say; 'Doesn't know she's being looked at' (*Ne sait pas être regardée*). There's no longer even the personal pronoun – it's 'she'[22] –, and then it's negative: 'Doesn't know', and then 'being looked at', that's passive. I'm wondering if there wasn't a sort of withdrawal there, a reworking of usual grammatical sense.

M.D. It's not conscious. It's blanks, if you like, that impose themselves. It happens like this: I'll tell you how it happens, it's blanks that appear, perhaps because of a sudden violent rejection of syntax, yes, I think, yes, I recognise something there.

X.G. And when you say 'blanks', is it also holes, or lacks?

M.D. Someone used the word: anaesthesia, suppressions.

X.G. I was wondering if that, if that wasn't a woman's thing, really a woman's thing, blank. If, for example, there's a grammatical chain, if there's a blank in it, isn't that where the woman would be?

M.D. Who knows?

X.G. Because that, that would be a break in the symbolic chain. And that's there in your books. I see exactly that, myself.[23]

And later:

X.G. Isn't it after *Le Ravissement* that the hole starts to come?

M.D. Experiments then, experimentation. That comes back to what you were saying; I was experimenting with the blank in the chain.

X.G. It happens as a forgetting at first, and forgetting is also a blank. It's a little bit based – if you can talk about base, because that's really not the word – in *Le Ravissement* on a forgetting of suffering.

M.D. It's an omission, really.

X.G. Yes, an omission. Perhaps that's the very thing that's frightening, because you're starting to enter into lack.[24]

---

22 The French would translate literally as 'Doesn't know to be looked at'; but this is ungrammatical in English, whereas the French is not.
23 Duras and Gauthier, *Les Parleuses*, pp 11–12.
24 ibid, p 15.

In citing this exchange at some length, I want to give an idea both of the importance of the 'blanks' in Duras's written work, hailed as 'the place of the woman', and also of the vagueness of their definition. For, at the risk of seeming cynical, I feel that in this conversation neither Gauthier nor Duras have a very clear idea of what the 'blanks' are, how they might affect the 'grammatical chain', or whether such an effect is really something to do with women; it's just a feeling. In this they are not alone. My own investigation into Duras's work arose partly out of the feeling that something that I could not quite put my finger on was being 'said' without being written and furthermore that this something had to do with women. So I want to take a closer look at these 'blanks'. However, before I go any further in my discussion of Duras's work itself, I want to clarify as far as I can the theoretical bases of the kinds of suggestions Gauthier and Duras are making here: how 'the feminine' has been defined by psychoanalysis, and, more specifically, by the Lacanians; and also to outline certain problems I have with the theories as they stand, and which make me a little wary of the way in which they are used to discuss the way that Duras writes.

THE FREUDIAN VIEW

The definition of what is meant by 'femininity' – and indeed 'masculinity' – has posed problems ever since the beginnings of psychoanalysis. The terms are used, but in conflicting ways; often in different ways within the work of a single author, so that it is impossible to ascribe a general meaning to them. Freud's own use of them varies from context to context, and he was well aware of the problems of their definition, which he discusses in a footnote to his 'Three essays on the theory of sexuality':

> It is essential to understand clearly that the concepts of 'masculine' and 'feminine', whose meaning seems so unambiguous to ordinary people, are among the most confused that occur in science. It is possible to distinguish at least *three* uses. 'Masculine' and 'feminine' are used sometimes in the sense of *activity* and *passivity*, sometimes in a *biological*, and sometimes again in a *sociological* sense. The first of these three meanings is the essential one and the most serviceable in psychoanalysis. When, for instance, libido was described in the text above as being 'masculine', the word was being used in this sense, for an instinct is always active even when it has a passive aim in view. The second, or biological, meaning of 'masculine' and 'feminine' is the one whose applicability can be determined most easily. Here 'masculine' and 'feminine' are

characterized by the presence of spermatozoa or ova respectively and by the functions proceeding from them. Activity and its concomitant phenomena (more powerful muscular development, aggressiveness, greater intensity of libido) are as a rule linked with biological masculinity; but they are not necessarily so, for there are animal species in which these qualities are on the contrary assigned to the female. The third, or sociological, meaning receives its connotation from the observation of actually existing masculine or feminine individuals. Such observation shows that in human beings pure masculinity or femininity is not to be found in either a psychological or a biological sense. Every individual on the contrary displays a mixture of the character-traits belonging to his own and to the opposite sex; and he shows a combination of activity and passivity whether or not these last character-traits tally with his biological ones.[25]

Freud takes the division of humanity into two sexes, male and female, as the basic fundamental difference between people, as it is generally considered to be in most, if not all, cultures. From this he proceeds to the widely held assumption that to the different biological sexes correspond different psychological makeup, the feminine and the masculine. That Freud was not entirely happy with this view is clear from the footnote cited above and from the thesis of bi-sexuality, which he developed when it became clear to him that biologically female individuals, particularly infants, could not be said to exhibit specific forms of sexuality and a specific psychological makeup that were not to be found in their male counterparts. However, the theory of bisexuality does not, in fact, resolve the problem of the meanings of 'femininity' and 'masculinity', since the term '*bi*-sexuality' implies a concurrence of feminine and masculine sexuality, and so we still have the binary division into what are seen as psychological sex characteristics. For Freud, and psychoanalysis as a whole, the problem remains of the definition of 'femininity' and 'masculinity', once their existence has been assumed.

The complications inherent in the use of these terms are clearly apparent in the footnote cited above. In the sentences: 'The third, or sociological, meaning receives its connotation from the observation of *actually existing masculine and feminine individuals. Such observa*tion shows that in human beings pure *masculinity or femininity is not to be found in either a psychological or a biological sense*'[26] the contradic-

---

25 Sigmund Freud, 'Three Essays on the History of Sexuality' (1905), in *The Standard Edition of the Complete Psychological Works of Sigmund Freud*, Vol VII, London, The Hogarth Press and the Institute of Psycho-Analysis, 1953, p 219, n 1.
26 My emphasis.

tion between the first and second appearances of the terms confirms that Freud's attempt at clarification of the terms has not, in fact, made things any clearer. For how are we to understand 'actually existing masculine and feminine individuals', when Freud goes on to say that the two points of reference he has thus far given us, the psychological and the biological, do not provide pure examples of the two types? How is it then possible to determine who is a feminine individual and who a masculine, particularly in the psychological sense?

What I think Freud is saying is that, although no observable individual exhibits pure femininity or pure masculinity, which are the essential characteristics corresponding to the sexes, in biological terms, observation of individuals who have predominantly the characteristics of one sex rather than the other will permit us to extrapolate a biological paradigm for each sex. Similarly, it would be possible to establish a corresponding psychological paradigm, since we can observe certain psychological similarities between individuals whose biological characteristics are predominantly those of the same sex. He then uses the term 'feminine' to designate the paradigmatic way of being of the paradigmatic biologically female human being – woman – as opposed to masculine, which is that of the paradigmatic man.

This, of course, does not remove the problem of the definition of the paradigm. In 'Three Essays on the Theory of Sexuality', Freud poses the problem of femininity as that of understanding 'how a little girl turns into a woman'[27], but this still raises the question of what is meant by 'woman'? Things are further complicated by Freud's disjunction of the biological and the psychological for the theory of bisexuality does not require hermaphroditism, as Freud himself illustrates when he replies to 'woman analysts' (i.e. biologically female), critical of his 'deep-rooted prejudices against the feminine' that they need not feel offended: 'This does not apply to you, you are an exception, in this respect you are more masculine than feminine.'[28]

However, Freud's theories can be used to solve the very problem they pose, since they provide a framework in the context of which it is possible to see femininity and masculinity as ideologically constructed meanings, which may vary greatly from context to context, rather than pre-existent essences which have to be sought out and isolated, like elements in a chemical compound. As Juliet Mitchell has suggested, rather than insisting upon biologically determined

27 Freud, op cit, p 220.
28 Freud, 'The Psychology of Women', in *New Introductory Lectures in Psychoanalysis*, London, Hogarth Press and the Institute of Psycho-Analysis, 1946, pp 149–50.

sex characteristics, psychoanalysis paves the way for a theoretical account of genderisation.

The Freudian theory of the sexual development of individuals describes how, in the first three stages, the oral, the anal and the phallic, the child takes the mother as its love-object, irrespective of whether it is male or female, and adopts both active and passive attitudes towards her:

> Now we should very much like to know what the libidinal relations of the little girl to her mother are. The answer is that they are manifold. Since they pass through all the three phases of infantile sexuality, they take on the characteristics of each separate phase, and express themselves by means of oral, sadistic-anal and phallic wishes. These wishes represent active as well as passive impulses; if one relates them to the differentiation of the sexes which comes about later (which one should avoid doing as far as possible), one can speak of them as masculine and feminine.[29]

Here then, Freud is arguing that biological sex difference does not, in itself, give rise to differences in psychic organisation (although quite why he finds it necessary to characterise passive and active wishes in terms of feminine and masculine, having said such characterisation should be avoided, is a matter for speculation), since he says that sex differentiation does not take place until later, i.e., the child does not identify itself or others as male or female until later. This change is instigated by the discovery of the anatomical distinction between the sexes.

In the phallic phase, says Freud, the little boy 'stands in the Oedipus attitude to his parents'[30]:

> The Oedipus complex offered the child two possibilities of satisfaction, an active and a passive one. He could put himself in his father's place in a masculine fashion and have intercourse with his mother as his father did, in which case he would soon have the latter as a hindrance; or he might want to take the place of his mother and be loved by his father, in which case his mother would become superfluous.[31]

Thus, according to Freud, identification with either sex of parent is possible and the child is at first unaware of anatomical complications. For the little girl in the phallic phase, whom Freud describes as being 'a little man',[32] since her attitude to her clitoris is the same

29   ibid, pp 153–4.
30   Freud, 'The Dissolution of the Oedipus Complex', in *Standard Edition*, Vol XIX, 1961, p 176.
31   ibid, p 176.
32   Freud, 'The Psychology of Women', p 151.

as that of the boy to his penis, the situation is the same. 'As we know, in the boy this phase is characterized by the fact that he has discovered how to obtain pleasureable sensations from his little penis, and associates its state of excitation with his ideas about sexual intercourse. The little girl does the same with her even smaller clitoris.'[33] At this time, children of both sexes are said by Freud to assume that all people have genitals like their own, girls and boys having the same attitude to their genitals. This assumption is destroyed by the child's sight of the genitals of the opposite sex. In the case of the little girl, Freud says this involves her realisation that the little boy has a penis, which is bigger and therefore better than her clitoris, so that in comparison she feels that she is castrated. For the little boy, the sight of female genitals brings on the fear of his own possible castration, since he perceives the female genitals as having once been like his own and having since been castrated. This realisation of the difference between the sexes means that the child has to identify itself in some way in relation to castration; it has to develop a way of dealing with the problem of the sexual difference of human beings.

This does not, for Freud, involve a simple division, whereby anatomically female children identify themselves as castrated and males as not castrated. Little boys who are unable to accept the sight of female genitals may disavow what they see and unconsciously cling to the belief that women have a penis. This, for Freud, is the root of fetishism, where 'the fetish is a substitute for the woman's (the mother's) penis that the little boy once believed in and – for reasons familiar to us (i.e. fear of castration) – does not want to give up'.[34] This is one example of the ways in which unconscious sexual identification of the self and others can become complex, since the fetishist's relation to castration and sexual difference is an ambivalent one; he at once knows and refuses to know. Hence his own position vis-a-vis the opposite sex, his own sexual identification must also be ambivalent.

For the little girl, Freud gives three options:

She acknowledges the fact of her castration and with it too, the superiority of the male and her own inferiority but she rebels against this unwelcome state of affairs. From this divided attitude, three lines of development open up. The first leads to a general revulsion from sexuality. The little girl, frightened by the comparison with boys, grows disatisfied with her clitoris, and gives up her phallic activity and with it her sexuality in general as well

33 ibid p 151.
34 Freud, 'Fetishism' (1927), in *Standard Edition*, Vol XIX, p 153.

as a good part of her masculinity in other fields. The second line leads her to cling with defiant self-assertiveness to her threatened masculinity. To an incredibly late age she clings to the hope of getting a penis some time. That hope becomes her life's aim; and the phantasy of being a man in spite of everything often persists as a formative factor over long periods. This 'masculinity complex' in women can also result in a manifest homosexual choice of object. Only if her development follows the third, very circuitous path, does she reach the final normal female attitude, in which she takes her father as her object and so finds her way to the feminine form of the oedipus complex.[35]

The 'normal female attitude' – i.e., 'femininity', or the attitude of 'a woman' – is achieved, according to Freud, when the little girl accepts 'the fact of her castration' and turns against her mother for not giving her a penis. She gives up clitoral masturbation and instead turns to her father, and later to male lovers, to give her a penis in the form of a child. Thus she takes up the passive attitude, waiting to be given what she does not have, with her main erotogenic zone transferred from clitoris, which she could stimulate herself, to vagina, which she cannot (without difficulty). So runs the theory.

In Freud's account sexuality is constructed rather than given, but he bases his theory on the view that the meanings attached to anatomical difference are fixed; that the little girl has to perceive her clitoris as inferior to because smaller than the boy's penis. Freud expresses this in terms of a teleological view of Nature (the Great Mother...):

If we now survey the stage of sexual development in the female which I have been describing, we cannot resist coming to a definite conclusion about female sexuality as a whole. We have found the same libidinal forces at work in it as in the male child and we have been able to convince ourselves that for a period of time these forces follow the same course and have the same outcome in each.

Biological factors subsequently deflect those libidinal forces (in the girl's case) from their original aims and conduct even active and in every sense masculine trends into feminine channels.[36]

and:

It is our impression that more violence is done to the libido when it is forced into the service of the female function; and that – to

35 Freud, 'Female Sexuality' (1931), in *Standard Edition*, Vol XXI (1961), p 229.
36 ibid, p 240.

speak teleologically – Nature has paid less careful attention to the demands of the female function than to those of masculinity.[37]

If the opposition 'female function/masculinity' is taken into account, it becomes apparent that, for 'female function', one might read 'femininity' and, for 'masculinity', 'male function'. Freud is here equating his view of 'femininity' as a specific psychic organisation in relation to the castration complex – a constructed gender identity – with that of a specific sexual function of Nature. He makes of his description of 'femininity' a norm, necessary for the continuance of the human species (thereby discounting the possibility that other forms of psychic organisation might also be conducive to heterosexual intercourse). However, this 'female function', which is pregiven (because bequeathed by Nature), involves constraint of the libido into forms which it would not otherwise take; it has been 'deflected' from its normal course (normal being in the male function).

Freud's view is that the process of deflection he describes does not always take place smoothly and indeed is most unlikely to be complete. He says on several occasions that women show greater tendencies towards bisexuality than men. Furthermore, the 'feminine' forms of psychic organisation which were present in the male child, manifested in desire for the father as well as for the mother, do not totally disappear from his account either. So that, whilst he regards 'femininity' in women and 'masculinity' in men as teleologically necessary, his own theories of sexuality undermine any biologist determinism. For he describes 'femininity' and 'masculinity' as identifications, or positions adopted by the individual, at the two poles of a spectrum along which there is any number of different positions that the individual can take up in relation to sexual difference. In saying this, I concur with Juliet Mitchell, who gives a reading of Freud which attempts to show that his theory is a lot less depressingly determinist than has been assumed, in particular by other analysts and by some feminist writers.

Post-Freudian analysts, as we shall see, have all too often interpreted 'this great antithesis' between the sexes to mean an absolute distinction between men and women for whom, indeed, therefore, anatomy was the *only* destiny. Nature had made the sexes essentially different and in social life thus diverse they must go forth. Obviously, on the contrary, what Freud meant was that *both* sexes in their mental life reflected this great antithesis; that in the unconscious and preconscious of men and women alike was echoed the great problem of this original duality. Without distinction,

37 Freud, 'The Psychology of Women', p. 169.

both sexes are preoccupied with the great distinction: in different ways they both flee from its implications. Both men and women live out in their mental life the great difficulty that there are men and women.[38]

In Mitchell's reading of Freud, sexual difference is seen as being primarily a question of the relation to symbolic castration. Freud's paradigmatic child finally comes to see all women as castrated, men as not castrated, though castratable. However, this castration is symbolic, it is a meaning attached to the genitalia. For himself, Freud appears to see this meaning as fixed: the penis is bigger, therefore, it *must* be better (indeed, Freud's concern with the size of genital organs seems to me eminently analysable, as, for example, in his superfluous description of the little boy's penis as 'little', and the little girl's clitoris as 'even smaller' in the passage cited above), the lack of penis *must* be seen as horrifying. He writes of the little girl's discovery of 'the fact' of her castration, and how acceptance of this 'fact' leads to the development of femininity.

Now, it is a fact that women are *not* castrated in a physical sense, or at least only very rarely in cultures other than those in which forms of clitoridectomy are practised systematically (although many little boys, and notably Jewish ones such as Freud himself, undergo the mutilation of their penises in the form of circumcision...). So to say that women are castrated is to place a meaning on women's genitals in a social context which takes the male genitalia as the standard.

From here it is possible to understand the concept of penis-envy in a different way, as Mitchell does. Patriarchal cultures such as ours are constructed around a power-relation between women and men in which the latter are in the superior position. In the paradigmatic nuclear family, the father is the highest authority and all the other members of the family take his name and submit to his will, including the mother, and though individual families, or groups of people, may be quite differently organised, the paradigm provides the norm against which other forms are measured.

It follows from this that the child's understanding of sexual difference creates the necessity for it to identify itself within the established power-relation between the sexes and the fundamental difference between the sexes is manifested in difference of genitalia, particularly in the case of children, in whom secondary sex characteristics are less apparent.

For the little girl, the discovery of sexual difference involves the

38　Juliet Mitchell, *Psychoanalysis and Feminism*, London, Penguin, 1974, p 50.

discovery of her own inferior position within that power-relation. Until this point she has, like the little boy, been able to identify either with mother or father, and been able to adopt either passive or active positions in relation to her object. Her fantasised relations to her object were hitherto accompanied by her auto-erotic pleasures – her clitoral masturbation – over which she has control. She then discovers that her genitalia require her to fall into the category of those who do not have (ultimate) control over anything, i.e., women. That her reaction might be to refuse to accept the meaning of her possession of female genitalia and identify with her father or with men as a whole, or to represent her desire to fit into the dominant category of human beings in terms of a wish for a penis, seems not unlikely, for the possession of the penis is, in the sexual hierarchy, the mark of power.

Similarly, for the little boy, who finds himself in the position of power by virtue of having a penis, fear of castration can be seen as a representation of fear of losing his eventual adult position of domin-ance and being pushed into the other category, the category of women, of those who do not possess a penis. And since the most powerful are those who set the rules, he needs adult penis-bearers (the father, for example), to acknowledge him as one of them; he must defer to the father in a struggle for the mother which, as a small child, he cannot win and so he has to relinquish his claims.

In both the case of the little girl and that of the little boy, it seems inevitable that a certain instability of identification in either the position of the castrated or that of the castratable – bisexuality – will be the result, given the disadvantages inherent in each, although the advantages of identifying with the castratable might attract the little girl more than those of the castrated position would attract the little boy. Freud seems to think bisexuality more common in women. Mitchell calls bisexuality 'a complex notion of the oscillations and imbalance of the person's mental androgyny'. She goes on:

> It is this dilemma, in which the subject is still resolving the precise point of the place he occupies in the world, in terms of his (and her) wish for it not to be the feminine place, which is the only, and ever-present alternative to where anyone really wants to be – in the male position within the patriarchal human order[39]

In Mitchell's reading, the term 'feminine' applies to the symbolic place of the woman in a patriarchal order: that of the castrated. The desire she describes not to be in that place does not arise from the innate physical or psychic inferiority of women, but from desires

39 Mitchell, op cit, p 51.

which cannot be reconciled with occupation of the symbolic position assigned to them. It is the desire to avoid impotence – castration –, which is a culturally ascribed meaning, if deeply entrenched.

I do not fully agree with Mitchell that no one wants to be in the feminine position, and I shall explain why later on. However, I find her reading of Freud and her understanding of the meaning of 'castration' convincing, since it avoids what seems to me to be a rather crude assumption on Freud's part that the penis is desirable in itself, an assumption, moreover, which, by fixing the meaning of the penis, denies the work of the unconscious as the place where meanings are produced. For Freud, however, it was apparently unthinkable that the order was not fixed, since he does not question it. Thus he avoids the hypothesis that his and other men's position in the sexual hierarchy is not necessarily a secure one and that the meanings of sexual difference might be subject to change.

To sum up then, Freudian 'femininity' is specific form of psychic organisation in which the feminine individual identifies her/himself in the position of the castrated in relation to the castratable masculine and, although Freud believes 'femininity' to be necessary to 'the female function' of reproduction and child-rearing, there is nothing in his theory to tie it to female human beings.

There is also nothing in Freud's theory about 'feminine language' or the suppression of 'femininity'. In fact he sees 'femininity' as being brought about by the deflection of the libido away from a 'normal' masculinity. This is clearly a very phallocentric view, and Freud was not surprisingly criticised for it, by both women and men analysts. It was in the attempts of these critical analysts to redress Freud's masculinist bias that anatomically-grounded 'femininity' first appears in psychoanalysis.

REDRESSING THE BALANCE: HORNEY AND OTHERS

During Freud's lifetime and since his death, many writers have objected to his depiction of femininity, frequently from the understandable point of view that he has been unfair to women. These writers have taken 'femininity' as Freud describes it, with its penis-envy and narcissistically passive sexuality, as a specific attribute of women. So in trying to get away from Freud's masculinist bias, they have sought to valorise what they see as women's attributes and to create a positive view of women's specificity, which they felt Freud had described in a restricted, negative light, simply as it deviated from the masculine.

Ernest Jones, for example, argued for the existence of a feminine libido – an idea rejected by Freud – which would be specific to women. It seems clear that Jones was trying to redress what he saw as an imbalance created within the work of Freud, which was due to the latter's masculine assumptions about the superiority of men and the 'normality' of the male function, and led him to portray women in the light of his masculine prejudice. However, as Mitchell and others have suggested, the idea of a 'feminine libido' potentially has the opposite effect from the positive one which Jones no doubt intended, and is furthermore theoretically untenable, if one follows the basics of psychoanalysis as set down by Freud.

In the first instance, the idea of a 'feminine libido' restricts women's (and men's) possibilities as regards psychic organisation with the constraints of a biologist essentialism, and produces implicit notions of 'normality', both for women and for men. On the theoretical level, as I understand Freud, libido is a force which finds many different expressions, depending on the phase of development of the individual, her/his history and unconscious wishes. It cannot as such have a sex, although the paths it follows might be termed 'feminine' or 'masculine' (once it has been decided what each term designates). In Freud's work, the ways in which libido is channelled are the results of the workings of the primary processes and the production of unconscious meanings; they are not fixed according to the anatomical division of the sexes. To attempt to gender the libido according to anatomy, therefore, seems to me to run counter to the psychoanalytic theory from which the concept of libido is taken, and also to block the radical potential of that theory as a way of accounting for the possibilities for change in the hierarchy of women and men.

Other criticisms of Freud's account of femininity have raised different objections. Certainly, the view of femininity as being in the place of the castrated, as Freud describes it, does not cover all the meanings carried by womanhood, or the feminine gender – the symbolic package attached to biological femaleness. Perhaps the most striking account of other meanings attached to womanhood is to be found in the work of Melanie Klein. Klein describes how the infant's early idea of its mother is of an all-powerful being, good or bad, but in no sense 'castrated', and these fantasies are never totally eradicated as the child grows older: 'This feeling that the mother is omnipotent and that it is up to her to prevent all pain and evils from internal and external sources, is also found in the analysis of adults.'[40] There are many cultural echoes of this early relation of the child to its mother; often they can be seen, reworked through later stages of unconscious

40 Melanie Klein, 'Envy and Gratitude', in *Envy and Gratitude*, London, The Hogarth Press and the Institute of Psycho-Analysis, 1975, p 185.

development, in the negative images of over-bearing, 'castrating' women: the domineering wife of a 'hen-pecked' husband, the mother-in-law, or the 'vagina dentata'. The feminine gender carries these meanings of power as well as that of being castrated.

On a more positive note, Freud's account of femininity excludes other meanings culturally built into the feminine gender: those echoes of the 'good mother', in Klein's terms, which Karen Horney points to in her work. Criticising psychoanalytic thinking on the strictly Freudian model, Horney notes:

> The first thing that strikes us is that it is always, or principally, the genital difference between the sexes which has been made the cardinal point in the analytical conception and that we have left out of consideration the other great biological difference, namely the different parts played by men and women in the function of reproduction.[41]

After describing the joys of motherhood, she continues:

> From the biological point of view woman has in motherhood, or in the capacity for motherhood, a quite indisputable and by no means negligible physiological superiority. This is most clearly re-flected in the unconscious of the male psyche in the boy's intense envy of motherhood. We are familiar with this envy as such, but it has hardly received due consideration as a dynamic factor.[42]

However, in spite of the importance of motherhood and mother-hood-envy in boy children, she states: 'The masculine envy is clearly capable of more successful sublimation than the penis envy of the girl'[43] with the result that many women take refuge in what she describes as a 'flight from womanhood' and a concomitant mascu-linity complex. Horney sees these as grounded in the oedipus com-plex, arising from infantile fantasies of sexual relations with the father. These involve 'fantasies that an excessively large penis is effecting forcible penetration, producing pain and haemorrhage, and threatening to destroy something'.[44] According to Horney, these fantasies produce fear in the little girl, which is exacerbated by her inability to inspect her internal organs for damage, and lead her to a desire to escape the feminine role altogether. However, besides the anxiety that these fantasies produce, Horney sees other forces at work: 'Now these typical motives for a flight into the male role –

41 Karen Horney, 'The Flight from Womanhood', in Jean Baker Miller (ed), *Psychoanalysis and Women*, London, Penguin, 1973, pp 9–10.
42 ibid, p 10.
43 ibid, p 11.
44 ibid, p 15.

motives whose origin is the Oedipus complex – are reinforced and supported by the actual disadvantages under which women labor in social life.'[45] She goes on to elaborate: 'In actual fact a girl is exposed from birth to the suggestion – inevitable, whether conveyed brutally or delicately – of her inferiority, an experience that constantly stimulates her masculinity complex.'[46]

I would further suggest that the intensely masochistic fantasies in relation to the father that Horney describes might be the result of the little girl's perception of the respective positions of the sexes, which constructs the father as all-powerful. For if he were not so seen, why should the little girl fantasise his 'forcible penetration' of her? However, this view is pure speculation on my part. The crucial point which Horney makes here is, I think, that even though women have the capacity to give birth, and even though men display envy of this capacity, it is the inferiority of womanhood in relation to manhood which is nevertheless constructed as fundamental, in Horney's account as in Freud's. The result is that many women seem to wish to escape the feminine gender – womanhood – in spite of the fact that it embodies the power of motherhood, as this power is outweighed for these women by the impotence of castration.

Horney uses the word 'femininity' in the sense of 'womanhood', or the meanings implicit in the feminine gender, as opposed to Freud's construction of 'femininity' as a relation to castration. Given this, her aim is to rehabilitate the feminine gender:

> To get beyond the subjectivity of the masculine or the feminine standpoint and to obtain a picture of the mental development of women that will be more true to the facts of her nature – with its specific qualities and its differences from that of man – than any we have hitherto achieved.[47]

However, it appears from her account that the positive meanings implicit in the feminine gender are, nevertheless and for whatever reason, undermined by the feminine position, that of being castrated. This has the effect of making women wish to be in the masculine position, translated into the wish to be a man.

Other writers who have seen a masculinist bias in the work of Freud, and I think rightly so, have, as Horney did, seen the development of penis-envy as related to the social structures in which the little girl grows up. There has been discussion of the archaic vaginal sensations which, as Horney described, were left out of Freud's

45 ibid, p 19.
46 ibid.
47 ibid, p 20.

account, since they did not fit into the picture. On another level, work has been done to show that the clitoris has as many nerve endings as the penis, and should therefore be equally good at producing pleasurable sensations (a rather mechanistic view, perhaps...). All this research has shown that the possibilities for a different view of womanhood, both on the part of women and men, are very great. Indeed, the fact that such work has been done at all is no doubt symptomatic of the process of change in the cultural content of the two genders which is underway. However, what is always apparent in work done on women's psychology is that women must always contend, in whatever way they choose, with the problem of femininity in the Freudian sense, that is to say, symbolic castration. Refusal of the position of the castrated leads, according to Freud, Horney and many others, to a 'flight' towards masculinity, in a conflation of 'masculinity' in the sense of 'castratable' with 'the masculine gender'. The reasons for this are well summed up here, I think, by Alfred Adler:

> The whole history of civilization [...] shows us that the pressure exerted upon woman, and the inhibitions to which she must submit today, are not to be borne by any human being; they always give rise to revolt. If this revolt now exhibits itself in the direction which we call masculine, the reason for it is simply that there are only *two* sex roles possible. One must orient oneself according to one of two models, either that of an ideal woman, or according to that of an ideal man. Desertion from the role of woman can therefore appear only as masculine, and vice versa. This does not occur as the result of some mysterious secretion, but because in the given time and place, there is no other possibility.[48]

As long as the most important meaning implicit in the feminine gender is that of castration (Freud's 'femininity'), refusal to accept that one is castrated (and why should we?) implies the rejection of femininity in the sense of 'womanhood'. At least such is the view not only of the phallocentric Freud, but also of those who, like Horney, have attempted a less biased account of sexual difference. But might it not be possible to shift the meanings attached to being gendered feminine so that acceptance of oneself as a female human being – a woman – does not also require an acceptance of 'castration', so that the 'castrated/castratable' dichotomy is abandoned altogether, to be replaced with an interplay of equality in difference, organised along other lines?

In psychoanalytic terms, the goal of most, if not all, the various stands of feminism can be formulated in this way. However, the

---

strands divide broadly into two in the paths they take to this goal: the first passes through a blurring of the differences between the categories of women and men, to looking at individuals as 'persons', whose particularities are influenced, but not fixed, by anatomical sex differences – Mitchell's reading of Freud, and my own position, fit somewhere here; the second aims to rehabilitate, and, where necessary, to uncover, the specificity of 'womanhood', and this is where I would place Jones and Horney. It is also, as I have indicated above, the fundamental approach of feminist critics of Duras's writing.

It may seem paradoxical, then, that what these critics praise in Duras's work should be its 'silence' and 'ambiguity', its hovering 'on the edges of madness'. At first sight, these may appear unpromising attributes to reclaim for womanhood. Certainly the pioneers of the rehabilitation of the feminine gender were interested in emphasising its more positive aspects, such as motherhood, or the existence of infantile vaginal sensations. Perhaps they would even have viewed silence, ambiguity and madness as symptomatic of the flight into masculinity. But the feminist claims have been made in the specific context of Lacanian theory, and Lacan had little time for the likes of Jones, Horney, or most of his psychoanalytic contemporaries. Instead he saw his own work as a 'return to Freud'[49] in the face of the false directions psychoanalysis was taking, and he drew on Freud's account of the unconscious, to develop an analysis of the psychic functions of language. For Lacan, the acquisition of language is the crucial structuring process of the human psyche, separating conscious from unconscious in the production of meaning, and he sees the process of signification itself as phallic, a process from which his version of femininity is by definition excluded. In such a context, feminists have hailed silence, ambiguity and madness as forms of rebellion.

Although the work of the Lacanian feminists diverges greatly from that of Lacan, they use his terminology and basic concepts, albeit in different ways from his own, and their views of femininity are based on an acceptance of his draconian pronouncements. So any evaluation of feminist claims for Duras's writing must also involve a discussion of Lacan's work, the more so since the way that some feminist writers have used Lacan raises important theoretical problems which are often overlooked in the application of their work to Duras's texts. I therefore now propose to discuss the Lacanian view of femininity and its relation to language in some detail.

49 Jacques Lacan, 'La Chose Freudienne' in *Ecrits I*, Paris, Le Seuil, Points series, 1966, p 209.

CHAPTER 2
The Lacanians

Lacan's position in the context of psychoanalytically-influenced debates on sexual politics is a strange one. His theories have been enthusiastically espoused by pro-feminist writers of both sexes, on the grounds that their accounts of mental processes deconstruct the individual as a separate and coherent entity, undermine authoritative, phallocentric discourses of knowledge and open the way to a theoretical understanding of how shifts can be made in the field of sexual politics. And yet some of the things Lacan has said about women seem, not only at first glance, but also at second and third and in context, mysogynistic to the point of being bizarre and no doubt he intended them to be so, for he clearly enjoys being provocative, in his writings as in his seminars. For example, in his seminar on, amongst other things, feminine sexuality, *Encore*, he says at one point: 'Woman does not exist' and a little later on:

> There is no woman who is not excluded by the nature of things, which is the nature of words; and it must be said that if there's one thing they themselves are complaining about enough at the moment, it is this – only, they don't know what they are saying; that's the whole difference between them and me.[1]

However, this second quotation also indicates why feminists have become interested in Lacan, for he tries to give a psychoanalytic account of what he sees as women's exclusion from the phallocentric order of things, an account which might offer an understanding of why, in spite of the child's experience of the all-powerful mother,

1 Lacan, *Encore*, Paris, Le Seuil, 1975, p 68.

and male envy of motherhood, it should be the castrated/castratable dichotomy that apparently orders relations between the sexes.

According to Lacan, the human psyche is structured by language, which brings about the split into conscious and unconscious and hence the existence of the 'subject' – the 'I' who understands and speaks or writes. This is, he says, made possible by the repression of a particular signifier and that signifier is the phallus. The result of this, in Lacan's theory, is that not only meaning, but also the existence of the subject and the desire of the subject in relation to objects, all are produced in relation to the phallus as a signifier.

Such a view, if one accepts it, has important implications for theories relating to sexual politics. But because of the constantly self-referential and just barely comprehensible nature of Lacan's work, anyone who wants to use his theory has to extrapolate her/his own version of it from all the texts s/he reads and the versions, and hence their implications, vary. So I want to go through my own version here in order to make it as clear as possible how I read Lacan, and also because my understanding of the role he ascribes to the phallus, and of his view of femininity and masculinity, raise problems in relation to the theoretical positions of other feminist or women-orientated writers using his theories, and notably those whose work is linked with that of Duras.

According to Lacan, the subject is fundamentally constructed in relation to lack, and her/his development is a continuing process of separation. The original lack arises at birth, when the infant loses 'his[2] anatomical complement'[3] with the loss of the security of the all-embracing mother's womb. The baby becomes transformed from the 'egg in the viviparous belly, where it has no need of a shell'[4] into 'Man, but also the *Hommelette*'.[5] *L'Hommelette* is a mythical organ, which turns out to be the libido.[6] So, according to Lacan, the libido is a product of this first separation, necessitated by the process of reproduction and the perpetuation of the species, for this is the point when needs, and their companion desire, begin.

The first needs, primarily for food, arise from the loss of the mythi-cal 'anatomical complement' – the all-enfolding mother's womb. In order to be satisfied, these needs must be articulated somehow in the

---

2   The French does not specify the gender of the infant here, but I have done so, since this (paradigmatic) infant goes on to become Man (see 52 below).
3   Lacan, 'Position de l'inconscient', in *Ecrits II*, Paris, Le Seuil, Points series, 1971, p 211.
4   ibid.
5   ibid. The French reads *L'Homme, mais aussi l'Hommelette*. The word 'Hommelette' would be most literally translated as 'little man'; however, Lacan is punning here, since the word is pronounced as 'omelette' in French, which continues the egg metaphor, and is also etymo-logically linked to the later *lamelle*, or 'lamina'.
6   ibid, p 213.

form of a demand, a demand first articulated to the mother, since she is the first fulfiller of needs. So the mother comes to occupy the position of the 'anatomical complement', the fantasised ultimate satisfier, which Lacan calls the 'Other.'

However, Lacan says that 'the demand turns on other things than on the satisfactions that it calls for. It is the demand for a presence or an absence'.[7] It is an absolute demand for total satisfaction, which is not satisfied by the satisfaction of a particular need. But as the underlying demand cannot be satisfied, there is a gap between the satisfaction and the real aim of the demand and it is this unfulfilled excess between the satisfaction of the need and the demanded love that Lacan terms desire. It is in the nature of desire that it can never be fulfilled, because the demand for love can never be met; it is a demand for the absolute satisfaction of every need, a demand for the 'anatomical complement', which alone filled the lack. '. . . the demand nullifies (*aufhebt*) the particularity of everything that can be given, by transmuting it into a proof of love; and the very satisfactions it obtains for the need are reduced (*sich erniedright*) to being nothing more than the quashing of the demand for love.'[8] The subject's desire constantly takes on new objects (and there may be fresh demands for the satisfaction of a need). Each time, the object takes the fantasised place of the Other but it does not fill that place, since it is never more than a partial satisfier in relation to particular drives.

Lacan calls these partial objects *objets a* for 'autre', where the lower case indicates that they are only partial in relation to the Other – *l'Autre*. The term *objet a* is often left untranslated, but I will translate it as 'o object', where 'o' stands for 'other'.

In the earliest stages of its life, the child does not experience itself as a distinct, unified whole. The orifices, which are the points where inside and outside meet and separation is felt, become points of excitation on the surface of the body – the erotogenic zones. They are the disparate focal points for the build-up of unpleasurable tension – the different drives – and this tension is relieved by absorption or expulsion of an object (milk, faeces).

Gradually, the difference between the body and its outside becomes established, and this makes possible the delineation of the ego as separate from 'the world'. Objects then propose themselves from outside as possible replacements for the 'anatomical complement' which the infant has lost at birth:

> The breast. . . well represents that part of himself that the individual loses at birth, and which may come to symbolise the most deep-

---

7　Lacan, *Ecrits II*, p 109.
8　idib, p 110.

seated lost object. I could evoke the same reference for all the other objects.[9]

It is in turning these objects to regain in them, to restore in him his original loss, that the activity within him which we call drive (*Trieb*) is employed.[10]

The objects themselves may not only be actual things, such as the breast, but also looks or voices, at first primarily those of the mother. They propose themselves to different areas of tension, different drives. The physical processes of absorption and expulsion of objects occur in what Lacan terms the order of the Real. This means that they actually happen in physical terms, but do not enter consciousness and are only represented indirectly, as in fantasies of introjection and projection, where the infant fantasises taking an object into its body, or expelling it. According to Lacan, 'the fantasm is only ever the screen covering up something which is absolutely primary',[11] but which remains concealed. This is because, unless they are reworked into representations, Real processes are incompatible with a unified subject, which can only exist in relation to other unified images and meanings. So the Real is always beyond the grasp of consciousness; 'the subject, inasmuch as he thinks, [...] does not encounter it'.[12]

However, the case of objects of the scopic drive, objects of the subject's vision, is different from that of other drives, for it is the scopic drive which makes possible the establishment of a unified subject in the order of the Imaginary. In Lacanian terms, Imaginary means something like 'in terms of a unified image'. The Imaginary is the relation of the subject to the world outside her/himself, which s/he can see, and in which s/he perceives objects as discrete and separate entities. According to Lacan, the child goes through what he calls 'the mirror phase', the time when it first recognises its own image in the mirror and spends time looking as it, and it is this which cements the subject in the order of the Imaginary, for this is when it first perceives itself as a discrete entity also. Of such activity Lacan says: 'From this we only need understand that the mirror phase *is an identification* in the full sense that analysis gives to the term: that is to say, the transformation produced in the subject when he takes on an image.'[13]

At this moment of looking at its image, the subject is said to be split in two. The act of looking at its own image gives the child an

9 Lacan, *Les Quatre Concepts fondamentaux de la psychanalyse*, Paris, Le Seuil, 1973, p 180.
10 Lacan, *Ecrits II*, p 215.
11 Lacan, *Les Quatre Concepts fondamentaux de la psychanalyse*, pp 58–9.
12 ibid, p 49.
13 Lacan, *Ecrits I*, p 90.

image of itself, whole and complete. This image of a whole, complete self is the *je idéal*,[14] or ideal ego. The assumption of this image – this 'I' – as itself is crucial to the child's development as a subject. It also constitutes the child's identity as an object – in this case of the scopic drive, i.e. it is the object of a desire to look. It is identification with/as this image which makes possible the illusion of a unified and temporally consistent subject.

The ideal ego, then, is the image with which, or as which, the subject identifies. At the same time as the ideal ego, the ego-ideal is produced, which is that aspect of the subject which looks at the ideal ego. So is established the narcissistic structure of the look, which the subject directs towards and receives from her/his image, in the dual relation of the split subject to her/himself. Lacan characterises this dual relation with the phrase, 'I see myself seeing myself'.[15] In this way, the mirror phase establishes the subject in terms of a fundamentally narcissistic relation to her/his own ego.

This narcissistic relation of the ego to her/his image is also present in the relation of the ego to other objects looked at:

> in the scopic field, the look is outside, I am looked at, that is to say, I am a picture.
>
> This is the function which is most intimately placed in the institution of the subject in the realm of the visible. The fundamental thing that fixes me in the realm of the visible is the look which is outside.[16]

The look of the subject captures the fantasised look of 'other things' and the look of 'other things', which is 'a look imagined by me'[17] – the look of the subject in its imaginary return – captures the mask, the ideal ego, the image assumed by the ego.

In this way, the illusion of a unified subject is produced by the division between the subject of the look and the image of the subject as looked at.[18] In the order of the Imaginary the subject is an alienated subject; in Rimbaud's words, 'I is another'.[19] The Imaginary relation of identification with the visual image is seen by Lacan as producing a certain fascination, a certain stasis and plenitude, which come

---

14   ibid, pp 90–1.
15   Lacan, *Les Quatre Concepts fondamentaux de la psychanalyse*, p 76.
16   ibid, p 98.
17   ibid, p 79.
18   One might speculate as to what would happen, following this account, in the case of a child born into a culture where mirrors do not exist; or, more interesting still, that of a child born blind. Unfortunately, if Lacan himself ever pondered these questions, I have never come across his thoughts on them.
19   Arthur Rimbaud, Letter to P Demeny, 15 May 1871, in *Oeuvres complètes*, Paris, Gallimard, 1972, p 250.

from the subject's fantasy of meeting the object's desire through the mutual identification of looking; the subject looks at the object, which looks back (either in fact, or in the fantasy of the subject) at the subject and makes the subject object.

However, for Lacan, the unification of the subject is always an Imaginary illusion. This is partly because it is a fantasised unity, constructed out of the divergent drives of the Real, but also, as I indicated at the beginning of my discussion, because of the effects of language. It is using language which splits the subject in the very process of her/his constitution and institutes her/him in a third order, that of the Symbolic. The subject moves into the order of the Symbolic because the plenitude offered by the Imaginary order is not in fact attainable as the fascination of looking cannot redeem the primary loss suffered at birth. However, Imaginary effects continue, inasmuch as the illusion of consistency and unity lent to the subject when it speaks or understands language arises in the Imaginary.

At first the child does not articulate its demands in the form of words and is helpless in the face of the mother's presence or absence, or of that of any other object to which its desire is directed. Lacan sees the mastery of language as a way in which the child changes its relation to its object from one of total powerlessness and dependency to one allowing it a measure of autonomy. Following Freud, Lacan exemplifies this process in the 'fort/da' game, in which a child throws a cotton-reel away from himself and then pulls it back, meanwhile saying *fort* ('gone') and *da* ('there'). Lacan fits this game into the category of 'repetitive games, in which subjectivity cooks up both the mastery of its dereliction and the birth of the symbol'.[20]

The child, in using the symbol to stand for the object, that is to say, to be the signifier of the object, changes the relation between subject and object, 'for his action destroys the object, which it causes to appear and disappear in the anticipatory *instigation* of its absence and presence. In this way [his action] reverses the field of the forces of desire, to become its own object'.[21] In this process, signifiers become objects of desire.

As I have mentioned above, Lacan says that in the act of speech, or in any process of signification, the subject speaking or understanding is split: 'I identify myself in language, but only to lose myself in it as an object'.[22] This sounds like the narcissistic splitting of the look, but in the order of the Imaginary, the subject also becomes a unified object in the rather static structure of the look. In the

20 Lacan, *Ecrits I*, p 203.
21 ibid.
22 ibid, p 181.

Symbolic order, the subject becomes a momentary locus of meaning, and the guarantor of that meaning is fantasised as the Other.

Following the linguist Ferdinand de Saussure, Lacan sees meaning as arising out of the relation of signifiers to each other, rather than through reference to extralinguistic, pre-existing objects or ideas. However, as it is possible for signifiers to go on referring to each other indefinitely in what Lacan calls 'the chain of the signifier', a fixed meaning can only be produced when this infinite possibility of reference and resonance is closed off. In order for the subject to be able to 'make sense', the potential for endless reference and production of meaning must be blocked, That is the signifier(s) being used must be 'pinned down' to an apparently unitary meaning (unless double meaning is specifically intended). According to Lacan, this happens when signifiers take on the role of 'o objects' for the subject. This is what is happening in the 'fort/da' game referred to above, where mastery of the signifier means the child can control the presence and absence of the object; the signifier takes the place of the object and becomes itself an object of desire.

When the subject uses language, and signifiers take on the position of 'o objects', the closing off of resonance to produce meaning is the process that makes them partial objects only, leaving an excess of desire for what is fantasised as the Other – the ultimate source of meaning and fulfiller of desire. So the Other's place is in the unconscious resonances of language, 'the chain of the signifier', out of which the particular meanings have arisen, or in which they have been 'pinned down', and from which the subject has become separated.

If there is talking in the Other[23], whether or not the subject hears it with his own ear, it is because that is where the subject, through a logical anteriority to any awakening of the signified, finds his signifying place. The discovery of what he articulates in this place, that is to say, in the unconscious, allows us to grasp at the price of what division (*Spaltung*) he has thus formed himself.[24]

In the unconscious, meanings go on being produced through the constant reference of signifiers to each other in all the ways described by Freud; references which arise out of the 'impersonal' linguistic and cultural contexts, but also from the individual's own personal history. Examples of open manifestations of these unconscious processes can be seen in puns, slips or jokes. The subject must, in order

---

23 *Si ça parle dans l'autre. Ça* is also the French rendition of Freud's *Es*, translated in English as 'id'.
24 Lacan, *Ecrits II*, p 108.

for identification and predication to be possible, split off from the these processes – from the Other, but cannot be completely separated, since the signifiers around which s/he forms her/himself are themselves ultimately Other:

> Inasmuch as his needs are subject to the demand, they come back to him alienated. This is not an effect of his real dependence [. . .] – but in fact because of their very consolidation into the signifying form, and because it is from the place of the Other that his message is put out.[25]

It is in this process of 'consolidation into the signifying form' that Lacan gives a crucial role to the phallus. For according to him, this process of splitting, and the production of fixed conscious meanings, is only possible because the subject has repressed the phallus as a signifier, and what the phallus signifies is *jouissance*. There is no single translation of *jouissance*; it can mean sexual pleasure in the sense of orgasm, but also has a more extended sense; so that as well as the '*jouissance* of the organ', or the '*jouissance* of the body', Lacan also refers to the '*jouissance* of (the) being' and the *jouissance* of the mystics. Lacanian *jouissance* seems in a general sense to refer to the effect of too much meaning, the dissolution of the division which is constitutive of the subject and the Other. And because it means dissolution, it is incompatible with the existence of the subject.

According to Lacan, this incompatibility is fantasised by the subject in terms of the Law of the Father, for in the fantasy of the subject, it is the existence of the father which prevents the child merging with the mOther in *jouissance*. However, what sets this whole edifice in place is the subject's awareness of the mother's desire, for desire arises out of lack, so the existence of the mother's desire signifies that she lacks. On becoming aware of the existence of the mother's desire, the child sees the father as having what she desires, this being (retrospectively?) fantasised as the phallus, the mark of difference between the sexes, on the child's discovery of the mother's 'castration'. Seeing her desire as desire for the phallus, the child then wants to be the phallus for her; but is unable to do so.

> If the desire of the mother *is* the phallus, the child wants to be the phallus to satisfy it. In this way the division inherent in desire already makes itself felt by being sensed in the desire of the Other, since it is already in opposition to the subject's satisfying himself with presenting to the Other the real thing he might *have* that corresponds to this phallus; for what he has is worth no more than

25 ibid, p 109.

what he does not have, for her demand, which would like him to be it.

... This establishes the conjunction of desire, in as much as the phallic signifier is its mark, with the threat or nostalgia of the failure to have (it).[26]

So the law is instituted by the inability of the mother to be phallic and the inability of the child to provide her with the phallus. Mother and child cannot form a complete, unified identity, both still lack. But it is the father whose existence, putative or otherwise, is seen by the child as breaking the unity of the mother/child relation and preventing the child's *jouissance* within that relation. 'The signification of the phallus, as we have said, must be evoked in the subject's imaginary by the paternal metaphor.[27] The 'paternal metaphor' is the name-of-the-father, which is the Symbolic representation of the father. It is the existence of the father which institutes the Law, for the child imagines him to be the object of the mother's desire and cause of her absence when she is not there. The father presents a threat to the child not to disturb the relations of desire between himself and the mother. The child is therefore excluded from these relations of desire, and this exclusion forms the Law, whose strong arm is the father. The law manifests itself as the taboo on incest and thus on the child's *jouissance* in its relation with the mother.

So the phallus takes up the position of signifier of *jouissance* when the child comes to perceive the mother as castrated. But it is repressed as a result of the father's intervention and the inability of the child to be the phallus for the mother. In this way, the missing phallus becomes the signifier of desire; in the first instance in the mother. For in the (retrospectively constructed) fantasy of the child, if the mother did not lack the phallus, she would have no desire which the child could not fill and she and child would be fused into a single whole. In any subsequent Imaginary relation of the subject to an object of her/his desire, the phallus is then fantasised as missing in the object as it was in the mother. If it could be present, the result would be *jouissance* and the end of desire, with subject and Other no longer split, and a complete merging with the object producing plenitude. This is not possible in the terms of the theory, (or perhaps momentarily so, in orgasm, or in mystic *jouissance*) and the missing phallus becomes the signifier of that impossibility. However, the phallus is present as the repressed signifier of *jouissance*, its repression providing the condition for the splitting of subject and Other without which signification itself would be impossible.

26 ibid, pp 112–13.
27 ibid, p 72.

Lacan makes it clear that he sees this paradigmatic process of separation, and the role of the phallus as a signifier, as the same for the subject of either sex: 'So Freud unveiled this imaginary function of the phallus as the pivot of the symbolic process, which perfects, *in both sexes* the undermining of the sexual organ through the castration complex.'[28] However, in the terms of his paradigm, subjects identifying themselves as feminine and masculine adopt different symbolic relations to the phallus, which come down to either having it or being it. The child at first sees the mother as lacking nothing, all-powerful, and this fantasy is translated, when the child reaches the phallic phase, into a fantasy of the mother as phallic. However, in the transfer of the phallus in the Imaginary of the subject from mother to father, the mother becomes what the father has: the phallus. This division is then extended to all women and men.

In heterosexual relationships, says Lacan,

> It is in order to be the phallus, that is to say the signifier of the desire of the other, that the woman will throw an essential part of her femininity, namely all her attributes, into the mascarade. It is for what she is not that she expects to be desired and loved at the same time. But she finds the signifier of her own desire in the body of him to whom her demand for love is addressed.[29]

For Lacan, then, femininity is an identification as the phallus, as the signifier of desire. According to him it then follows that women, who he assumes to be in the position the phallus, are not subjects of desire – and therefore of speech – in the way that men are. This is because following his theory, the speaking subject is constructed in relation to castration, to the problem of having the phallus or not. Lacan sees this problem as one for men, whose penises provide them with a possible Imaginary version of the Symbolic phallus; but women's relation to the phallus is constructed around being it or not, since with no penises, there is nothing, he says, to make them think they have it. So Lacan calls women 'not-all-there',[30] incomplete in terms of the phallic function. This is why he says that they are 'excluded from the nature of things, which is the nature of words' and 'do not know what they are saying'. In relation to the phallic function he sees women as a gap, taking the place of the Other in the

---

28 ibid, p 70.
29 ibid, p 113.
30 Lacan describes women as *'pas-toute*, which means 'not-whole', or 'not-complete', and has been rendered into English as 'not-all'. However, I have translated it as 'not-all-there', which I think works better in English and also conveys both the idea of psychic incompleteness in relation to the phallic function, and the idea that the woman is somewhere else – in her 'other *jouissance*'.

fantasy of the (masculine) subject. In phallic terms, it then follows
for Lacan that women do not have a specific sexuality for they do
not either 'have' the phallus or not, as men symbolically do, they
'are' it, object rather than subject. This is why he says: 'The sexed
being of these not-all-there women does not come through the body,
but through that which results from a logical requirement within
speech'.[31] From this, Lacan continues to say that woman 'does not
exist', but is instead a gap in meaning, so that '"Woman" can only
be written if it is crossed through'.[32]

However, in the same section of *Encore* as that from which the
above quotations are taken, Lacan goes on to suggest that women
in fact do have a specific form of *jouissance* (and so of sexuality)
'beyond the phallus'[33]. This he very briefly and confusingly opposes
to clitoral *jouissance* in a way which implies that the latter is in fact
in some way phallic, masculine, or at least, not specific to women.
Clitoral *jouissance* looks all set to disturb Lacan's account of how
Woman is 'not-all-there' in relation to the phallic function, but
Lacan mentions it only to ignore it and return to 'the other' *jouissance*. This, he says, is what Freud was getting at when he asked
his famous question, 'What does Woman want?' However, Lacan
suggests that women themselves do not actually know anything
about it; firstly he says: 'There is a *jouissance* which is specific to her,
to this *her* that doesn't exist and signifies nothing. There is a *jouissance*
specific to her about which she perhaps knows nothing, except that
she feels it – she knows that.'[34] Then he suggests that perhaps the
woman does not even know she feels this *jouissance*: 'If it was simply
that she feels it, but knows nothing about it, that would make it
possible to raise plenty of doubts about that famous frigidity.'[35]
Exactly what this might mean is something that has greatly
excercised the minds of subsequent Lacanian women writers, as
I shall discuss in the next section.

To sum up here though; Lacan's version of femininity is, essentially, an identification *as* the phallus, in relation to masculine
subjects, who are fantasised as possibly *having* it. The result is that
there is no such thing as a feminine subject, since the subject comes

31 Lacan Ecore, p 15.
32 ibid, p 68. This is particularly difficult to translate, because of the differing use of the
    definite article in French and English. Lacan actually says that the definite article *La* of
    La femme should be crossed through, because it is indicating what he regards as an
    impossible universal: '*La femme, ça ne peut s'écrire qu'à barrer* La. *Il n'y a pas* La *femme,
    article défini pour désigner l'universel*'. In English the universal is marked by a capital letter –
    here the 'W' of Woman – and I have translated it as such to avoid confusion.
33 ibid, p 69.
34 ibid.
35 ibid, p 70.

into being only in relation to the phallus, in an always failing attempt to find it in the object, in which it is always missing. This means, for Lacan, that a putative 'feminine sexuality', which is not about a having or not of the phallus, must be off-limits to the subject; and women, both in relation to their putative 'other *jouissance*', and in terms of phallic language, are 'not-all-there', not subjects.

I think there are problems with this rather strange theoretical position, not least since the view that women are not full subjects of desire would seem to be undermined by the role of the mother's desire, so important elsewhere in the Lacanian edifice. In the first place, Lacan sees mothers (who are after all, still women) as desiring subjects in relation to their children, the child being in the position of the 'o object'. But more importantly, the mother must also be the subject of more general desires. For without the mother's desire for other objects besides the child, Lacan's whole account of the institution of the Law and the role of the phallus would be prevented.

From this it would seem that, even following Lacan exactly, there is more to being a woman than simply being in the position of the phallus. After all, only women are mothers and, given all the other relations between women and the world, I would suggest that no woman identifies in the place of the phallus all the time. Furthermore, if the subject is only ever a provisional, and not quite separate entity, instability of identification seems the most likely result, for any subject of either sex. Even Lacanian men have been children, with the desire to be the phallus for the mother; effects of this might subsist in the most masculine of positions. Lacan does not discuss such things, but he does allow for the possibility that an individual of one sex might identify her/himself in the place of the other, and makes the odd brief reference to it; of the 'side where the man stands' he says: 'One stands there, in short, by choice – women are free to stand there if it gives them pleasure. Everyone knows there are phallic women.'[36] And the same goes for the women's side: 'when any speaking being stands under the women's banner, it is because of the fact that he bases himself on being not-all-there, on placing himself in the phallic function.'[37]

However, his view is that the potential of the penis to be the Imaginary representative of the phallus leads men towards masculinity, women to femininity. And following Freud, Lacan takes as obvious the role of the phallus as prime signifier, basing this upon an unquestioning idea of visibility. As Stephen Heath points out in his article

36 ibid, p 67.
37 ibid, p 68.

on 'Difference': 'The function of castration as the articulation of the subject in difference is brought down to a matter of sight, the articulation of the symbolic to a vision.'[38] To put it another way, the penis is visible, women's genitals are not, therefore, Lacan argues, the penis can be used to make a Symbolic signifier of *jouissance* – the phallus, whereas the 'invisible' organs of women cannot. The penis becomes erect and then limp again, a constant reminder of lack, says Lacan. Furthermore, the father has one and the mother does not, this being the most striking visible difference between them. Heath takes issue with Lacan over his use of the sight of the genitals of the opposite sex as being the sole basis for the castration complex without situating it in any cultural context. As he argues:

> a recognition of lack is given outside of any signifying process as a fact of each individual subject with a return in the symbolic – the phallic function – that ties process to vision. What is at stake and shut off in the logic of the penis/phallus is the history of the subject in as far as that history might include effects of social organization, and, for example, of patriarchal order.[39]

A point which Lacanian psychoanalysis certainly seems to have left unanswered, and which is the more telling when one considers that, in spite of so many writings to the contrary, there is nothing inherently invisible about women's genitalia unless one happens to be looking for a penis. Women may lack a penis, but men lack clitoris, labia, vagina. It is only in terms of a lack of penis that women's genitals can be said to be invisible, except, perhaps at some distance. But it is never specified how close the child must be to the person whose genitals s/he sees in order for the sight to spark off the castration complex. This raises the problem of why so many psychoanalysts have written of women's genitals as invisible. I suggest that these organs have had invisibility thrust upon them. As Heath says: 'The vision, any vision, is constructed, not given; appealing to its certainty, psychoanalysis can only repeat the idological impasse of the natural, the mythical representation of things.'[40]

Ironically, however, Lacanian theory does leave a space for exploration of the cultural determination of the meanings of the genitalia of the different sexes. Indeed it almost demands one, since it lacks any analysis of why – or when – 'any speaking being stands under the women's banner'. 'One stands there, in short, by choice',

38 Stephen Heath, 'Difference', in *Screen*, Vol 19, no 3, London, Society for Education in Film and Television, Autumn 1978, p 54.
39 ibid, p 53.
40 ibid, p 55.

with its casual voluntarism, is an empty phrase in the context of psychoanalysis. It seems to me that one must begin to look outside the limits of psychoanalytical enquiry in order to explore questions of how individuals come to take up particular gender positions, how the meanings attached to gender are formed and whether and how they might be changeable. Such problems require discussion of a wider context than simply that of the individual subject. However, much of the subsequent Lacanian work on femininity and women has not really explored these questions, concentrating instead on 'what women want'; the secret of which, it has been assumed, lies in the silence of Lacan's 'other *jouissance*'.

'THE RUIN OF REPRESENTATION'

Undeterred, or in some cases perhaps spurred on by Lacan's assertion that 'they do not know what they are saying', several women analysts in France have armed themselves with his theories and set off to explore what Montrelay, quoting Freud, refers to as the 'dark continent' of femininity, the place of the 'other *jouissance*'. Montrelay herself follows Lacan quite closely. Like him, she sees femininity as a place of silence, which undermines all meaning, and compromises the position of the woman as a speaking subject, making her 'not-all-there'. However, starting from this position, she then goes on to give an account of what she understands by 'femininity' and why it has the effects she describes.

Montrelay uses the work of Jones, Klein and Françoise Dolto to discuss the pre-oedipal phases of the little girl's development. Freud had already indicated the significance of those phases for female sexuality, but Lacan described them as 'not of course non-existent, but analytically unthinkable'[41] (although his own theories clearly owe a debt to those of Klein, whose work was largely concerned with precisely these phases). Montrelay takes up the idea of 'the archaïc experiences that the girl has of the vagina' in the order of the Real, which 'organise themselves according to pre-established oral-anal schemas'. In *L'Ombre et le Nom* she says: 'femininity will be understood as the "feminine" drives (oral, anal, vaginal) taken as a whole and insomuch as they resist the process of repression.[42] According to Montrelay, these feminine drives do not undergo repression through the castration complex in the way that masculine (phallic) drives do, because of their concentric nature:

41 Lacan, *Ecrits II*, p 70.
42 Michèle Montrelay, op cit, p 67.

It could be said that early sexuality 'turns' around a single orifice; an organ which is both digestive and vaginal, which aims to absorb, to appropriate, to devour, indefinitely.

...If this insatiable organ-hole is at the centre of early sexuality, if it orientates every psychic movement, according to circular and closed schemas, it compromises woman's relation to castration and to the law: to absorb, to take, to take in, is to reduce the world to the most archaïc 'laws' of the drives. It is a movement diametrically opposed to the one on which castration is based: where the *jouissance* of the body is lost 'for' speech which is Other.[43]

This is Montrelay's version of Lacan's 'other' *jouissance*. For her, women lack lack because of the uninterrupted workings of the feminine drives. They lack the lack that constitutes a separation from *jouissance* in the order of the Real and that lies at the root of representation. To the extent that their libidinal economy is concentric and closed off, she says, the feminine drives are sufficient unto themselves and do not undergo the workings of the primary processes. This means that they are unrepresented in the unconscious and are, indeed, unrepresentable: 'Feminine sexuality is a dark, unexplored continent, not as the result of some provisional inadequacy of research: it is unexplored to the extent that it is unexplorable.'[44] This lack of lack occurs in the order of the Real. However, Montrelay also describes women as potentially lacking lack in the order of the Imaginary and the Symbolic, at least after puberty. This, she says, is because of the woman's Imaginary relation to her mother.

For the woman enjoys her body as she would that of another woman: it is the fascinating actualization of the Femininity of every woman; but also, above all, of the mother. Everything happens as if 'becoming a woman', 'being a woman', gave access to a *jouissance* of the body as feminine *and/or* maternal. In the 'self-love' she has, the woman is not able to differentiate between her own body and the body which was the 'first object'.[45]

It is this relation to the mother that Montrelay sees as producing the other side of Lacanian femininity: the identification *as* the phallus. For the *jouissance* she equates with femininity here is not the self-sufficient satisfaction in the Real of oral-anal-vaginal drives, it is an Imaginary and Symbolic identification of the woman sub-

43 ibid, p 68.
44 ibid, p 66.
45 ibid, p 69.

ject with and as the Other as represented by the mother and the Maternal respectively. She goes on:

> The real of the body, taking shape at puberty, taking on density, weight and presence, as the (male) lover's object of desire, re-actualizes, reincarnates the real of another body, the one which, in the first moments of life, was the substance of words, the organ-iser of desire; the one which, in the time that followed, formed the stuff of archaïc repression. Recuperating herself as the maternal body (and also the maternal phallus), the woman can no longer repress, 'lose', the first thing that was at stake in representation.[46]

Montrelay stresses that changes occur in the order of the Real, but she is talking about the body taking on new Imaginary and Symbolic meanings in relation to the maternal here, and although the little girl's body could be Symbolically identified, by herself and/or others, as being on the side of the mothers before puberty, such being one of the meanings of the female gender, the woman's body comes to signify a new Imaginary relation to motherhood when the changes of puberty take place.

It seems plausible that physical similarity might make it possible for women to experience being both object and subject in the rela-tions of maternal desire, but I think a degree of confusion surfaces in Montrelay's theory here. For in her discussion of the woman's Imaginary and Symbolic identification with/as the mOther, and resulting fascination and lack of lack, she leaves aside the effects of the mother's desire for objects other than the child, which, in the Lacanian theory she uses, construct the (phallocentric) subject in relation to castration and the Law. It is unclear, in Montrelay's theory, how far, if at all, she sees the Real loss of the 'anatomical complement', and the superimposed Imaginary and Symbolic lacks of the phallus, as bringing about a fundamental constitution of the woman subject in relation to lack and the Law, as she accepts that it does in the case of men, and if not why not, for there seems no reason for such a basic difference. The 'self-sufficient' feminine drives she describes are not in themselves enough to account for such a difference, since all the others would still be operating in the realm of lack.

But Montrelay avoids this issue altogether, concentrating instead on the identification of daughter with mother, and seeing pregnancy and particularly the moment of giving birth as conducive to the *jouissance* of merging with the mOther. However, she says that the father may contribute to the daughter's possibility of *jouissance*, by

46 ibid.

putting her in the position of the (maternal) phallus, thereby setting up an identification with maternity for both of them:

> Thus the father seduces the daughter; not with the penis, which he keeps for the son, but by procuration, with a maternal phallus, which he marks out for her. Operating in this way, he succeeds only too well. The phallus around which he turns, which is supposed to be veiled, is her: the little girl.[47]

So, in Montrelay's work, femininity in its phallocentric Imaginary and Symbolic manifestations is an identification with both the (phallic) mother and with maternal phallus, which threatens to produce plenitude and a lack of the lack which is necessary for the woman subject to come into being; meanwhile, the workings of the unrepresentable feminine drives continue in the order of the Real. The result of all this, she says, is that femininity produces anxiety: women feel 'fear of the feminine body as an unrepressed, unrepresentable object'.[48] In the order of the Real, Montrelay sees a way round this problem in heterosexual intercourse, where the action of the penis breaks up the constant *jouissance* of the woman's concentric sexuality:

> it could be said of the penis, of its throbbing, of its rhythm and of the gestures of love, that they produce the most elementary, the purest form of signifying articulation. That of a series of strokes, which mark a limit.
> ...Paradox: the penis gives pleasure because it incarnates finitude.

So that: 'pleasure is the meaning of the metaphor by which the penis 'represses' the feminine body, feminine sexuality'.[49] But this is a temporary effect. In the Imaginary and Symbolic orders, she finds another, more permanent way of staving off the anxiety produced by femininity and making entry into the Symbolic possible. This lies in the simulation of a lack:

> It is a question of organising a representation of castration which is no longer symbolic, but imaginary: a lack will be simulated and through it, the loss of some stake. This enterprise is made all the easier precisely because feminine anatomy shows a lack; that of the penis. Whilst remaining her own phallus, the woman will dress up in this lack, making the dimension of castration suddenly appear as an optical illusion.

47 ibid, p 143.
48 ibid, p 70.
49 ibid, p 78.

...In this way the woman's sexual organ, a vagino-oral organ which sets up an obstacle in the way of castration, at the same time 'falsely' represents the latter through effects of illusion, which create anxiety.[50]

So Montrelay apparently sees phallocentric sexuality in women as a secondary formation, 'set up to maintain the phallic power of the father',[51] and to maintain the woman subject within the Symbolic order. This it does by contradicting her self-sufficient, static identification with/as the mOther, and thereby instituting Imaginary castration, in relation to which a (phallic) subject of desire can come into being. The problem of how she understands the role of the 'anatomical complement' and the mother's desire crops up again here, for according to Lacan these two between them ground the subject in a relation to castration; but again, Montrelay does not broach this question.

However, secondary formation or not, she sees an irresolvable difference between women's phallocentric sexuality and their femininity. The two forms of sexuality remain, as she sees it, 'two heterogeneous, incompatible territories', which 'coexist within the feminine unconscious: the territory of representation; the one which remains a "dark continent"'.[52] This view is not without its difficulties; for if some forms of 'feminine drives' remain unrepresentable processes in the order of the Real, in what sense can they be said to 'exist' in the unconscious? The whole phrasing of 'coexist within the unconscious' would seem to imply a black box theory of the unconscious, in which it might be possible to put all sorts of things. However, Montrelay, following Lacan, states that 'the unconscious is a structure or configuration of desires which are articulated in representations'.[53] If this is the case, and the unconscious exists in terms of representations, it is unclear to me how the unrepresentable can be said to exist within it. It is also hard to see how feminine sexuality as Montrelay describes it could create 'blind spots' in the chain of representations of a masculine unconscious, since it would presumably be operating on a totally different and closed circuit; after all, they are 'heterogeneous territories'.

However, Montrelay does not seem to see a theoretical problem here. She goes on to describe two slightly different results of what she sees as women's dual sexuality. It happens, she says, that the feminine erupts into the masculine at certain points to bring about 'the

50   ibid, pp 70–1.
51   ibid, pp 59–60.
52   ibid, p 70.
53   ibid, p 63.

ruin of representation' 'Femininity "according to Jones", experienced
in a real and immediate way, makes a blind spot in the symbolic
processes analysed by Freud.'[54]

She describes this effect as occurring periodically in the discourse
of her analysands during the course of an analysis, at points when
the woman subject does not separate from the Other, so that her
speech has no unconscious resonance. 'The spoken word can no
longer be heard as anything but an extension of the body which is
there, speaking. It no longer seems to be hiding anything. Nothing
is latent, everything is manifest.'[55] Elsewhere in her discussion,
Montrelay generalises this effect, saying that, as Lacan implied in
his description of women as 'not-all-there', women do not become
separated subjects in language as men do. 'When he writes, a man
separates himself from the Other with words, with their feminine
matter, making sure that a little bit of it stays on the paper.' Women
have an other relation to words. They are the extension of themselves. '. . . A woman is not separated from words. They live through
her and contain no secret which has been hidden from her'.[56] Again
there is a confusion in Montrelay's theory here, as it is not really
clear whether she sees femininity as erupting periodically into
women's language as a point of non-sense, or whether she thinks it
compromises women's relation to meaning and the Symbolic all the
time. She never discusses her personal experience of using language,
or her own relation to femininity, and indeed when she is writing
about Woman, or women, she tends to give the impression that she
does not include herself in the category. However, she does mention
Duras's work in this context, as an example of writing which gives a
place to femininity:

> In Marguerite Duras's novels the same world of amazement and
> silence unfolds. One could show how this silence, this non-speech,
> always reveals the fascinating dimension of feminine lack:
> whether Duras wants to make it 'speak' in an inarticulate cry
> (*Moderato cantabile*), or as 'music'. Let us simply remember here
> what is said in *Le Ravissement de Lol V. Stein*: 'It would have
> required a word-absence, a word-hole [. . .] it could not have been
> spoken, it could have been made to resound'.[57]

The 'feminine lack' here is the lack of lack. Montrelay praises
Duras's work for making femininity manifest, for she wants to see
the non-sense of femininity recognised, in order that women's rela-

54   ibid, p 70.
55   ibid, p 66.
56   ibid, p 152.
57   ibid, p 71.

tion to language, and the workings of human mental processes in general, might be better understood. But, as I mentioned in Chapter 1, she sees the process of reading Duras as one of 'anihilation' for the reader, who must allow her/himself to 'grow stupid' and to be 'ravished'. Montrelay wants the non-sense of femininity to be heard resounding, but she does not seek to hear it speak, since for her, by definition, it has nothing to say.

'WOMAN-SPEAK'

However, such a view is not shared by all, and the most notable dissenting voice is that of Irigaray. Irigaray writes explicitly as a feminist, that is, she sees women as oppressed by relations between the sexes, and she wants to change this state of affairs. For her this means rediscovering women's specific sexuality, which she sees as having been suppressed by the dominance of men, and in opposition to the position of Montrelay, she puts forward the view that it is this masculine – or male – sexuality, that threatens women's relation to language, rather than the feminine.

Like Montrelay, Irigaray began as a Lacanian, and uses a neo-Lacanian framework, although she fell from grace from the Lacanian school, and she reworks Lacan's concepts to fit her own theories. In *Ce sexe qui n'en est pas un*, in the section entitled 'Cosi fan tutti', she sets out the Lacanian (she says psychoanalytic) view of feminine sexuality, a view she criticises for its refusal to take account of its historical and political context, although she accepts it as an accurate and adequate description of the way things are at the moment.

So psychoanalytic theory speaks the truth about the status of feminine sexuality, and about the sexual relation. But it sticks there. Refusing to interpret the historical determinants of its discourse [. . .] and notably what is implied by the sexed quality, until now exclusively masculine, of the application of its laws, it remains caught in phallocentrism, which it claims to make into a universal and eternal value.[58]

Besides a Lacanian background, Irigaray shares with Montrelay a stress on the importance of the mother/daughter relation and the duality (or plurality) of feminine – women's – sexuality. However, unlike Montrelay, she sees women's sexuality as something which has been forced (one is reminded of Freud) into a form which it would not otherwise take by the imposition on to it of men's

58 Luce Irigaray, op cit, p 99.

sexuality. Irigaray is concerned to look at women's sexuality both as she thinks it has been constructed by the relations of power between the sexes and as it might be outside those relations of power. This last, she says, can only be guessed at, for women do not know exactly what a society in which feminine sexuality was not suppressed would be like, because they have been made to fit the place created for them in a culture dominated by masculine sexuality.

She starts from the point of view that women's specific sexuality has been denied and silenced because the patriarchal culture in which women find themselves is based on the exchange of women between men, a structure which Claude Lévi-Strauss saw as basic to human societies. In Irigaray's view, this structure reduces women to the role of commodities, and this is how they are currently seen and treated. However, she thinks that an economy based on the exchange of commodities between individuals is, in fact, foreign to women's nature.

For Irigaray, as for Lacan, men's sexuality is organised in terms of unity, which in turn produces a culture organised in terms of 'the *one* of form, of the individual, of the proper noun, of specific meaning'.[59] This, she says, is because masculine sexuality is centred on one organ, the penis, which is, here again, visible and potentially detachable; it also requires active stimulation by something other than itself in a way that, according to her, is unnecessary for women's eroticism; the ultimate effect of these attributes being a logic of 'the prevalence of the look and discrimination of form, of the individualisation of form.'[60] Whereas Montrelay's view was that what she saw as women's self-sufficient, concentric sexuality was a problem, requiring the intervention of a unified subject in the shape of the father or male lover to give the woman back to herself, for Irigaray a similar idea of self-sufficiency is seen in a positive light and the constraints forcing women into the order of 'the One' then become the problem.

For in the terms of the order of 'the *One*', according to theories circumscribed by 'masculine parameters',[61] 'the erogenous zones of the woman are never more than a sexual-organ-clitoris, which does not bear comparison with the valorous[62] organ, or a hole-envelope, which provides a sheath and a rubbing round the penis during

---

59   ibid, p 26. The French reads, '*le un de la forme, de l'individu, du sexe, du nom propre, du sens propre*. The word *propre* also carries the sense of 'property' and 'ownership' here.
60   ibid, p 25.
61   ibid, p 23.
62   *Valeureux*, meaning 'valliant', 'brave', or 'valorous', also carries within it the word *valeur*, 'value'. As it seems to me that Irigaray also uses it in the sense of 'having value', as opposed to women's sexual organs, which are not valued in the patriarchal order, I translate it in this second sense in the quotation that follows.

coitus: a non-sexual organ, or a masculine sexual organ turned inside out around itself, to self-stimulate itself'.[63] She continues:

> Of the woman and her pleasure, nothing is said in such a conception of the sexual relation. Her lot is supposed to be that of 'lack', of 'atrophy' (of the sexual organ), and of 'envy of the penis' as the only sexual organ recognised as having value. She is therefore said to try, by all possible means, to appropriate it for herself: by her slightly servile love of the father-husband who might give it to her; by her desire for a child-penis, preferably a boy; by access to cultural values still reserved by right for men alone and as a result always masculine, etc. So the woman is said to experience her desire only as a waiting until she can at last possess the equivalent of the masculine sexual organ.[64]

Following this account, in the conditional tense (the tense used to give an unproven version of facts, for example, of the prosecution case before the defendant has been proved guilty), Irigaray then goes on to describe what she sees as the reality of female sexuality; that is, when it is not seen purely in terms of that of men. She makes women's auto-erotic pleasure into a standard, in relation to which that of men, who require 'an instrument to feel themselves with', is seen as inferior:

> The woman, for her part, feels herself by herself and in herself without needing any mediation, and before any possible splitting up between activity and passivity. The woman 'feels herself' all the time, without anyone being able to forbid her, moreover; for her sexual organ is made up of two lips which continually kiss. Thus within herself, she is already two – but not divisible into one(s) – which stimulate each other.[65]

This leads Irigaray to the view that women's bodies are erotically sufficient unto themselves. However, because she gives this a positive value, her view of heterosexual intercourse is a striking contrast to that of Montrelay. She sees it as a brutal interruption of this auto-erotic pleasure:

> The suspension of this auto-eroticism is carried out in a violent breaking and entering: the brutal parting of these two lips by a penis rapist. This takes the woman away, leads her astray from

63 ibid.
64 ibid.
65 ibid, p 24.

her 'auto-stimulation', which she needs if she is not to incur the disappearance of her pleasure in the sexual relation.[66]

In a culture based on heterosexuality and phallomorhism,[67] she continues:

> The *one* of form, of the individual, of the sexual organ, of the proper noun, of specific meaning...supplants, by parting and dividing, this touching of *at least two* (lips) which keep the woman in contact with herself, but without any possibility of distinction between that which touches itself.
>
> This is behind the mystery that she represents in a culture which claims to enumerate everything, to number everything by units, to make an inventory of everything by individualities. *She is neither one nor two.*[68]

Women's sexuality, says Irigaray, 'always at least double, is also *plural*'.[69]

> Well, *the woman has sexual organs just about everywhere*. She feels pleasure just about everywhere. Without even mentioning the hysterisation of her whole body, the geography of her pleasure is much more diversified, multiple in its differences, complex, subtle, than is imagined...in an imaginary which is a little too centred around Sameness.[70]

The result of this plural sexuality, says Irigaray, is that women's relation to desire and language is 'multiple'. According to Lacanian theory, the speaking subject is always split from the Other – the infinite chain of meaning – but nevertheless is a unified, single moment of identification, speaking from one place. It cannot be plural in the Lacanian orthodoxy. Irigaray accepts this as far as the masculine subject is concerned, because, following Lacan, she sees men's desire as organised in terms of unity, the unity of a relation to the phallus. This means, she says, that when men speak (or write), it is as unified subjects from a single position, produced by the unidirectional movement of their phallic desire, and the words they utter have a fixed meaning insofar as they are uttered from a single place, a single subject position. However, for Irigaray, women's sexuality is not purely phallic. Indeed it is only phallic at all by imposition. In itself it is multiple and, therefore, she says, women's relation to meaning

66 ibid.
67 ibid, p 26.
68 ibid.
69 ibid, p 27.
70 ibid, p 28.

is also multiple. Instead of seeing this as producing non-sense, 'the ruin of representation', as Montrelay might have done, she proceeds to the view that women's relation to the symbolic – to language – is simply different from that of men; and possibly better.

In what she says too – at least, when she dares – the woman keeps feeling herself all the time. She just barely draws back from herself, from a babble, from an exclamation, from a half-confidence, from a phrase left hanging... When she comes back to it, it's to set off again from another direction. From another point of pleasure or pain. This should be listened to with another ear, as *an 'other meaning' always in the process of weaving itself, of kissing itself with words, but also of shedding them, so as not to become fixed, frozen in them.*[71]

Women's relation to the Other, according to Irigaray, is different from that of men because 'the other is already within her and is auto-erotically familiar to her'.[72] This must be a rather different other from Lacan's Other, which arises as a result of the loss of the 'anatomical complement' and is a fantasised Other, constructed out of the subject's constitution in relation to fundamental lack. Lacan's Other is by definition that which the subject is cut off from, and to that extent it must be separate. In contrast, Irigaray's other seems to be a sort of genital version of the 'anatomical complement'. She seems to view the rubbing together of the labia as sufficient to fill the lack produced at birth, so that, instead of splitting into subject and Other, the woman subject is formed as a plurality, whose fluid divisions are constantly shifting. However, although Irigaray asserts this to be the case, it is not really clear in her account how the physiological effects and Symbolic meanings of the sexual organs interact, be they plural (labia) or single (penis), because although she uses Lacanian theory, her usage differs from that of Lacan in ways which she does not clarify.

The effect of women's plurality is, she says, to undermine the bases of phallocentric culture, with its constructions of identity around property:

Ownership, property, are doubtless quite foreign to the feminine. Sexually, at least. But not *closeness*. Such closeness that any distinguishing of identity within it becomes impossible. And therefore any form of property. The woman takes pleasure in one *so close that she can neither have [this other] nor have herself.* She constantly

71 ibid.
72 ibid, p 30.

exchanges herself with herself, with no possible identification of one or the other.[73]

This fluidity and lack of appropriation, which is essential to women's nature, is, in Irigaray's description, suppressed and denied by 'masculine discourse'.[74] Masculine discourse is the dominant, indeed the only, form of discourse now available, she says. In this discourse, 'the dimension of desire, of pleasure, is untranslatable, unrepresentable, it cannot be brought into the 'seriousness' – the appropriateness, the univocity, the truth...of a discourse which claims to speak the meaning of it... *to tell the truth is to forbid woman's 'jouissance', and therefore the relation between the sexes'.*[75]

Irigaray suggests that work should be done on language 'to return the masculine to its own language, making possible an other language',[76] and she stresses that this work has political implications; it would be part of the political struggle of women for equality in difference, as fundamentally different beings from men. However, in the current state of relations between the sexes, Irigaray sees no possibility for women to explore their sexuality, or their language. For the only place she sees patriarchal culture as offering us is one of identification with/as the merchandise exchanged between men. If women occupy this place, she says, they are then subordinated to men's judgements and fantasies and placed in competition with other women, forced to vie for status as commodities and thereby perpetuating the status quo. To her, the solution to the problem of women's oppression lies in the development of (sexual) relationships between women, in which it would be possible for them to escape the constraints placed upon them by the need to conform to masculine desire. *'And what if the 'commodities' refused to go to 'market'?* Maintaining an 'other' trade between themselves?'[77]

Irigaray does not try to say exactly how women's plural sexuality would manifest itself, or what the 'other' language would be, for they are suppressed at present, and the utopia she describes as yet out of reach. She gives no examples of this 'feminine' language in other women's work, although she indicates that she tries as far as possible to use it herself, and describes how a woman can bring femininity into language in the following passage, quoted by Marini in relation to the work of Duras:

73   ibid. I have translated *le propre* as 'ownership' and *le proche* as' closeness here. *Un si proche* – 'one so close', is gendered masculine in French. However, later Irigaray writes, *sans identification possible de l'un(e) ou l'autre*, so I have tried to keep the gender open in English.
74   ibid, p 138.
75   ibid, p 158.
76   ibid, p 77.
77   ibid, p 193.

Well...She should turn every meaning upside down, inside out, round and round. *Radically convulse it,* bring to it, bring back to it, the attacks suffered by her 'body' in its incapacity to say what moves it. She should also deliberately insist on these *blanks* in the discourse which evoke the places where she has been excluded, spaces which ensure, with their *silent plasticity,* the cohesion, the articulation, the coherent expansion of established forms. Rewrite them *as gaps,* otherwise and elsewhere than where they are expected, in *ellipses* and *eclipses* which deconstruct the logical grids of the reader-writer, make her/his reason go off the rails, disturb her/his sight until the very least result is incurable double vision...[78]

Irigaray's own style tends to be expansive, allusive and metaphorical. It is full of puns and words, or parts of words, in brackets, she often proceeds by asking questions, although equally often she answers these with assertions, and her theoretical expositions often take the place of a dialogue with the texts of another writer – Freud, for example, in *Speculum* – or with questioners, or a second-person singular addressee, as in *Ce sexe qui n'en est pas un.* She does what she can to put her theories into practice, to undermine the unities of phallocentrism; and she calls on others to do the same:

It is better to speak only in double-meanings, allusions, inuendos, parables...Even if they ask you for a few explanations. If they tell you that they don't understand at all. No one has ever understood anyway. So why not redouble the misunderstandings to the point of exasperation? To the point where ear grows used to an other music, where the voice begins to sing...[79]

This, says Irigaray, and with her Marini and many others, is how to let the multiplicity of the feminine speak.

78 Irigaray, *Speculum*, Paris, Editions de Minuit, 1974, pp 176–7.
79 ibid, p 178.

CHAPTER 3
Femaleness, Femininity and Feminism

THE FEMININE AND THE FEMALE

Irigaray's femininity might be a multi-faceted, fluid sexuality and relation to meaning, but in one respect it is fixed for it is, like Montrelay's feminine *jouissance*, tied to anatomy. Irigaray states this to be the case, however, her vaguely sketched, neo-Lacanian version of why it should be so does not make sense in terms of the Lacanian theory she apparently thinks 'speaks the truth' about current relations between the sexes; for she reworks Lacan's concept of the Other into something quite different, gives genital sensation a simple one-to-one correspondence to the woman's relation to meaning, and seems to eschew any understanding of the workings of desire, or whether or not women should be considered as conscious subjects in the Lacanian sense, separated from unconscious meanings. Irigaray does not seem to feel the need to go into any explanatory detail on these or any other points. She asserts that her account is correct, with her own womanhood as implicit ultimate guarantor of the truth of what she says (although explicitly, she says truth has no part to play in feminine language). She writes vehemently, sometimes wittily, but beyond the strength of personality that comes through her writing, she offers no solid reasons why anyone should believe what she says.

Following Irigaray's lead, Hélène Cixous, another influential writer on femininity in language, also makes femininity a result of being female. Cixous is probably more interested in the literary applications and implications of psychoanalytic theory than in the precise formulations of the theory itself. Nevertheless, in an interview for the journal *Sub-stance*, she states her viewpoint quite categorically: 'It is beyond doubt that femininity derives from the body, from the anatomical, the biological difference, from a whole system

of drives which are radically different for women than for men.'[1]
However, this leads Cixous into deep water when she says a little
later on: 'The fact that bisexuality subsists in a certain number of
individuals implies the presence of femininity in men, femininity
which is always massively repressed. What it means to be a man,
'being-a-man', consists first of all in eradicating femininity.'[2] There
seems to be some contradiction here. Possibly Cixous and her sym-
pathisers would argue that, as no one is ever totally either male or
female in the anatomical sense, it is the residual anatomical femininity in men which leaves traces of psychic femininity. Some might
want to argue that the femininity to be found in men is hormonal,
although no mention of hormonal effects is to be found in any of the
Lacanian work on femininity, the emphasis being always on anatomical features. But, if one accepts that it is residual anatomical
femininity in men that produces psychic femininity, such a position
begs all sorts of questions: for example, what sort of drives would
make up the hidden femininity in men? They could not be associated
with the vaginal sensations which Montrelay, Irigaray, and before
them Horney and Jones regard as essential to femininity, and why
should there be a need to repress them? Cixous does not address
such questions, and as it stands, her theoretical edifice looks rather
shaky.

Elsewhere, Cixous's position leads her into the dangerous territory
of generalisation, when she discusses women's speech.

In some ways, feminine writing constantly resounds with the
tearing that using words orally is for women – 'using' which is
more like tearing, dizzy leaping, hurling oneself forward, diving.
Listen to a woman speak in a meeting (if she hasn't painfully lost
her breath); she doesn't 'speak', she launches her trembling body
into the air, she lets herself go, she flies, the whole of her goes into
her voice, she upholds the 'logic' of her speech with her living body;
her flesh speaks truly. She exposes herself. To tell the truth, she
materializes her thought in flesh, she signifies it with her body. She
inscribes what she says, because she does not refuse the drive its
undisciplined and passionate participation in speech. Her speech,
even if it's 'theoretical', or political, is never simple or linear, or
'objective', generalized, she brings her own history into history.[3]

1 Interview with Hélène Cixous, conducted by Christine Makward, translated by Ann Liddle
  and Beatrice Cameron, *Sub-stance*, Madison, University of Wisconsin Press, no 13, 1976,
  p 20.
2 ibid, p 22.
3 Cixous, *La Jeune Née*, pp 170–1.

Notwithstanding the vivid and almost lyrical nature of this description, and its reiteration of commonplaces about women's speech, such as the placing of the word 'logic' in inverted commas and the idea that the 'truth' of a woman is in her body, never mind what or how she speaks, I do feel that Cixous has got a little carried away here, in what seems a rather sweeping generalisation. The more so when she goes on:

> Every woman has experienced the torment of starting to speak, her heart beating fit to burst, sometimes collapsing, losing her tongue, the ground and language slipping away, because for the woman speaking – I would even go so far as to say: opening her mouth – in public is such recklessness, such a transgression.[4]

But is this really every woman's experience? The names of powerful women speakers spring instantly to mind. And are there no men who feel anxious about public speaking? Possibly men are assumed to be less nervous and are therefore less often questioned on the matter, but I have met plenty of men who have exhibited symptoms of the kind of feelings Cixous describes here. Various sociolinguists have carried out research which indicates that women do tend to speak differently from men, using different vocabulary or pitch, and Spender's research has shown that men tend to dominate discussions in mixed groups. Cixous says that 'there is something in women's libidinal organization which doesn't like this kind of discourse'[5] but I think it is a little rash to assume that the effect she describes, when it occurs in women, is a manifestation of women's libidinal organisation, without first investigating other possibilities. It is true that most public speakers (with notable exceptions) tend to be men: perhaps lack of experience is a factor in many women's anxiety. It is also true that many men are somewhat dismissive or even hostile when asked to listen to what women have to say. Women are familiar with this, consciously or unconsciously, and speaking to an unreceptive audience can be an intimidating business. However, Cixous does not stop to dwell on such possibilities, and follows the Irigarayan tradition of assertion rather than argument.

In contrast to Irigaray or Cixous, Montrelay approaches femininity through a more traditional theoretical exposition. She fixes her version of femininity to female anatomy by tying Real feminine *jouissance* to concentric oral-anal-vaginal drives, whose unrepresentable nature is, she says, established in early infancy, and is a feature of women's psychic processes in general. However, although

---

4 ibid, p 171.
5 ibid, p 269.

she takes pains to explain how and why this comes about, her account raises certain problems which, left unaddressed, threaten to undermine it.

The oral-anal dimension is of course present in men as well as women; but, according to Montrelay, it does not produce the same effects. This, she says, is because women's vaginal drives are not repressed in the way that other drives are. But, on closer inspection, her reasons for saying this seem rather unsatisfactory.

The first is that 'the girl is less subject than the boy to the threats and defences which punish masturbation'.[6] Montrelay does not make clear whether she is here referring to clitoral or vaginal masturbation, but since the clitoral is equated with the phallic in psychoanalytical terms, she must be referring to some form of vaginal masturbation, otherwise it would surely be irrelevant to a discussion of 'feminine drives'. Montrelay goes on to say that this comparative freedom enjoyed by little girls means that 'the girl, the woman, can experience a protected sexuality'.[7] Presumably what she means by this is that the little girl's (or woman's) vaginal sensations go unnoticed and unrepresented by adults, and therefore can be enjoyed without prohibition, or threat of interruption.

This may be true in individual cases, particularly if Montrelay is talking about the kind of invisible pleasure Irigaray describes of 'two lips touching'. But, if what is in question is masturbation in the sense of manipulation, then this is an observable activity and there seems no reason why Montrelay should assert that little girls are less subject to threats against it than little boys. The touching of one's genitals is generally taboo in Western culture, for persons of both sexes (in other cultures, where clitoridectomy and infibulation are practised, the idea of a 'protected' female sexuality seems even more difficult to sustain. However, Montrelay is not explicitly making claims for the universality of the effects she discusses). In this context she does mention 'the rape, the penetration anxiety' which 'is evoked' as figuring in the fantasy life of little girls, but dismisses them with 'in reality...the girl runs few risks'.[8] However, I would suggest that any threats of castration made to the little boy, or, more importantly, his own fantasies and fears, bear no closer relation to reality than those of the little girl. The little boy's fears are – certainly in the Lacanian theory which Montrelay uses – symbolically motivated through the institution of the Law of the Father and are not a response to actual threats. For the phallus which is missing in the

6 Montrelay, op cit, p 67.
7 ibid.
8 ibid, p 68.

Imaginary of the Lacanian subject is not that of the little boy in the equation penis-phallus. Rather it is the symbol representing the condition of desire, the mother's lack which the child cannot fill. This relation to the mother's desire and the phallus is, in Lacanian terms, that of children of both sexes and, whilst Lacan himself says that the phallus is 'because of its turgidity, the image of the flux of life as it is manifested in generation'[9] his theory nevertheless makes of it a (repressed) signifier of *jouissance*, extrapolated out of the relation between mother's desire, father and child. It is not the image of a particular penis which may or may not be threatened with removal.

Montrelay also describes how the little boy's anatomy exposes him 'very early to understanding that he is not master of either the manifestation of his desire, or the extent of his pleasures';[10] but is the little girl's experience different? The possibility that little girls might also find that their genital organs fail to work exactly as and when they would wish does not seem ever to be discussed in this context, although they are doubtless as much subject to the vaguaries of unconscious processes as their penile counterparts and such experience of lack of control would surely apply to either sex. Montrelay simply states that the feminine drives are excluded from the Lacanian economy of need, demand, desire and lack, since they operate on a different, concentric circuit. However, there seems no reason why the 'feminine drives' should automatically be any more concentric and closed than any others. They would surely be as subject to lack of satisfaction as any other, given that the vagina is not constantly being filled, as is its aim according to this view. Montrelay's very description of this 'organ-hole' as 'insatiable' implies a lack of satisfaction. And where there is a lack of satisfaction, one would expect desire, and some form of representation, to be produced.

In fact, Montrelay does acknowledge the existence of unconscious or conscious representations in relation to the vaginal drives and indeed, as I have cited above she mentions them briefly, but explicity, in the form of rape and penetration fantasies. Such fantasies must involve representations of the vagina, or of vaginal drives, but Montrelay does not seem to have noticed this contradiction to her theory.

Another hiccup in Montrelay's account of femininity arises when, like Cixous, she mentions that there is a form of femininity in men. In a footnote to *L'Ombre et le Nom* she says:

> One must avoid establishing a sharp distinction between the sexuality of the man and that of the woman. Without re-posing

9 Lacan, *Ecrits II*, p 111.
10 Montrelay, op cit, p 68.

the whole problem of bisexuality here, we will simply note that every masculine subject is invested as the object and product of his mother: he was 'part' of the maternal body. *A propos* of the masculine body and unconscious investment, one could also speak of 'femininity' implicated in maternal femininity.[11]

Unfortunately, since she does not go into the 'problem of bisexuality', it is not very clear how she integrates it into her theory. In an analysis of Freud's 'Wolf Man' case, which she gives in *L'Ombre et le Nom*, she seems to use the term 'femininity' in the sense of a merging with the Other, available to subjects of either sex. It is the effect of 'too much sense' that occurs when the separation between subject and Other is broken down in the order of the Symbolic. The separated (phallic) subject is re-established when an 'offspring' is produced – word, orgasm, dream, symptom – that soaks up the too much sense and releases the subject from the meaninglessness of femininity. Elsewhere Montrelay says the that the father makes a phallus out of the daughter's 'feminine substance, with which [he] identifies'.[12] So her view of femininity in men would appear to be analogous to the Symbolic identification of women with the maternal (phallus) and the resulting disappearance of the phallic subject. However, if this is the case, it is hard to see in what sense such an effect can be regarded as specific to women – or indeed, why it should be gendered feminine.

Overall, the view that femininity is attached to femaleness via self-sufficient, feminine drives seems fraught with contradictions – when it is not simply forcefully asserted. Both Freud and Lacan reject the idea of a specific, anatomical femininity, and their theories cannot simply be beaten into shape to accommodate the existence of something they expressly deny. If women (or men) want to elaborate a theory or theories of a feminine sexuality with its own drives and organisation of those drives, it will be necessary to start from that assumption and build a new theoretical framework, rather than simply trying to change the foundations of the old one whilst leaving the superstructure intact. However, there are other explanations that link a specific psychic makeup – femininity – to being a woman, without making them the result of anatomy – via identification with the mOther for example, which Montrelay and Irigaray also discuss, but do not seem to think enough by itself.

Eugénie Lemoine-Luccioni, another Lacanian analyst, tries to do establish a version of psychic processes specific to women, which are nevertheless not fixed anatomically, in her book *Partage des femmes*.

11 ibid, p 80, n 27.
12 ibid, p 143.

Lemoine-Luccioni takes the Lacanian view of the penis as providing an Imaginary representative of the phallus. However, unlike Lacan, she deduces from this that women lack a Symbolic representation of loss. Like Montrelay, she says that men can take the penis as the representation, on their own bodies, of the missing phallus, for the penis is a visible and separate organ which could be removed. But 'the woman, on the other hand, lacks nothing, at least in the sense that no organ can fail her, unless through a symptomatic surgical operation.'[13] Of course, penises do not just fall off of their own accord either, but I assume that Lemoine-Luccioni is here referring to the external visibility of the penis and to Freud's oft-used view that the little boy's fear of castration is fed by his inability to produce erections at will. Lemoine-Luccioni concludes that the phallus as symbol of impossible *jouissance* does not take up its place as prime signifier in the unconscious of women. The effect of this, she says, is that: 'Rather than castration anxiety, the woman thus experiences *partition* anxiety. She really lives under the sign of abandonment: mother, father, children, husband, penis, everyone leaves her.'[14]

Lemoine-Luccioni uses the word *partition*, which can be translated as 'division', 'partition', or 'splitting', but also has the sense of 'share', or 'lot', to describe what she sees as a division inherent in women's sexuality. 'Woman participates in creation; and it is this that makes her split, since she is also a creature. Herein lies her lot and her suffering; that which comes back to her as her lot and divides her.'[15] Like Montrelay, Lemoine-Luccioni sees women existing in an 'order of the double':

> She has two sexual organs, dissimilar, it is true: the vagina and the clitoris; she is of the same sex as the parent who gives birth to her. This *double* order, this order of the double, becomes more clearly double as a result of pregnancy and childbirth; the woman who becomes a mother is not one, but two. From the point of view of the woman, it is she who becomes double and splits in two; not the father.[16]

Her view is that, instead of Symbolic castration, it is Imaginary 'partition' that structures women's psyches: 'the woman lives with the fear of losing a part of herself'[17] but, 'the loss of a part of herself should not be assimilated in women to the man's fear of losing the

---

13 Eugénie Lemoine-Luccioni, *Partage des femmes*, Paris, Le Seuil, 1976, p 70.
14 ibid, p 71.
15 ibid, p 8.
16 ibid, p 80.
17 ibid, p 81.

penis'.[18] Instead, it is 'a phenomenon of imaginary partition...a specifically feminine psychic order'.[19]

Not only does Lemoine-Luccioni see women's relation to castration as different from that of men, as Lacan does, but the position she has developed is that women lack a castration complex altogether, and therefore lack the basis of entry into the Symbolic. Here, of course, she runs up against empirical observation: 'However, [the woman] talks and she stands upright'[20]. So the theoretical problem for Lemoine-Luccioni then becomes, 'how does she pass from Imaginary partition to the Symbolic castration which controls entry into language?'[21] This passage, she says, is brought about by a process of identification.

> In order for there to be a symbolic chain, there must be a lack, which gives rise to demand. For the woman there certainly is a real loss or a casting off of something which she experiences in the imaginary as a part of herself; that is to say, of herself as *one*. So her demand is to be given back to herself. When she comes to make love, the detumescence and withdrawal of the penis quite naturally represent and sum up (while waiting for the future birth) all these losses. They mark them retroactively with the sign of sex. Still, in the sexual act, the part from which the woman is separated and which does no more than overlay a loss which is always more ancient, has – let us repeat it – never been part of her. So she moves from the real loss of an imaginary half of herself to the imaginary loss of an organ which becomes superimposed on these lost parts.[22]

After this 'natural' assimilation of the withdrawal of the penis as the archetype of all other losses has produced Imaginary castration, says Lemoine-Luccioni, it then becomes Symbolic castration when 'it is grafted on to the symbolic partition which has already come into being'.[23] Before this happens, she implies, the woman (or girl) has no relation to castration.

Following her account, partition arises in the order of the Symbolic as a result of the desire of the mother for the Other. The interchange of looks between mother and daughter potentially makes it possible for the latter to identify herself totally with her Imaginary image, in a narcissistic relation to her ideal ego. If this happens,

18 ibid.
19 ibid.
20 ibid, p 70.
21 ibid, p 100.
22 ibid, p 82.
23 ibid, p 100.

says Lemoine-Luccioni, the daughter 'merges with this figure that is full and has no cracks, no holes and which preserves and is preserved by parental power'[24] and 'all that is left are reflections of the Same, and a hole in the palce of the subject, as of the object'.[25] If this happens, then, the daughter still lacks lack, and so has no basis on which to form herself as a subject of desire.

However, Lemoine-Luccioni sees a way out of the impasse; 'if, on the other hand, the Mother's Other has the function of an interrupter, the girl loses a deceptive image, but rediscovers her desire. It is to the Father that she now displays herself... Now she offers herself as an (*o*) object and incites the Other's response, avoiding alienating identification.'[26]

Thus Lemoine-Luccioni describes women's accession to the order of the Symbolic via the gap left in her narcissism by her mother's desire for the Other. There is then room for her to establish herself in a different position in relation to her father. But the effect of this process, continues Lemoine-Luccioni, is to place the woman in a dependent relation to the father, or to the male lover who comes to take his place.

> Deprived of an exterior love object, the woman wanders 'like a soul in torment' and in fact turns back to her father: the only man who has loved her, or whom she has been able to love. It is in him that she finds her ideal, that is to say, the unity that she lacks, since she is split. And when she loves another man, she loves him as she loved her father. She makes a Father out of him; a Father-mother in actual fact. She wants him to desire her and to give her life. She expects everything from him...This is because she is entirely suspended on the desire of the Other, as long as she has not discovered her own desire. And there is no other way for her to discover her desire than via the desire of the Other.[27]

The effect of this relation of dependency is, according to Lemoine-Luccioni, to make women appear as the origin of the (presumably male) subject's desire. For, by placing herself in the position of object of desire, she invites and stimulates that desire. At the same time, her own position as subject – and Lemoine-Luccioni makes her a purely narcissistic subject – is very tenuous and threatened with dissolution.

> She becomes spontaneously alienated following the mode of coupling of master and slave. She has always been placed within

24 ibid, p 85.
25 ibid, p 87.
26 ibid.
27 ibid, pp 88–9.

an alternative: life or death. It is the Lacanian *vel*; either she settles into the death of Narcissus; or she gets recognition for herself from the Other and loses herself as a subject, because she identifies with the desire of the Other.[28]

For Lemoine-Luccioni, women's position within the symbolic order is thus unstable, as it is for Montrelay, Irigaray or Cixous. However, Lemoine-Luccioni is careful not to pin this to 'vaginal drives', or the rubbing together of labia; indeed she is very critical of Irigaray. Instead, she stresses the importance of the processing through language of anatomical difference:

So the man and the woman are provided with different sexual organs; and they are certainly anatomically different, although genetics is far from categorical on this point; and nature, with its variations, even less categorical. But the essential thing is to show that these differences are taken up, or re-taken up, on the level of language, and this with the sole aim of maintaining the difference between the sexes. Freud is far more revolutionary than Luce Irigaray, despite appearances, when he posits fundamental bisexuality and significatory differenciation.[29]

Nevertheless, she derives her view from women's role in reproduction, where the baby moves from being 'part of' the woman to something separate and also from women's capacity for identification with the mother. Her femininity is not a direct result of anatomical features but like Lacan's, it rests heavily on the universalising role of vision and Imaginary identification.

It also leaves me with several unanswered questions. For example, Lemoine-Luccioni lays great stress on the role of heterosexual intercourse in the constitution of the woman as a subject in relation to castration. But what does this mean about the woman's gender identity before she has sexual intercourse with a man? Or if she never does, is a lesbian, or simply celibate all her life? Moreover, an explanation is needed of how the woman articulates her demand 'to be given back to herself' if she is not already constituted somehow in the Symbolic. Clearly, if one takes Symbolic castration as the necessary condition for entry into the Symbolic order, one must assume that the little girl develops a relation to Symbolic castration when she starts to speak. It is also unclear to me why the sense of loss 'of a part of herself', which Lemoine-Luccioni calls 'partition' and describes as overlaid by Imaginary castration, differs from Lacan's view of lack of the 'anatomical complement', on to which subsequent

28 ibid, p 90.
29 ibid, p 65.

fantasised lacks are grafted. For they seem fundamentally identical, both constituting a subject in relation to lack.

Overall, then, I think there are theoretical problems with all the accounts of femininity I have discussed here. All use Lacanian terminology and implicitly or explicitly refer to Lacanian theory, without adequately explaining how their use differs from that of Lacan. All make reference to the 'doubling' of mother and daughter, stressing the relationship of fascination established between mother and daughter, who mirror each other, but all seem to ignore the role of the mother's desire as instituting the castration complex *'in both sexes'*. All place great emphasis on women's self-sufficiency and auto-eroticism, and describe the woman as being in some sense her own other, but ignore the loss of the 'anatomical complement', out of which Lacan's Other is formed. Nevertheless, in themselves, I think both Freudian and Lacanian theory point to an understanding of both self-sufficiency and duality in the sexuality of women, without fixing these in a biologically set 'nature', nor making them inevitable results of finding oneself anatomically female.

Freud describes three possible ways forward for the little girl upon the discovery of her 'castration': rejection of sexuality, 'normal' femininity (acceptance of castration) and disavowal. It is evident from Freud's case histories that any individual takes up different positions in relation to different wishes at different times, indeed, different wishes clash within the same individual at the same moment: of such things are symptoms made. So it seems hardly likely that the girl or woman would adopt any of the three paths exclusively. Freud points to this himself:

> Bearing in mind the early history of femininity, I will emphasize the fact that its development remains open to disturbance from traces left behind by the previous masculine period. Regressions to fixations at these pre-oedipal phases occur very often; in many women we actually find a repeated alternation of periods in which either masculinity or femininity has obtained the upper hand. What we men call 'the enigma of woman' is probably based in part upon these signs of bi-sexuality in female life.[30]

In Freud's account women are more likely to take the path of identification with the position of the paradigmatic mother, which he calls 'normal femininity', although not all do. However, the little girl does not usually reject her old phallic position completely, and I would suggest that this might lead to a duality, or more probably

30   Freud, 'The Psychology of Women', p 168.

a confusion, possibly a loss of any coherent position ('a hole', 'emptiness').

Lacanian theory makes inherent duality in the sexuality of both sexes seem inevitable. For Lacan, desire is a phallic process, an active desiring in relation to the (missing) phallus. His theory makes the active subject of desire at the same time the fantasised object of the Other, represented by the 'o object' ('I watch myself watching myself' for example). Desire goes out to the object and returns to the subject, making the subject object of a fantasised desire of the Other. This boomerang movement of desire produces a partial identification with the 'o object' for the subject is striving after the impossible *jouissance*, of merging with the Other, in whose place the 'o object' stands.

Once sexual difference has been established, the subject must always identify her/himself as having a place within it, whatever other relations s/he may also identify within. In heterosexual relations as described by Lacan, the man takes woman as his object and thus identifies partially with her (the phallus/mother), whilst also identifying himself as a man (with the father), who desires a woman or women. This is the Lacanian version of bisexuality. Irigaray poses it as the fundamental (male) homosexuality underlying patriarchal culture, where-the only way in which the man can have his father as his object is to identify with/as him in his desire for women (the mother).

> Reigning everywhere, but forbidden in practice, *l'hom(m)o-sexualité* plays itself out through the bodies of women, be it in their materiality or as signs, and until now heterosexuality has been nothing but an alibi for the smooth running of the relation of man to himself, of relations between men.[31]

Be that as it may, for Lacan the role of the male (masculine) subject in heterosexual relations is in harmony with the process of subjectification itself, which is active and phallic. For the paradigmatic woman, however, the situation appears more complex; in terms of this theory, she is in the position of identifying as object of desire, as phallus, for the man. Lacan takes a provocatively simplistic view of this, saying she is thus not able to be an active phallic subject of desire and hence 'does not exist'. This seems to me to be a rather crude dismissal of the complexities of the position of the woman-subject. The woman-subject cannot simply be conflated with ~~Woman~~ (*La femme*), whose position is that of the castrated and of

---

31 Irigaray, *Ce Sexe Qui n'en est pas Un* p 168. *L'hom(m)o-sexualité* is a pun on *l'homosexualité* – 'homosexuality – and *l'homme* – 'man'.

being the phallus, the object as opposed to the subject of desire. This position is an abstraction, a point in Lacan's schema of the construction of positions in relation to sexual difference, but as a description of actual women's pscyhes it is hardly adequate, even if one accepts Lacan's highly schematic description of heterosexual relations. Things are always more complicated.

My own view is that in cultural terms, any woman is almost inevitably seen both by herself and by others in terms of the feminine position as object of desire for men. We might accept it or reject it, but it does not go away. However, this means that in terms of heterosexual relations, the woman also partially identifies with the masculine source of the desire of which she is object: her narcissism passes via a fantasised or actual masculine desire for her. Furthermore, desire is phallic in Lacanian terms, it arises from a relation to the mother as Other. That process constitutes the woman as phallic subject at the same time as she identifies herself as phallus/mother/object. If to this duality is added the position of woman as phallic subject in relation to a man object of her desire (a phenomenon Lacan did not seem to think possible), things become more complicated still, even in the most schematic of scenarios. Life itself is never so simple.

The Lacanian boomerang of desire and exchange of identification might also provide a way of accounting for Irigaray's view of the fluidity of relations between women, without making it a theoretically dubious effect of labial touching. For one might argue that in the case of homosexual relations between women, each woman's identification as subject and object of desire could be more fluid than those established within a heterosexual relation, since the assignation of positions in terms of those already culturally established for the different sexes might weigh less heavily on the protagonists. Of course, even Lacan slips in the idea that the division between the sexual ranks may not be so sharply drawn as all that: 'you stand there by choice', but whatever you choose, it does make a difference how others choose to see you too. So possibly Irigaray's description of the fluidity of women's sexuality in isolation from men, the blurring of difference and the similarity and identification of women lovers with each other described in the section *Quand nos lèvres se parlent* in *Ce sexe qui n'en est pas un* might result from the comparative freedom of members of the same sex to define themselves in relation to each other. In passing, though, it should be said that Irigaray's vision of fluidity might not appeal to all women, bearing in mind the long-standing lesbian tradition of division into 'butch' and 'femme', which sets up a symbolic 'sexual' differenciation. For, as human beings have always known, without a degree of separation and difference there is no desire. However, Irigaray's concerns appear to lie elsewhere than with the maintenance of the conditions of desire.

To sum up, for both Freud and Lacan, 'femininity' and 'masculinity' are symbolic positions in the context of theories which see all psychic phenomena as in a certain way secondary, as indirectly related to the underlying event or trauma, but subjected to the primary processes in their very constitution as psychic phenomena. The libido is described as masculine, not because it is 'male', but because both Freudian and Lacanian theory see desire as caught up in the relation to the phallus for both women and men. And the phallus is *not* the penis. 'Phallic' sexuality concerns a relation to a symbol – Jane Gallop calls it 'the general relation of subject to signifier';[32] it is not the result of energy-flow through a specific organ. Furthermore, the relation to the symbol which constitutes the desiring subject is not immutable as even Lacan's theory gives scope for variation from individual to individual, 'by choice'.

This dimension of individual variation should never be overlooked, as Lemoine-Luccioni points out when she says, 'Anyway, what interests the analyst is the "subjective declaration of belonging to a sex"'.[33] In accordance with this, her own theoretical standpoint in *Partage des femmes* is built up using case histories, although her project appears to be to describe the psychic workings of Woman. This use of case histories is very important; for it means not only that one can extrapolate generalisations from the individual stories, but also that their ever-unfolding differences tend to undermine fixed accounts of what the unconscious produces, since they show such variations of detail.

Furthermore, they represent the stories of a particular group of women, i.e. those who have chosen to go into analysis. This does not set them in opposition to 'normal' people (although it probably means they are richer than the majority), but it does mean that laws of psychic functioning extrapolated from this particular group might be unreliable when generalised. Of course this point has been made many times before in relation to psychoanalysis; it has been said, for example, that Freud's theories of psychic development are not generally applicable and merely reflect his observations of rich, hysterical, Viennese women at the turn of the century who were, like him, obsessed with sex. There is probably some truth in this view; after all, everyone is to some extent a product of her/his context. Of course, to suppose that Freud's views were coloured by his own and his patients' preoccupations, does not in itself undermine his theory

32 Jane Gallop, *Feminism and Psychoanalysis*, London, Macmillan, 1982, pp 19–20.
33 Lemoine-Luccioni, op cit, p 65.

of how unconscious processes produce meanings, but it might, however, have some effect on what, or how universal, those meanings are assumed to be.

I would level an analogous criticism at many accounts of the psychic processes of Woman. For example, Lemoine-Luccioni develops her theory of 'partition' using analyses of women going through pregnancy and childbirth, and what she says might indeed be relevant to many women's experience of that process. But should we therefore assume that Imaginary and Symbolic 'partition' and dependency on the desire of a man rule every woman's psychic life? Or again, in the case of Montrelay, who describes how, over and over again, she finds a lack of repression of anal-oral-vaginal drives in her woman analysands. Clearly she hears something in these women's speech which leads her to the conclusions she draws. Perhaps such psychic organisation triggers something in Montrelay herself for, as Lemoine-Luccioni says, 'one only hears what one might say oneself, but which, without the other, would remain unsaid'.[34] But must we take such lack of repression as inevitable in all women's mental processes? There seems no reason to do so; equally, it may well be true of some women.

One might object here that there is a suprising degree of basic similarity in the accounts of femininity given by Irigaray, Montrelay and Lemoine-Luccioni, even if their theoretical understandings differ. Why resist the conclusion that women's sexuality really is dual, that we really are in some sense our own Others, that our relation to meaning and language really is fundamentally different from that of men, more fluid, more ambiguous?

My response to this is that it may well tend to be so. Perhaps, to quote another analyst, Béla Grunberger, these are '*tendencies* which exist in a sufficiently large number of people for me to say that they are characteristic of women (as opposed to men)'. Grunberger, on whose work Montrelay draws for her theories, is interested in narcissism as a formative factor in both men and women, and he is discussing women's narcissistic tendencies here. He goes on, 'these tendencies have their origin in women's unconscious, thus characterizing all women, *at least in our society*' (my italics).[35] For me, the the words in italics are very important. Although Grunberger is writing an account of psychic organisation specific to women, he limits his universalisation to a tendency, in our society. Women and

34 ibid, p 11.
35 Béla Grunberger, '*Outline for a Study of Narcissism in Female Sexuality*', in *Female Sexuality*, J Chasseguet-Smirgel Ed, Michigan, University of Michigan, 1970, reprinted London, Maresfield Library, 1985, p 78.

men occupy different positions in our society and to these correspond different psychic tendencies. Yet anything, he implies, is possible.

Grunberger's view is that mothers tend to give their sons a great deal of narcissistic confirmation, but that, because they cannot fulfill their oedipal desires, little boys tend to grow into men who 'despise their narcissistic needs'. Women, he says, tend to lack the same degree of narcissistic confirmation in infancy, and their desires in relation to the mother are always frustrated. This means, says Grunberger, that the little girl, and later the woman, *'attempts to give* [this narcissistic confirmation] *to herself, thereby becoming essentially narcissistic'.*[36] He suggests that this may lead to an identification with the phallus, but he sees such an identification as 'pathological', as opposed to Lacan, for whom such an identification represents the feminine position. At the same time as she becomes narcissistic, says Grunberger, the woman 'rejects her *component instincts'*,[37] she may have 'a feeling of narcissistic integrity (symbolized by the phallus)',[38] but her disparate drives may be badly incorporated into this narcissistic unity. Perhaps a lack of narcissistic integration might lie behind Montrelay's disturbing, unrepresentable femininity, or behind Irigaray's feminine plurality and fluidity.

Personally, I find Grunberger's work on narcissism very interesting, but I do not propose to discuss it in detail here, partly because it is irrelevant to the context of criticism of Duras, and partly because my expression of preference has brought me to the final point of this section, which is that ultimately, psychoanalysis does not offer a single, satisfactory account of femininity, or of masculinity for that matter. There are almost as many variations as there are analysts, and they are often mutually exclusive. Personally again, I am neither surprised nor sorry at this, but it does mean that, if one is to accept the validity of psychoanalysis at all, one must consciously or unconsciously choose which versions to uphold.

And to return now to the original orientation of this book, the choice of any strand of psychoanalysis as a tool for understanding human beings is also potentially a political choice, notably as regards sexual politics. My project here is to discuss Duras's writing in relation to the claims made by psychoanalytically-orientated feminists that it manifests 'femininity' in a psychoanalytic sense and that it is, therefore, feminist. I have tried thus far to point to some internal problems with the psychoanalytic theories these feminists have espoused. I now want to turn my discussion to look at the

36 ibid, p 73.
37 ibid, p 74.
38 ibid, p 77.

political aspects of their psychoanalytic choices, and at the more general relations of politics to psychoanalysis. In the process I hope also to explain my own choices of analytical tools, before going on to use them on Duras's texts.

PSYCHOANALYSIS AND POLITICS

Duras's work has generated much interest and enthusiasm amongst Lacanians and neo-Lacanians, and, as I have said above, a large proportion of criticism of her writings and films contains either implicit or explicit reference to lacanian theory.

> Le Ravissement de Lol V. Stein, in which Marguerite Duras shows she knows what I teach without me.[39]

> In one way Marguerite Duras's writing follows the course which Lacan has rightly called that of psychoanalytic method: when 'the subject takes up her/his own history as it is constituted in speech addressed to the other'[40]

> If *India Song* proposes to us a reading of psychoanalytic theory, it is insofar as the film, like the fantasy, is the *mise en scène* of desire.[41]

That Duras's work lends itself to a Lacanian or a Lacan-influenced reading is undeniable, as the critics quoted above, and many others, reveal. Duras herself seems to have a certain inclination towards the standpoint according to which her work is an exposition of Lacanian theory. For example, she says to Xavière Gauthier: 'And who brought Lol V. Stein out of her coffin? After all, it was a man, it was Lacan.'[42] thus implying that only Lacan *really* understood. Lacan's reciprocal view of Duras's understanding is revealed in the first quotation above. He pays tribute to Duras for her manifestation of his theory in all its truths and splendour, but in fictional form. This is also how Montrelay reads *Le Ravissement de Lol V. Stein* in the section she devotes to analysing the novel in *L'Ombre et le Nom*, and Elizabeth Lyon sees *India Song* as proposing 'a reading of psychoanalytic theory', where 'psychoanalytic' means 'Lacanian'. Her whole article is a description of how the film

39 Lacan, 'Homage à Marguerite Duras pour *Le Ravissement de Lol V. Stein*', in *Marguerite Duras*, Paris, Albatros, 1979, p 133.
40 Marini, op cit, p 157.
41 Elizabeth Lyon, 'The Cinema of Lol V. Stein' in *Camera Obscura*, no 6, Berkeley, Camera Obscura inc., Fall 1980, p 37.
42 Duras and Gauthier, op cit, p 161.

'take(s) up and interrogate(s), within the terms of a fantasmatic, the question of desire'.[43] Meanwhile, other, more explicitly feminist critics stay in the Lacanian vein, but, as I have indicated above, tend to see Duras's work as manifesting (particularly Irigarayan) femininity.

The overall effect is one of critical symbiosis: Duras's fictional works reinforce Lacanian theory by concretising its constructions, whilst the theory 'explains' and enhances the films and writings by giving them a little more credibility as having a relation of truth vis-a-vis the 'real world'. That the Lacanian and the Durassian can coexist so harmoniously is not a coincidence for there are similarities between them which I shall discuss later on, both in what they have to say and in the way in which they set up a position for the reader to adopt. That the enthusiasts of the one should also appreciate the other is therefore not particularly surprising. However, this symbiosis is not just a *folie à deux*, it represents a general approach to understanding human beings, and the possibilities for changing relations between them, particularly those between the sexes.

Those who see Duras's work as feminist because it opens the way for Irigarayan femininity to resound and speak have made certain choices about how to think about the kind of change that is possible in relations between the sexes, and how to bring it about. Irigaray takes Lacan's provocative account of women's identification with the phallus at face value,[44] sees this version of femininity as an attribute of women (confusing Symbolic with Imaginary?), and from there chooses to make being 'not-all-there' into a positive value, and to remonstrate with Lacan for his derogatory and ignorantly dismissive attitude to women's sexuality. She takes one identification (amongst many possible ones) and ties it to one sex, as an absolute definition of the present possibilities.

Montrelay and Lemoine-Luccioni are concerned with accounting for the workings of patriarchy and its concomitant forms of heterosexuality, and the feminist implications of their work lie in the fact that they have both written books whose main concern is women's sexuality – a kind of gynopsychoanalysis. Irigaray, however, is explicitly calling for a change in the structure of patriarchal society, in order that women might find a place as something other than commodities. Whereas Lacan, Montrelay and Lemoine-Luccioni, take the phallic, masculine subject as the standard and see heterosexuality as the means by which women reach this position, Irigaray makes a standard out of what she sees as the supressed and as yet

---

43 Lyon, op cit, p 37.
44 For an illuminating discussion of Lacan's provocativeness, see Gallop, op cit, Chapter 2.

unexplored sexuality of women. Her refusal to see the nature of women's sexuality as the problem makes her place relations between the sexes in a political context, seeing them as something which can be changed if women reject their role as objects of exchange between men, 'maintaining an "other" trade between themselves'. If this were to happen, then women would be able to be as they really are, speaking a different kind of language, no longer subordinated to men; or so she says.

It is no doubt because of its avowedly feminist perspective that Irigaray's work has appealed to those who want to develop theories of political change using psychoanalysis, whilst rejecting the latter's implicit or explicit masculinist bias. Irigaray powerfully states her feminism and any theoretical problems tend to be buried in the difficulty of her language, a difficulty which she upholds as a virtue, on the grounds that it is an attempt at the plurality and non-fixity of 'woman-speak'.

I have tried to indicate some of the internal theoretical problems with Irigaray's work in previous sections, but I also think her approach, and the approach of those who use her work, leads to a theoretical impasse for feminism, because it is anchored in the idea of essential female and male sexualities. The combination of this basic division and her feminism leads Irigaray to an implicit asser- tion that feminine sexuality and 'woman-speak' are in some way better than their masculine counterparts, certainly for women. Unity is bad, she implies, because it is phallic and for her the phallus refers to the penis, which women do not have, and the authority of the father, which is the cause of all our woes. So she exhorts us to inu- endo and allusion, and she tries to set us an example.

But are women really any more at home with double meanings and 'blanks' than men? Do we really want to stop trying to assert 'truths' (which are unified, however temporary) and to relinquish any positions of separated authority we may have available to us, in favour of fluidity and ceaseless exchange of identity? And, even if we did do all these things, would it improve our lot? For if the sexuality of women and men is biologically fixed, thereby fixing the respective relations of the sexes to signification, and if the present situation is one where the male or masculine form is dominant over the feminine to the total exclusion of the latter, might we not have to accept it as a natural consequence of the difference between the sexes?

The question of the origin of the status quo is always pressing in theories of one-to-one cause and effect since any theory which posits a fixed essence for something also implies that the state in which it is found, or finds itself, is somehow the inevitable consequence of its nature. Irigaray calls on women to cease to allow men to use them as objects of exchange, yet if this is seen not as implying a transformation of the separation between 'woman' and 'man', but as a way of allowing women to revert to their 'natural' state, the state they might have been in in a putative 'state of nature', then what is to stop recolonisation by men, who could similarly only be the same as before, but lacking women? Boys will be boys...Such a view seems to me to lead into a political cul-de-sac, where the best that can be hoped for would only be a kind of state of siege, in which women huddle together 'without men', whilst constantly fending off the marauders, either psychologically or physically. This may be some women's choice, but to me it has always seemed a rather illusory form of liberation.

My own position is that there is nothing alien to women, or inherently wrong, with unity, be it of subject positions, meanings, or anything else. The problem lies with the monopoly that particular meanings have as truths, rather than their singleness as meanings. Whether or not one accepts the Lacanian view of subjectification as a phallic process, it is clearly not necessary to have a penis to be a subject, to use language, to think and to understand. So rather than undermine the authority of our own utterances with double meanings, thereby rendering them incomprehensible to all those who have not had a rigorous training in 'woman-speak', I think we are far more likely to bring about change by asserting our own meanings as truths, understood from our own positions, and by implicitly or explicitly showing that dominant truths also come from specific positions. In fact, this is what Irigaray herself does when, for example, she enters into a dialogue with Freud's texts in *Speculum*, asking questions and making suggestions from a different point of view from Freud's, with the incisiveness of a single blade. It is also what I am trying to do in this book.

However, I think it is possible that women do have a greater tendency than men to psychic manifestations of duality: as subject/object, phallic/phallus, mother/daughter. Indeed the psychic consequences of the possibility for women of identification with/as the mOther might play an important role in the foundation of a feminine narcissism that bypasses masculine desire (as the work of Horney and Klein, as well as that of Montrelay, Lemoine-Luccioni and Irigaray, suggests) and why not regard this in a positive light, as Irigaray does, rather than the negative view of the more explicitly phallocentric Lacanians? But perhaps too women can get stuck in their dualities, and men in their unities. We need to be able to be subjects without also always being primarily constructed as objects of (masculine) desire, perhaps thereby making men more aware of their own status as objects, and evening out the distribution of power that re-

sults from the relation of subject to object. If the fluidity of identification that Irigaray sees as an immutable feminine essence is viewed
as one possible form of unstable identification in one of many potential relations between the sexes, where the meanings produced in
terms of those identifications are not fixed but in process, then it
might offer an option to explore, without catching women in the
impasse of fixity.

It is possible to read Irigaray's work in this way, as I have indicated above, if one reads it in terms more orthodoxly Lacanian than
her own. However, Irigaray herself rejects process in favour of
essence and, implicitly, politics in favour of psychoanalysis. For she
makes the universal psychic structures of the sexes as she sees them
into an absolute opposition, on to which the power relation between
them, the political, is then grafted. In so doing she represents as fixed
the fluidity of identification between the sexes which was at least
implicit in the work of Freud and Lacan, and undercuts the possible
political implications of her own theory.

But if Irigaray's openly feminist work leads to a political impasse,
what use can more phallocentric, masculinist psychoanalytic theory
be to feminism? Many feminists have said none, but is this the only
response?

The relation of psychoanalysis to politics seems to elude any
definitive formulation, although many attempts have been made.
That the gap should be hard to bridge is not really surprising when
one considers the nature of the objects of study of each field. Psychoanalysis deals in the specificity of the individual in terms of structures which are seen as universal in human societies. Politics, on the
other hand, is concerned with specific relations of power between
specific groupings, and their shifts. There is a difference of level
between the political and the psychoanalytical which makes a
simple link between the two seemingly impossible to forge; at the
same time, some writers (including myself) have obviously felt the
need for such a link, particularly in the area of sexual politics, as
titles such as Mitchell's *Psychoanalysis and Feminism* and Gallop's
Feminism and Psychoanalysis would indicate. This is hardly surprising, since psychoanalysis has always concerned itself with sexuality,
or in Heath's terms, was a major factor in 'the establishment of the
concept of "sexuality" and its modern "discovery"'.[45] So a political
approach to questions of sexuality and sexual relations would seem
obliged to refer to psychoanalysis in one way or another.

However, the problem of their incompatibility remains, and its
effect appears to be that one is usually subordinated to the other

45　Heath, *The Sexual Fix*, London, Macmillan, 1982, p 32.

when they appear together. Examples of this can be seen in the two books I have mentioned above. Gallop, in *Feminism and Psychoanalysis*, criticises Mitchell, saying that 'perhaps the "and" suggestive of peaceful coexistence in the title *Psychoanalysis and Feminism* betrays Mitchell's wish that psychoanalysis should not disrupt feminism as she knows it',[46] and arguably, this is so. However, Gallop in her own writing, never mentions feminism as it exceeds psychoanalysis, thereby falling into the same trap, but on the other side, the subordination of feminism to psychoanalysis.

My own view is that psychoanalysis, particularly the work of Freud and Lacan, and political theories are not incompatible but that to use them together constructively it is necessary to distinguish between two different facets of psychoanalytic theory. The first is its account of the structuring of human mental processes: the production of the unconscious, the way that it produces meanings, and the relation of unconscious meanings to the conscious individual. The second aspect is psychoanalysis as a general account of the positions adopted by types of individuals in relation to particular meanings, which are seen as universal: castration, or the phallus.

There have been many objections to both Freud and Lacan on grounds of phallocentrism, and these cannot be ignored if their theories are to be used in a discussion of sexual politics. As I have already mentioned, objections to Freud tend to centre on the second aspect of psychoanalysis, the what and why of unconscious meanings, as manifested in Freud's concept of 'penis-envy', his tendency, in practical terms at least, to equate 'femininity' with 'passivity' and his ultimate basing of his theoretical positions on the idea of fixed meanings of the anatomical features of the sexes. These aspects of Freud's work have been considered deleterious to women on the grounds that they theorise a socially constructed position of inferiority assigned to us in the sexual hierarchy into a biological necessity.

However, as I have indicated (with Juliet Mitchell), because of its other aspect, its account of the structuring of the human psyche, Freudian theory can be read in a way that undermines such a simple equation of anatomy with destiny. Indeed it lends itself to such a reading, since the whole theory contradicts any idea of a simple one-to-one correspondence of psychic and organic phenomena. That psychoanalysis as an institution might be politically reactionary, and that attempts might be made to use it to 'normalise' 'patients', and thus to prevent them from threatening a status quo that is in fact a contributing factor in their problems, these things do not in

46 Gallop, op cit. p 14.

themselves deny the potential as a factor in political change of a theory which can be used to undermine ideas of normality.

Accusations of phallocentrism levelled at Lacan touch on both facets of psychoanalysis; for not only does he tend to describe the meanings of being female (identification as the phallus, being 'not-all-there') as fixed, he also has a phallocentric view of the structuring of the subject, saying this comes about in relation to the phallus as the prime signifier. I have already referred to some of the objections raised to this view by Irigaray and Heath, both Lacanian fellow-travellers.

However, as with Freudian theory, it is possible to extract ideas from Lacan's work which are useful to feminist theory, whilst taking into account the undeniable phallocentrism of its author, for I would agree with Anthony Wilden that 'what results from the Lacanian analyses of the lack of object and the primordial relationship to difference, from the fact that the breast is the primary symbolic "object", and from the distinction he makes between need and desire, is not precisely what he intended. It is not simply that we must remember to distinguish penis (need) from phallus (demand, desire). The logical consequence of [Lacan's] position is in fact the refutation of his own phallocentrism'.[47] Wilden's argument is that 'all questions relating to the phallus in our culture depend upon the Imaginary confusion of penis (an entity) with phallus (a relation)'.[48] This, he argues, and I agree with him, is Lacan's confusion too, which motivates the latter's 'metaphysics of the phallus'.[49] This confusion of Symbolic and Imaginary is also what Heath is referring to when he objects that Lacan does not question the role of the sight of the penis and the meaning of that vision in the construction of the subject in relation to castration.

Like Freud's phallocentrism, that of Lacan can be undermined using his own theoretical constructs. The theory exceeds the limitations of the man whose name it bears and can be used to challenge the ideological positions which it ostensibly upholds. However, Lacan's phallocentrism does make problems for those who do not wish to subscribe to it whilst still using the theory, since it provides the solid basis for the fixing of meanings. The role of the phallus cannot be simply taken away; if the meaning of a vision is to be seen as something which is changeable, then some explanation must be found for the production and reproduction of that particular meaning.

47 Anthony Wilden, *System and Structure*, London, Tavistock, 1980, pp 286–87.
48 ibid, p 286.
49 ibid, p 288.

This is where political analysis come in. As I said above, politics is about relations between people seen in terms of group identities, it is about the shifting power relations between identifiable social groupings, or representatives of those groupings, the complex ways these groupings refer to each other, and the relations of power which are set up between them. If, in the combination of psychoanalysis and politics, the latter is subordinated to the former, then the range of groupings and references between them which can be encompassed theoretically is limited to those explicitly dealt with by psychoanalysis, that is, family or sexual relations. As a result, ways in which the political, or the socio-historical, might exceed the field of psychoanalytic interest become unmentionable within the confines of the theories.

The unmentionable excess of the political has not gone unnoticed by writers on psychoanalysis. It is what Wilden is calling on when he says, 'the role of the phallus in digital, Imaginary exchange is a product of our socio-economic system, not a product of human psychology as such',[50] and it is what Heath is evoking when he says, 'Psychoanalysis looks to and ceaselessly fails – in its theory – the unconscious, and that failure is history, the social relations of production, classes, sexes'.[51] However, the work of both Freud and Lacan (being the basic forms of psychoanalysis with which I am concerned here) lacks a theoretical account of the historical and socio-economic context in which the construction of the subject and the unconscious might take place, even if, in Freud's work at least, the importance of such a context is implicit. The model for the process of the construction of the subject is one of a paradigmatic family, where the desiring subject is produced in relation to parental, and more specifically maternal, desire. The fantasies, desires and positions which are then described in the elaboration of the theories are seen only in terms of familial relations, where the paradigmatic family is taken as the universal structure upon which any other, more fleeting moments of social organisation are conditional. In this way, any determinants which lie outside the structure of familial positions or positions in relation to sexual difference are neither accounted for nor have any explicit reference made to them as determinants. Freud says at the beginning of the 'Dora' case history: 'It follows from the nature of the facts which form the material of psychoanalysis that we are obliged to pay as much attention in our case histories to the purely human and social circumstances of our patients as to the somatic data and the symptoms of the disorder.'

50 ibid.
51 Heath, 'Difference', p 61.

However, he continues: 'Above all, our interest will be directed towards their family cirumstances.'[52] The family is taken as the microcosm in which basic human relations can be discerned, rather than as a specific form of social relations amongst others, potential or actual. The effect of this, and perhaps its motivation, is a pronounced phallocentrism. For the signifier which provides the pivotal point in the adoption of positions within the paradigm of the family is...the (father's) phallus. The phallus is the prime signifier (according to Lacan) of a patriarchal culture.

To say that a culture is patriarchal is to say that it has a hierarchical structure based on the model of the nuclear family, in which the father occupies a position of power in relation to the mother and child(ren). This structure must by definition also be one in which there is a hierarchical relation between the sexes; whether or not one can be a biological mother is above all a matter of whether or not one is biologically female, whilst the father is always male. It then follows that if, for whatever reasons, power accrues to the producer of the sperm which impregnates the mother, in the paradigm at least, then power will accrue to the potential father, the extrapolation from the father, men, as opposed to women.

Various theories have been advanced throughout history as to how this state of affairs arose, ranging from the view of women's innate inferiority to notions of women's need for protection, or general incapacitation, due to motherhood and the (biological) need to nurture children. I do not intend to evaluate these theories here, not only because to do so would require a book in itself, but also because psychoanalysis, in the first of its two manifestations, renders the search for the origin as a means to finding a way out of the present situation slightly less urgent than it seems in relation to other theories, since it gives an account of how individual subjects are constructed in relation to structures of ever-changing meanings, rather than being fixed effects of some essential aspect of being. However, a general patriarchal structure seems to have been in evidence throughout the history of Western culture, and is arguably found in all human societies, give or take a few variations, such as matrilineage. To this extent, it is perhaps possible to speak of the phallus as prime signifier; the mark of the first separation.

At the same time, the cultural context in which psychoanalysis has developed its account of familial relations also manifests hierarchical structures based on differences of, for example, class, race, wealth and health, as well as sex, all of which operate at the

52 Freud, 'Fragment of an Analysis of a Case of Hysteria', (1901), in *Standard Edition*, Vol VII, p 18.

same time as and interconnect with the patriarchal. Such structures are the object of political, rather than psychoanalytic study but since psychoanalysis offers an account of patriarchal structure as an interplay of the ideological and the biological, where meaning accrues to sexual difference, it also opens the way to understanding the workings of analogous interplays of ideology and biology, or, in the case of wealth, of ideology and money. On the model of the Lacanian account of patriarchy, where the prime signifier, the mark of power in difference, the phallus, is the 'elevation' to the role of symbol of the mark of maleness, the penis, one might be able to describe similar relations to a symbol at work in other structures of power in difference, working at the same time as, and possibly in conflict with, the patriarchal. For it is clear that the subject is constructed in relation to other structures besides *and at the same time as* the patriarchal; that desire is generated in relation to other objects besides the 'sexual' or the 'parental' in their restricted senses.[53]

I am not going to try and theorise here the way in which these differing desires might intersect in any general sense. But, in terms of feminist politics, I think it follows that the most effective way to shift power relations between the sexes is by placing more emphasis on women's position in other relations of difference, that is, to alter what 'being a woman' means in terms of all social structures, not merely concentrating on (hetero)sexual or family relations but structures such as those of work, or productive (as opposed to reproductive) processes in general. Of course, this alteration is already well under way. For example, little girls growing up in Britain in the eighties know that 'woman' and 'Prime Minister' are not the mutually-exclusive terms they seemed when I was a child. These children have a different starting point as gendered subjects from mine, or Mrs Thatcher's. I cannot see how such changes can fail to influence power relations between the sexes generally; opening up new areas for negotiation besides the purely sexual and familial, new conflicts, new meanings and new individual variations, irrespective of whether or not one accepts the phallus as the only possible prime signifier. Psychoanalysis can offer a theoretical understanding of how individual subjects are constructed in relation to meanings, and it can describe the positions they tend to adopt at given moments; but it should not ignore its own discovery that subjects, meanings and relations between them are always in process.

It is in the light of their relation to the process of change in the meaning of the feminine gender – being a woman – that I want to

---

53 Gallop points out an example of such an intersection when she discusses the role of the maid in the 'Dora' case, op cit Ch 9.

evaluate the feminist claims for Duras's texts. For example, is there any reason why the 'blanks' in her writing should be seen as 'the place of the woman', and if so, what does that say about what 'woman' means within the text? What is the relation of woman figure to men figures, and to the narratee, or to the reader? What aspects of the feminine gender are stressed, and what denied?

So in my discussion I shall be looking at the 'what' as well as the 'how' of the meanings that the texts produce, and one of the tools I shall use to do this will be psychoanalysis, both as a way of understanding the processes involved in reading, and as a descriptive account of certain psychic structures which are mirrored in Duras's work, such as fetishism, or narcissism. However, my concern is not so much to show how Duras's texts reveal psychoanalytic 'truths', but to look at the resonances of these structures, and the way that they are constructed in the texts, in the context of sexual politics. For this reason, my investigation will call on other frameworks, besides the psychoanalytic.

PART II

CHAPTER 4
The Blanks

I want to start my investigation of Duras's work by looking at the 'blanks', which Gauthier calls 'the place of the woman', and which are so crucial, if ill-defined to the view that Duras's writing is 'feminine'. I shall try to analyse how they are produced and to establish in what ways, if any, they relate to ideas of 'femininity'. Duras's writing practice has changed considerably over the years, so I shall analyse passages from several texts which mark what I see as different stages. I start with a passage from one of her early novels, *Un barrage contre le pacifique*, which is written in a more conventional style of psychological realism than most of her later work, so to that extent, this passage can serve as a 'control', with which the later, more experimental forms can be compared. The passage follows the account of M. Jo's first meeting with Suzanne, Joseph and their mother, and informs the reader as to who M. Jo is, before the story of his pursuit of Suzanne gets under way.

Voilà donc quelle avait été leur rencontre.
M. Jo était le fils unique d'un trés riche spéculateur dont la fortune était un modèle de fortune coloniale. Il avait commencé par spéculer sur les terrains limitrophes de la plus grande ville de la colonie. L'extension de la ville avait été si rapide qu'en cinq ans il avait réalisé des bénéfices suffisant pour investir à nouveau ses gains. Au lieu de spéculer sur ses nouveaux terrains, il les avait fait bâtir. Il avait fait construire des maisons de location à bon marché dites 'compartiments pour indigènes' qui avaient été les premières du genre dans la colonie. Ces compartiments étaient mitoyens et donnaient tous, d'une part sur de petites cours également-ment mitoyennes et, d'autre part, sur la rue. Ils étaient peu coûteux à construire et ils repondaient alors aux besoins de toute une classe de petits commerçants indigènes. Ils connurent une grande vogue. Au bout de dix ans, la colonie pullula de compartiments de ce genre. L'expérience

démontra d'ailleurs qu'ils se prêtaient très bien à la propogation de la peste et du choléra. Mais comme il n'y avait que les propriétaires pour avoir été avertis du résultat des études que les dirigeants de la colonie avaient fait entreprendre, il y eut des locataires de compartiments en toujours plus grand nombre.

Le père de M. Jo s'intéressa ensuite aux planteurs de caoutchouc du Nord. L'essor du caoutchouc était tel que beaucoup s'étaient improvisés planteurs, du jour au lendemain, sans compétence. Leurs plantations périclitèrent. Le père de M. Jo veillait sur elles. Il les rachetait. Comme elles étaient en mauvais état, il les payait très peu de chose. Puis il les mettait en gérance, les remontait. Le caoutchouc faisait gagner beaucoup, mais trop peu à son gré. Un ou deux ans plus tard, il les revendait à prix d'or à de nouveaux venus, choisis de préférence parmi les plus inexpérimentés. Dans la plupart des cas, il put les racheter dans les deux ans.

M. Jo était l'enfant dérisoirement malhabile de cet homme inventif. Sa très grosse fortune n'avait qu'un héritier, et cet héritier n'avait pas une ombre d'imagination. C'était là le point faible de cette vie, le seul définitif: on ne spécule pas sur son enfant. On croit couver un petit aigle et il vous sort de dessous le bureau un sérin. Et qu'y faire? Quel recours a-t-on contre ce sort injuste?

Il l'avait envoyé en Europe faire des études auxquelles il n'était pas destiné. La bêtise a sa clairvoyance: il se garda de les poursuivre. Lorsqu'il l'apprit, son père le fit revenir et tenta de l'intéresser à quelques-unes de ses affaires. M. Jo essaya honnêtement de réparer l'injustice dont son père était victime. Mais il arrive qu'on ne soit destiné à rien de précis, même pas à cette oisiveté à peine déguisée. Pourtant, il s'y efforçait honnêtement. Car, honnête, il l'était; de la bonne volonté il en avait. Mais là n'était pas la question. Et peut-être ne serait-il pas devenu aussi bête que son père même se résignait à le croire s'il n'avait pas été élevé à contresens. Seul, sans père, sans le handicap de cette étouffante fortune, peut-être aurait-il remédié avec plus de succès à sa nature. Mais son père n'avait jamais pensé que M. Jo pouvait être victime d'une injustice. Il n'avait jamais vu d'injustice que celle qui l'avait frappé, lui, en son fils. Et cette fatalité étant organique, irrémédiable, il ne pouvait que s'en attrister. Il n'avait jamais découvert la cause de l'autre injustice dont son fils était victime. Et à celle-là, pourtant, il aurait pu sans doute remédier. Il lui aurait suffi peut-être de deshériter M. Jo; et M. Jo échappait à cette hérédité trop lourde qu'était pour lui l'héritage. Mais il n'y avait pas pensé. Pourtant, il était intelligent. Mais l'intelligence a ses habitudes de pensée, qui l'empêchent d'apercevoir ses propres conditions.

Ce fut là l'amoureux qui échut à Suzanne, un soir à Ram. On peut dire qu'il échut tout aussi bien à Joseph et à la mère.[1]

1 *Un barrage contre le Pacifique*, Paris, Gallimard, Folio series, 1950, pp 62–5.

So this was whom they had met.

M. Jo was the only son of a very rich speculator, whose fortune was a paragon of colonial fortunes. He had begun by speculating on plots of land on the outskirts of the largest town in the colony. The growth of the town had been so rapid that in five years he had made sufficient profits to reinvest his gains. Instead of speculating on new plots, he built on them. He built houses to be let at low rents, called 'native compartments', which were the first of this type in the colony. These compartments were terraced, they all had little adjoining yards at the back and gave on to the street at the front. They were cheap to build and at that time they answered the needs of a whole class of native shopkeepers. They were very popular. After ten years, compartments of this type were springing up all over the colony. Experience proved, moreover, that they lent themselves very well to the propagation of bubonic plague and cholera. But as only the owners had been informed of the results of the studies that had been commissioned by the colony's governors, the number of compartment tenants continued to grow.

Next M. Jo's father became interested in the rubber planters in the North. The rubber boom was such that many had quickly set themselves up as planters, from one day to the next, without knowing anything about it. Their plantations failed. M. Jo's father kept an eye on them. He bought them up. As they were in a bad state, he payed very little for them. Then he appointed managers, got them back in business. Rubber made a lot of money, but too little for his liking. One or two years later, he sold them off at astronomical prices to newcomers chosen preferably from among the least experienced. In most cases, he was able to by them back within two years.

M. Jo was the pathetically inept child of this inventive man. His very large fortune had only one heir, and that heir had not a flicker of imagination. There lay the weak point of this life, the only definitive one: you cannot speculate on your child. You think you are hatching a little eagle, and what crawls out from under your desk is a cuckoo. And what can you do about it? What steps can you take against this injustice of fate?

He had sent him to Europe to pursue studies for which he was not destined. Stupidity has its own clairvoyance: he took care not to pursue them. When he learned of this, his father brought him back and tried to interest him in a few of his businesses. M. Jo tried in all decency to make up for the injustice to which his father had fallen victim. But it can happen that one is not destined for anything definite, not even for that form of thinly disguised idleness. Nevertheless, he made a decent effort. For, decent, he was; willing, he was. But the problem lay elsewhere. And perhaps he would not have become as stupid as even his father resigned himself to believing he was, if he had not been brought up against the grain. Alone, without a father, without the handicap of that stifling fortune, perhaps he would have been able to amend his nature with more success. But it had never occurred to his father that M. Jo might be the victim of an injustice. He had never seen any injustice other than the one by which he had been struck himself, in his son. And as that fate was organic, irremediable, he could only be saddened by it. He had never discovered the cause of that other injustice to which his son was victim. And yet it was nevertheless one for which he could no doubt have found a remedy. It would perhaps have been enough for him to disinherit M. Jo; M. Jo would then have escaped the too heavy legacy that his inheritance had proved to be. But he had not thought of it. He was intelligent enough. But intelligence has habits of thinking, which prevent it from perceiving the conditions of its own existence.

This was the admirer who fell to the lot of Suzanne, one evening in Ram. It could be said that he fell just as much to the lot of Joseph and their mother.

This passage is written in a style which could be called 'common-sense' or 'naïve' realism, where the narration purports unproblematically to construct a fictional world in imitation of extratextual 'reality'. A separate section at the end of its chapter, it forms a break in the unravelling of the story, during which the character and background of M. Jo are established. It sets up M. Jo as a referent in the fantasy of the 'real world' which the reader is invited to build up around *Un barrage contre le Pacifique*. The relation of realist fiction to reality is ambiguous; the reader knows that the events and characters described are not 'real' in the sense that they do not exist other than as a product of the text, or at least not exactly in the form in which they appear there. Napoleon Bonaparte is a real historical figure and the battle of Borodino actually took place in 1812 but the reader of Leo Tolstoy's *War and Peace*, which describes them both, reads it as a work of fiction set at a particular historical period, whose portrayal of people and events that could be described as 'real' may or may not be 'accurate'. The ambiguity arises out of the way in which the fiction produces a 'real world'. The discourses it uses and the form of a narrative in the third person are not confined to fiction. They are similar to, or the same as, discourses used in biography or history, for example, where the text is assumed to be 'accurately' describing 'real' persons and events. This overlapping of discourses allows both 'real' and fictional worlds to be rendered intelligible in similar terms, so that the fictional is produced as 'real', and constructs a narratee who accepts it as real. The reader is invited to take the place of the narratee whilst reading, although at the same time of course s/he knows that what is recounted is not 'real'.[2]

In order for realist writing to portray a coherent 'reality' purporting to correspond to Reality, the language it uses must not in itself be problematic. So contradictions between or within discourses are avoided, allowing the language to become 'transparent' and appear referential or expressive. The above passage is an example of this type of writing. The first part takes the form of a biography, recounting, in chronological order, the stages of the process by which M. Jo's father made his money. The main tense in French is the past historic, which is almost exclusively a written form, used to describe a completed action in the past. It is the tense of History, Biography and Literature, which Roland Barthes describes, in *Le Degré zéro de l'écriture*, as 'the ideal tool for all building of universes'.[3] The sentences in this part of the passage are simple in structure and relate the events in sequence and without embellishment. The passing of time is marked at appropriate intervals, with notations such as *en cinq ans* ('in five years'), *au bout de dix ans*, ('after ten years') and *ensuite* ('next'). The sequence of events described resembles accounts of the accumulation of wealth by colonialists to be found in both fictional and non-fictional works concerning colonialism, and it is possible to 'situate' them both historically, in the first half of the twentieth century, and geographically in what was then Indo-China, although the country is not specified other than as *la colonie* ('the colony'.)

The second part of the passage is concerned with M. Jo's character. It describes him in terms of the convention according to which the individual has fixed psychological traits. The narration defines M. Jo in terms of the interaction between his personal 'nature' and the context into which he is born and in which he grows up, following the view that human psychology is produced in the action of the individual's environment on certain innate and genetically determined dispositions. M. Jo is the innately stupid son of a very shrewd and wealthy man, rendered even more foolish than he might otherwise have been by the wealth with which he is surrounded. The result is a man who is *honnête* ('decent'), with *de la bonne volonté*, ('willing'), but who is at the same time *dérisoirement malhabile*

---

2 A crossing over between fiction and 'reality' would seem to be even more complete in the cinema, judging by the disclaimer carried by some films, to stress the fictional nature of what is being shown.

3 Roland Barthes, *Le Degré zéro de l'écriture*, Paris, Le Seuil, Points series, 1972, p 26.

('pathetically inept'). It is in the light of this established character
that the reader is invited to understand M. Jo's actions on reading
this passage.

The passage then tells the reader/narratee 'what happened' and
'who M. Jo is' in an uncomplicated way, leaving little room for uncertainty in either case. However, it would be misleading to describe
the language as purely 'expressive' in effect. It also produces a personalised 'point of view', a specific attitude to events and persons
on the part of the narrator. The use of third person narration in the
past historic has for effect the production of an omniscient narrator,
who is outside the story, knows the meaning of each event in relation
to whole, and gradually reveals it all to the narratee. The conventions of realist fiction permit such a narrator's intrusion in a more
personal capacity into the narration, and examples of 'intervention'
in the narrative by the narrator are legion. The forms it takes may
differ. In *War and Peace*, for example, the narrator launches into
long discussions of philosophical questions relating to cause, effect
and the individual. In the passage under discussion here, the narrator's presence is undoubtedly felt but this occurs more indirectly, in
the ironic tone of the writing.

The ironic tone of the passage is produced at the points of conflict in its discourse. The coherence of the discourse is not seriously
threatened, but it is not without cracks. It is the presence of these
cracks which creates an implicit criticism of M. Jo's wealthy father
and of the whole colonial system within the description of the
former's rise to riches.

M. Jo's father's accumulation of wealth is described as 'a
paragon of colonial fortunes' – my translation of *un modèle de fortune
coloniale.* A *modèle* ('paragon') in its usual sense is something which
provides a pattern for other examples of the same type of thing.
Then follows the account of how he made his money building houses
for the native (colonised) population, houses called *compartiments*
('compartments'), rather than *appartements* ('appartments', 'flats'),
or *maisons* ('houses'), these being words more usually employed to
describe the dwelling-places of human beings – those of the colonisers,
for example. The exploitative nature of the enterprise is confirmed
when we are told that these 'compartments' '*se prêtaient très bien à la
propagation de la peste et du choléra. Mais comme il n'y avait que les
propriétaires pour avoir été avertis du résultat des études que les dirigeants
de la colonie avaient fait entreprendre, il y eut des locataires de compartiments en toujours plus grand nombre*' ('lent themselves very well to the
propagation of bubonic plague and cholera. But as only the owners
had been informed of the results of the studies that had been commissioned by the colony's governors, the number of compartment

tenants continued to grow'). The ironic effect is produced here first by the use of *très bien* ('very well') to qualify the way in which the plague and cholera spread in the 'compartments', since the usual connotations of the names of these diseases are in direct opposition to anything being 'very well'. There is further irony in the use of *comme* ('as'), which gives a logical link to the two halves of the sentence. The reader is thus led to infer that it is logical that, if only the owners know that the 'compartments' are dangerous, they will not tell the people who might rent them, since such a step would prejudice their chances of making money, even though it might also prevent the deaths of their prospective tenants. The implication is, of course, that to the coloniser, money is more important than the lives of the colonised people.

The story of M. Jo's father's rise continues with the description of how he played on the inexperience and ineptitude of would-be rubber plantation owners, fellow colonialists, encouraging or at least facilitating their failure for his own profit. The whole story is one of exploitation as the source of M Jo's father's money. And this is the 'paragon of colonial fortunes', which others should take note of and follow. The irony then springs from the use of *modèle*, which connotes something good, worthy of immitation, to refer to a story of greed and exploitation.

Our Western capitalist culture carries the idea that wealth accumulated is not to be frittered away by the person who accumulates it, but should instead be reinvested, increased and passed on to the son (*sic*) and heir. This assumption is firmly entrenched in dominant ideology and as there is nothing in the story of M. Jo's father's rise which contradicts it, it will be shared by the narratee – the reader who is constructed by the text. This means there is a certain irony in the description of the wily speculator's 'pathetically inept child' for the father is obliged to confer the money he used such ingenuity to acquire on an imbecile who would have been better off without it. Given the teleological nature of the process of accumulating wealth, that is, that its final aim is the foundation of a wealthy dynasty, M. Jo's imbecility and general unworthiness render all the efforts of his father vain as he is obviously incapable of taking over the business. There is irony in the contrast between the naratee's expectations concerning the bestowal of wealth, expectations arising from the context of capitalism, and the impossibility of those expectations being fulfilled, due to a quirk of fate beyond the control even of M. Jo's father: 'you cannot speculate on your child'. Further ironic effect is produced by the use of 'injustice' and 'handicap', since these words are usually used to refer to the effects of grinding poverty, such as that of Suzanne's family, rather than to that of a 'stifling for-

tune'. Since it is the acquistion of wealth which is usually considered
beneficial to the individual, the idea that M. Jo's father could best
have ended the injustice by disinheriting his son reverses the
convention and disturbs the smoothness of the discourse. Moreover,
after the story of M. Jo's father, it is impossible to regard him simply
as the victim of injustice, when he also perpetrates it; so there is an
ironic disturbance here too.

It is this disturbance of the discourse which sets up the point of
view of the narrator. According to Tzvetan Todorov's 'principle of
pertinence' (*principe de pertinence*), 'following which, if an utterance
exists, there has to be a reason for it',[4] unexpected incongruities in a
discourse must be interpreted: a 'receiver' – hearer or reader – must
assume an intention to mean on the part of the utterer. To put this in
Lacanian terms, the receiver assumes that the utterance represents
a desire on the part of another subject, which has meaning and can
be interpreted. In a text, it is what Wayne C Booth calls the 'implied
author' who is constructed as occupying the place of the ultimate
source of meaning, but this author 'speaks' through the narrator. In
the case of a third person narration where the narrator's attitude is
implied rather than specified, as is the case in *Un barrage contre le
Pacifique*, the reader/narratee can easily assume that the author
named on the cover and the narrator are the same, so that the narrator and implied author merge. In this passage, then, the reader
makes sense of the (albeit slight) contradictions in the discourse by
assuming a narrator (who may be Duras), who controls that discourse and is using it to mean, whose desire shapes its form and is
present in the conflicts in the discourse of the text.

The production of the narrator is reinforced by the ironic asides of
the narration, the generalisations about the nature of things, such
as 'you cannot speculate on your child', or 'intelligence has its habits
of thinking, which prevent it from perceiving the conditions of its own
existence'. Such comments imply a superior knowledge and produce
the omniscient narrator as something Lacan terms a *sujet supposé
savoir* or subject supposed to know. The narrator is the locus of
authority and guarantor of the truth – the 'accuracy' in relation to
the 'real world' both inside and outside the text – of what is being
recounted. In Booth's terms, s/he is a reliable narrator.

The narrator is constructed as relating events with a purpose in
mind and from a point of view. In this passage, the point of view
would seem to be that colonialism fosters the enrichment of the cun-
ning coloniser at the expense of the weak colonised and the foolish in
general, plus the view that wealth is not the answer to every pro-

4 Tzvetan Todorov, *Symbolisme et interpretation*, Paris, Le Seuil, 1978, p 26.

blem. The narrator is produced as separate from the characters, M. Jo and his father, and this has the effect of distancing the narratee from them as well. The reader is invited to take the position of the narratee and to look at the characters in the light of the narrator's insights. So the narrator tells the reader what to think, whether or not the latter accepts the offered viewpoint.

The only ambiguity lies in those parts of the passage which are ironic. There is one example of free indirect style, where the narrator's voice and that of M. Jo's father merge: 'you think you're hatching a little eagle and what crawls out from under your desk but a cuckoo? And what can you do about it? What defence have you got against this unjust fate?' The narrator is generalising here ('you' is my translation of *on*) from the point of view of those, such as M. Jo's father, who have been smitten by 'injustice' in the form of children who are not worthy of them. However, this invitation to see it from M. Jo's father's point of view has an ironic ring to is, as the 'unjust fate' follows an account of the injustice perpetrated by him. As with other ironic parts of the passage, the disturbance of the overall point of view of the narration serves to produce an ironic narrator, rather than simply a shift of the point of view of the text to that of M. Jo's father. The shift occurs in only three lines of the whole passage, and is done in free indirect style, which produces both narrator and character at the same time, thus keeping the narrator as an entity separable from the character.

This strengthens the narrator's position as the place from which the text is to be understood. The desire to mean something on the part of the individual narrator, as inferred by the reader/narratee, is both produced by and guarantees the possibility of the latter's interpretation of the text. The reader assumes that events related mean something in relation to each other, that questions will be answered and that s/he will be able to follow the movement of the narrator's desire from the beginning of the text to the end, where the 'point' or 'meaning' of the text will be graspable.

Un barrage contre le Pacifique ends with the answer to the question 'will Suzanne leave the plain and, if so, who with?' Suzanne's desire to leave the plain and how she conceives of doing it are established early in the text: 'One day a man would stop, perhaps, why not? because he had caught a glimpse of her by the bridge. Maybe he would be attracted to her and he would ask her to go to the town with him.'[5] There follows M. Jo's arrival on the scene and the growing inevitability of his not being the man with whom Suzanne will leave the plain. After the final rejection of M. Jo comes the story

5 *Un barrage contre le Pacifique*, p 21.

of the selling of the diamond, which proves difficult and effects no great change in the lives of the characters. Then, with their mother's death, comes the final solution: Suzanne leaves the plain not with a lover, but with her brother.[6] Her life is irredeemably altered and the question 'will she escape from the plain?' has been answered. The ending of the text coming as it does with the answer that she will leave with Joseph makes that question appear to have been the motive force behind the text, giving a retrospective coherence to the whole although many other questions are generated, or potentially generated, by the novel.

The sequence of events provides a structure which assures the reader that s/he is following a progression to an ultimate end. The most immediately obvious reading of works of realist fiction is one which privileges the unfolding of the plot. The reader is invited to read to find out 'what happened next' until s/he reaches the end. In *Un barrage contre le Pacifique*, the story is fairly slow-moving and there is a large number of passages which are to a greater or lesser extent extraneous to the progression of the plot, which is itself quite loose. There is the description of 'old Bart',[7] for example, who is a very minor character, or the story of the rise of M. Jo's father cited above, or the description of Suzanne's visit to the cinema.[8] The basic structure of a progression of events ties these diverse passages together. It provides a coherence for the text. However, the reader reflecting on the text, or the critic, who differs from the latter in that s/he writes her/his reflections down, might also extrapolate certain 'themes' from the diversity of these passages, inferring a coherent desire motivating the presence of different aspects of the text and seeing them as related to each other in terms of 'what they are trying to say'. For example, one could link Suzanne's experience of the cinema and the film she sees of lovers kissing to the story of the mother's attempts to build dams against the Pacific, in terms of a theme of the interplay of fantasy and reality. 'Old Bart' and M. Jo's father are both examples of corrupt colonialists, and can both be read as part of a general indictment of colonialism, which I would see as one of the themes of the novel.

To sum up then, *Un barrage contre le Pacifique* is a realist novel, which lends itself to being read in a relatively unproblematic way as the coherent manifestation of the desire(s) of a narrator, who can be easily conflated with the implied author. The reader attributes to the author/narrator both knowledge of the psychology of the characters,

6 For a more detailed discussion of the relationship between Suzanne and Joseph, see pp 213–16 below.
7 *Un barrage contre le Pacifique*, pp 40–1.
8 ibid, pp 188–9.

of the significance of the events described, etc., and a reason for relating them to others. The desire of the author/narrator sometimes appears to be moving in different directions at once, allowing the text to be read in terms of themes as well as plot. The narrator and implied author might sometimes become separate, or, as when free indirect style is used, the narrator might become partially merged with a character. However, overall the text appears coherent and authoritative. It tells the reader what there is to know, that is the plot, the psychology of the characters, and 'what the author meant', or 'was trying to say' in the text, through its themes, or the point of view of the narration.

In some types of realist fiction, the plot appears as the most important aspect of the narration. In many thrillers, for example, the reader reads for the pleasure of suspense, waiting for the questions posed by the text to be answered by the progression of events. In other texts, the themes will seem more important. This is arguably the case in *Un barrage contre le Pacifique*, where the story in itself is simple and there is little sense of suspense. The plot here seems to be the vehicle which allows certain problems to be explored as diverse in nature as those of relations within the family and the effects of colonialism. The reader or critic can extrapolate such themes from the accounts of events and characters, although it is possible just to read for the plot, which unfolds bit by bit in chronological sequence, from the point of view of an interested, and not entirely detached, observer.

★   ★   ★

I now want to look at *Moderato cantabile*, which is a very different piece of writing. As opposed to *Un barrage contre le Pacifique*, which recounts events and gives insights, usually through free indirect style, into the psychology of the characters, 'in *Moderato cantabile*, not only does it not say what happened, but it may be that nothing happens at all'[9] and, even supposing something is happening, 'who can give a name to what happens between strangers, to what is happening now between Anne Desbaresdes and Chauvin?'[10] In this text, according to one critic, Duras refuses 'to name, to recount, to entertain, to fill the blanks'.[11] It is possible, however, to give a brief reconstruction of the events described, as Jean Mistler does:

9 Gaëton Picon, 'Moderato cantabile dans l'oeuvre de Marguerite Duras', in *Moderato cantabile*, Paris, Minuit, 10/18 series, 1958, p 169.
10 ibid, p 171.
11 Madeleine Alleins, 'Un langage qui recuse la quiétude du savoir', in ibid p 159.

Anne Desbaresdes was a chance withness to a crime of passion in a quayside café, whilst her little boy was having his piano lesson. She goes back to this café several times and questions a man whom she meets there each time. We have the impression that the man knóws no more about it than Anne and moreover that she scarcely listens to what he tells her. After five or six meetings, there has been no action, but we have a vague feeling that the psychological positions have been transformed.[12]

Mistler, as his article clearly shows, is not impressed. But those who are praise Duras's ability to produce silence and 'blanks' in her writing. So what is happening in this text, and how does Duras do it?.

Perhaps the first point to make is that a large part of *Moderato cantabile* is taken up with a reconstruction of events which culminate in the shooting at the end of the first chapter. This reconstruction is undertaken by two figures, Anne Desbaresdes and Chauvin, neither of whom 'know what really happened' and will never be able to know, since one of the protagonists is dead and the other mad. Because of the way in which the text is narrated, this story is always out of reach of the authoritative narration and is equally out of reach of Anne and Chauvin. It has already happened before the chronological point where the text begins and is thus produced as an unattainable object of knowledge a 'blank'.

However, even in the events actually narrated by the text, there are gaps and silences. I have taken two passages for analysis in order to see how Duras produces effects of silence; the first is representative of the dialogue which makes up much of the text and the second is taken from the section recounting the dinner party, which contains little dialogue, but where a similar process is at work as in the first passage. The first passage is taken from the end of Anne Desbaresdes's first conversation with Chauvin:

Les premiers hommes entrèrent. L'enfant se fraya un passage à travers eux, curieux, et arriva jusqu'à sa mère, qui le prit contre elle dans un mouvement d'enlacement machinal.

– Vous êtes madame Desbaresdes. La femme du directeur d'Import Export et des Fonderies de la Côte. Vous habitez boulevard de la Mer.

Une autre sirène retentit, plus faible que la première, à l'autre bout du quai. Un remorqueur arriva. L'enfant se dégagea, d'une façon assez brutale, s'en alla en courant.

– Il apprend le piano, dit-elle. Il a des dispositions, mais beaucoup de mauvaise volonté, il faut que j'en convienne.

12 Jean Mistler, 'Un essai non une oeuvre achievée', in ibid, p 162.

Toujours pour faire place aux hommes qui entraient regulièrement très nombreux dans le café, il se rapprocha un peu plus d'elle. Les premiers clients s'en allèrent. D'autres arrivèrent encore. Entre eux, dans le jeu de leurs allées et venues, on voyait le soleil se coucher dans la mer, le ciel qui flambait et l'enfant qui, de l'autre côté du quai, jouait tout seul à des jeux dont le secret était indiscernable à cette distance. Il sautait des obstacles imaginaires, devait chanter.

— Je voudrais pour cet enfant tant de choses à la fois que je ne sais pas comment m'y prendre, par où commencer. Et je m'y prends très mal. Il faut que je rentre parce qu'il est tard.

— Je vous ai vue souvent. Je n'imaginais pas qu'un jour vous arriverez jusqu'ici avec votre enfant.

La patronne augmenta un peu le volume de la radio pour ceux des derniers clients qui venaient d'entrer. Anne Desbaresdes se tourna vers le comptoir, fit une grimace, accepta le bruit, l'oublia.

— Si vous savez tout le bonheur qu'on leur veut, comme si c'était possible. Peut-être vaudrait-il mieux parfois que l'on nous en sépare. Je n'arrive pas à me faire une raison de cet enfant.

— Vous avez une belle maison au bout du boulevard de la mer. Un grand jardin fermé.

Elle le regarda, perplexe, revenu à elle.

— Mais ces leçons de piano, j'en ai beaucoup de plaisir, affirma-t-elle.

L'enfant, traqué par le crépuscule, revint une nouvelle fois vers eux. Il resta là à contempler le monde, les clients. L'homme fit signe à Anne Desbaresdes de regarder au dehors. Il lui sourit.

— Regardez, dit-il, les jours allongent, allongent...

Anne Desbaresdes regarda, ajusta son manteau avec soin, lentement.

— Vous travaillez dans cette ville, Monsieur?

— Dans cette ville, oui. Si vous reveniez, j'essayerai de savoir autre chose et je vous le dirai.

Elle baissa les yeux, se souvint et pâlit.

— Du sang sur sa bouche, dit-elle, et il l'embrassait, l'embrassait.

Elle se reprit: ce que vous avez dit, vous le supposiez?

— Je n'ai rien dit.

Le couchant était si bas maintenant qu'il atteignait le visage de cet homme. Son corps, debout, legèrement appuyé au comptoir, le recevait déjà depuis un moment.

— A l'avoir vu, on ne peut pas s'empêcher, n'est-ce pas, c'est presque inévitable?

— Je n'ai rien dit, répéta l'homme. Mais je crois qu'il l'a visée au coeur comme elle le lui demandait.

Anne Desbaresdes gémit. Une plainte presque licencieuse, douce, sortit de cette femme.

— C'est curieux, je n'ai pas envie de rentrer, dit-elle.

Il prit brusquement son verre, le termina d'un trait, ne répondit pas, la quitta des yeux.

– J'ai dû trop boire, continua-t-elle, voyez-vous, c'est ça.

– C'est ça, oui, dit l'homme.

Le café s'était presque vidé. Les entrées se firent plus rares. Tout en lavant ses verres, la patronne les lorgnait, intriguée de les voir tant s'attarder, sans doute. L'enfant, revenu vers la porte, contemplait les quais maintenant silencieux. Debout devant l'homme, tournant le dos au port, Anne Desbaresdes se tut encore longtemps. Lui ne paraissait pas s'apercevoir de sa présence.

– Il m'aurait été impossible de ne pas revenir, dit-elle enfin.

– Je suis revenu moi aussi pour la même raison que vous.[13]

The first men came in. The child pushed his way through them, curious, and reached his mother, who pulled him against her in an automatic clasping movement.

'You are Madame Desbaresdes. The wife of the head of Import Export and of Coastal Foundries. You live on Sea Boulevard.'

Another siren sounded, quieter than the first, from the other end of the quay. A tugboat came in. The child freed himself, quite roughly, ran off.

'He's learning the piano', she said. 'He's got ability, but I must admit, he's very unwilling.'

Again to make space for the men entering the café at regular intervals and in very large numbers, he drew a little closer to her. The first clients left. Still more came in. Between them, in the play of their comings and goings, one could see the sun setting in the sea, the sky which was aflame and the child who, on the other side of the quay, was playing all alone at games whose secret was indiscernible at that distance. He was jumping over imaginary obstacles, must have been singing.

'I want so many things at once for that child that I don't know how to go about it, where to begin. And I go about it very badly. I must go home because it is late.'

'I have often seen you. I never imagined that one day you would come up here with your child.'

The café owner turned up the volume of the radio a little for those of the later clients who had just come in. Anne Desbaresdes turned towards the counter, made a face, accepted the noise, forgot it.

'If you knew all the happiness that one wants for them, as if it were possible. Perhaps it might be better sometimes if they took them

13 ibid, pp 30–4.

away from us. I can't seem to be reasonable about this child.'

'You have a beautiful house at the end of Sea Boulevard. A large walled garden.'

She looked at him, perplexed, brought back to the present.

'But these piano lessons give me great pleasure,' she stated.

The child, harried by the dusk, came back towards them once more. He stayed there contemplating all the people, the clients. The man gestured to Anne Desbaresdes to look outside. He smiled at her.

'Look, he said, the days are getting longer, longer...'

Anne Desbaresdes looked, rearranged her coat carefully, slowly.

'Do you work in this town, Monsieur?

'In this town, yes. If you come back, I'll try to find out something more and I'll tell it to you.'

She lowered her eyes, remembered and grew pale.

'Blood on her mouth,' she said, 'and he was kissing her, kissing her.'

She pulled herself together: 'what you said, you were just supposing it?'

'I said nothing.'

The sun had sunk so low now that it touched the man's face. His body, standing, leaning slightly on the counter, had already been catching it for some time.

'Having seen it, one can't stop oneself, don't you think, it's almost inevitable?'

'I said nothing', the man repeated. 'But I think he aimed for her heart, as she asked him to do.'

Anne Desbaresdes groaned. A soft, almost licentious moan came from the woman.

'It's odd, I don't want to go home,' she said.

He took up his glass abruptly, finished it at one go, did not answer, turned his eyes away from her.

'I must have drunk too much,' she went on, 'you see, that's it.'

'That's it, yes', said the man.

The café had almost emptied. People came in more rarely. As she washed her glasses, the owner watched them out of the corner of her eye, intrigued, no doubt, at seeing them stay on so long. The child, who had gone back to the door, was contemplating the now silent quayside. Standing in front of the man, turning her back on the harbour, Anne Desbaresdes stayed silent for a long time more. He did not seem to notice her presence.

'It would have been impossible for me not to come back', she said at last.

'I also came back for the same reason as you.'

This passage, like the rest of *Moderato cantabile*, is written in the past historic, constructor of universes and of the observer who records them. However, unlike the passage from *Un barrage contre le Pacifique* which I have discussed above, it does not produce a narrator with a point of view in the sense of an attitude, such as irony, with regard to what is narrated. The discourse is not disturbed in the way that it was in the previous passage by conflicting meanings. This makes the style appear almost hyper-realist, like the transcription of a photograph. It appears to be a simple description of the events, a recording, as if by a kind of verbal camera, with no comment on the part of the narrator. This allows the language to appear 'transparent', with none of the colouring or 'distortion' which can be read into a text where the reader infers a narrator with a 'personality' who is directing the former's perception of events.

So the 'impersonal narrator' is reduced almost to transparency, disappearing into the language, only seeming to encroach on the recording of events at points of uncertainty ('whose secret was indiscernible at that distance', 'must have been singing'). This encroachment does set up a point of view, but in a spatial sense. The passage is written in such a way as to make it possible for the reader to construct a fantasised image of the café by the quay, with workers coming and going, and where two people, Anne Desbaresdes and Chauvin, are talking by the bar. This is all put forward with little or no apparent mediation or interpretation on the part of the narrator. An unthreatened illusion of reference is maintained throughout.

Anne and Chauvin are produced as 'real people', seen as if by a camera. But 'real people' are more than surfaces; Anne and Chauvin have names, a vaguely defined social status, and by realist implication, psychology and desires. The main thread running through the passage is the dialogue between them. Nevertheless, their conversation does not proceed unproblematically. In the first half of the passage they do not appear to be talking about the same thing. Anne is talking about her child, whilst Chauvin is talking about Anne. Furthermore, the dialogue is punctuated by descriptions of the child's actions, the café owner turning up the radio, or Anne's own actions. These actions are, for the most part, written in the past historic, the tense used to mark the speech of Anne and Chauvin, the tense of definite, completed action. The effect of this is that the utterances of Anne and Chauvin and the actions or descriptions which punctuate them are given equal importance and appear to follow each other chronologically. The difference this makes to the flow of the narration can be seen when the above passage is compared to the following exchange between Suzanne and M. Jo in *Un barrage contre le*

Pacifique, when M. Jo is trying to get Suzanne to open the door and let him see her washing.

– *Dire que vous êtes toute nue, dire que vous êtes toute nue, répétait-il d'une voix sans timbre.*

– *Vous parlez d'une affaire, dit Suzanne. Si vous étiez à ma place j'aurais pas envie de vous voir.*

Quand elle évoquait M. Jo, sans son diamant, son chapeau, sa limousine, en train par exemple de se balader en maillot sur la plage à Ram, la colère de Suzanne grandissait d'autant.

– *Pourquoi vous ne vous baignez pas à Ram?*

M. Jo reprit un peu de sang-froid et appuya moins fort.

– *Les bains de mer me sont interdits, dit-il avec toute la fermeté qu'il pouvait.*

Heureuse, Suzanne se savonnait. Il lui avait acheté du savon parfumé à la lavande et depuis, elle se baignait deux et trois fois par jour pour avoir l'occasion de se parfumer. L'odeur de la lavande arrivait jusqu'à M. Jo et en lui permettant de mieux suivre les étapes du bain de Suzanne rendait son supplice encore plus subtil.

– *Pourquoi les bains vous sont-ils interdits?*

– *Parce que je suis de faible constitution et que les bains de mer me fatiguent. Ouvrez, ma petite Suzanne...une seconde...*

– *C'est pas vrai, c'est parce que vous êtes mal foutu.*

Elle le devinait, collé contre la porte, encaissant tout ce qu'elle lui disait parce qu'il était sûr de gagner.

– *Une seconde, rien qu'une seconde...*[14]

– 'To think that you're completely naked, to think that you're completely naked', he repeated in a toneless voice.

'Some bargain', said Suzanne. 'If we swapped places, I wouldn't want to see you.'

When she pictured M. Jo, without his diamond, his hat, or his limousine, walking along in a swimming costume, for example, on the beach at Ram, Suzanne's anger grew all the greater.

'Why don't you go bathing at Ram?'

M. Jo recovered his cool a little and pushed (against the door) less hard.

'I am not allowed to bathe in the sea', he said, as firmly as he could.

Suzanne was soaping herself, happily. He had bought her some

---

14 *Un barrage contre le Pacifique*, pp 104–5.

lavender scented soap and ever since she had been bathing two or three times a day so that she could cover herself in perfume. The scent of the lavender floated out to M. Jo and, by allowing him to follow the stages of Suzanne's bathing more easily, rendered his torture all the more subtle.

'Why aren't you allowed to bathe?'

'Because I have a weak constitution and bathing in the sea tires me. Open up, my sweet little Suzanne...just one second...'

'That's not true, it's because you're ugly.'

She could imagine him, pressed up against the door, swallowing everything she said to him because he knew he would win.

'One second, just one second...'

In this exchange the dialogue is interrupted by two fairly long passages, the one beginning *Quand elle évoquait*...('When she pictured...') and the other beginning *Heureuse, Suzanne se savonnait* ('Suzanne was soaping herself, happily'). However, both these passages have their main verbs in the imperfect tense, the tense of indefinite time. This means that the actions described in the imperfect do not interrupt the actions described in the past historic, but can be read as happening at the same time, providing a background for the words. In the *Moderato cantabile* passage this is not the case. The result is that the reader/narratee assumes a gap between two parts of the dialogue in which, for example, the café-owner turns up the radio, Anne turns towards the bar, makes a face, resigns herself to the noise and forgets it, before speaking. This produces a gap in the dialogue, when neither speaks while these actions are performed. Thus a dialogue full of silences can be produced without the narration having to make this explicit; the silences arise in the spaces between the utterances of the figures, made by the intercalation of narration in the past historic between instances of direct speech.

The passage also produces effects of silence in what the speakers actually do say, by creating the impression that there is something they are not saying, or are avoiding saying. In the first part of the passage it would appear that what Anne and Chauvin each say bears no relation to the words of the other. Alone, this section of the dialogue would appear absurd(ist). The speeches of Anne and Chauvin would appear to be lacking in 'pertinence'; the reason for their existence would at best be obscure in terms of accepted conventions of dialogue, which uphold the view that when two people talk together their utterances have some relevance to each other. For here, whilst each independently appears to be capable of coherent thought, they seem unable to follow each other's drift. However, after Anne asks Chauvin if he works in the town, the conversation picks up and each speech appears to be connected in some way to the previous one. Although the connexions may not be immediately obvious, the reader can assume that when Chauvin says, 'I'll try to find out something more', he is referring to the shooting, that the memory of the latter event makes Anne turn pale and that it is the man's kissing of the dead woman to which she refers when she says 'Having seen it'. 'One can't stop oneself' can be referred back to a previous speech of Anne's: 'I've thought about it more and more since yesterday evening...since my child's piano lesson. I couldn't have stopped myself from coming today, you see.'[15] 'It' here refers to the shooting. After Chauvin has said he will try to find out more, both figures appear to be talking about the incident, after the disconnected conversation they had been having before. The reader can then reasonably infer that that shooting is of interest to both of them, following the idea that these are 'real people', whose utterances are not completely random. Continuing in this vein, the reader can also assume that Chauvin's words about the shooting have the effect of making Anne groan in a way which was 'almost licentious', since the groan immediately follows them. The proximity of the two suggest cause and effect. The reader might then assume that Anne's loss of desire to go home is also something to do with what has just been said and the 'almost licentious' sound that she has just made. Because, with a little effort, the reader can find or invent a 'pertinence' in this part of the dialogue, s/he can continue to read Anne and Chauvin as 'real people', and assume that there is something which Anne is trying to justify when she says, 'I must have drunk too much...That's it', even if it is totally unstated what 'it' might be. Such an assumption is also possible in relation to Chauvin's words: 'I also came back for the same reason as you'. No reason has been given but 'real people' have reasons for doing things, or say they do, or even say they have not when they really have. So runs the convention. From the vantage point of the all-seeing, but not necessarily all-comprehending eye of the narrator, the reader may not know exactly what the reason that Chauvin refers to is; but since the latter apparently does, s/he assumes it exists.

It is then by compelling the reader to make the associations necessary to find the 'pertinence' of the utterances attributed to Anne and Chauvin that the text produces an effect of things left unsaid. The reader supplies the associative links, but notices they are missing. With the hindsight of Anne and Chauvin's exchange on the subject of the shooting, the reader can also infer a suppression of this topic during the disconnected part of the conversation, since their willing-

15 *Moderato cantabile*, p 30.

ness to talk about it has apparently carried over from an earlier exchange. Perhaps, the reader might think, it was that suppression which made their conversation so fragmented and disconnected. Perhaps not. We cannot know for sure.

The second passage from *Moderato cantabile* that I want to discuss also relies on the reader's desire to find the 'pertinence' of the words s/he reads. However, here it is not the utterances of the figures in the text which require interpretation, it is the narration.

Le pétale de magnolia est lisse, d'un grain nu. Les doigts le froissent jusqu'à le trouer puis, interdits, s'arrêtent, se reposent sur la table, attendent, prennent une contenance, illusoire. Car on s'en est aperçu. Anne Desbaresdes s'essaye à un sourire d'excuse de n'avoir pu faire autrement, mais elle est ivre et son visage prend le faciès impudique de l'aveu. Le regard s'appesantit, impassible, mais revenu dèjà douloureusement de tout étonnement. On s'y attendait depuis toujours.

Anne Desbaresdes boit de nouveau un verre de vin tout entier les yeux mi-clos. Elle en est déjà à ne plus pouvoir faire autrement. Elle découvre, à boire, une confirmation de ce qui fut jusque-là son désir obscur et une indigne consolation à cette découverte.

D'autres femmes boivent à leur tour, elles lèvent de même leurs bras nus, délectables, irréprochables, mais d'épouses. Sur la grève, l'homme siffle une chanson entendue dans l'après-midi dans un café du port.

La lune est levée et avec elle voici le commencement de la nuit tardive et froide. Il n'est pas impossible que cet homme ait froid.[16]

The magnolia petal is smooth, with a naked grain. The fingers crush it, tearing it, then, forbidden, stop, lie on the table once more, wait, adopt an attitude of composure, which is illusory. For one has noticed. Anne Desbaresdes tries a smile of appology for having been unable to do otherwise, but she is drunk and her face takes on the shameless appearance of confession. The look grows heavier, impassive, but it has already painfully recovered from all astonishment. One has always expected this.

Anne Desbaresdes drinks another glass of wine all at once her eyes half closed. She has already reached the point of being unable to do otherwise. She discovers, in drinking, the confirmation of what had been until then an obscure desire and a shameful consolation in this discovery.

Other women drink in their turn, they likewise raise arms which are naked, delectable, irreprochable, but are those of wives. On the beach, the man whistles a song heard in the afternoon in a quayside café.

16 ibid, pp 97–8.

The moon has risen and with it here is the beginning of the cold, late-coming night. It is not impossible that the man is cold.

Here the first link to be made is between the magnolia flower worn by Anne as a corsage at the dinner-party and the one Chauvin has described her as wearing when he saw her before:

> – *Vous étiez accoudée à ce grand piano. Entre vos seins nus sous votre robe, il y a cette fleur de magnolia.*
> *Anne Desbaresdes, très attentivement, écouta cette histoire.*
> – *Oui.*
> – *Quand vous vous penchez, cette fleur frôle le contour extérieur de vos seins. Vous l'avez négligemment épinglée, trop haut. C'est une fleur énorme, vous l'avez choisie au hasard, trop grande pour vous. Ses pétales sont encore durs, elle a justement atteint la nuit dernière sa pleine floraison.*[17]

'You are resting your elbows on the grand piano. Between your breasts, which are naked beneath your dress, is that magnolia flower.'
Anne Desbaresdes, very attentively, listened to this story.
'Yes.'
'When you lean over, the flower brushes against the outline of your breasts. You have pinned it carelessly, too high. It is an enormous flower, you chose it at random, too large for you. Its petals are still hard, in fact it reached its full flowering just the night before.

In Chauvin's description, the magnolia is associated with Anne's breasts. The reader is encouraged to infer Chauvin's sexual interest in Anne from his clear memory of how the flower touched her breasts. The magnolia flower worn by Anne during the dinner-party scene carries the weight of this earlier magnolia with it. The very use of the word 'magnolia', followed by *grain nu* ('naked grain'), echoing the earlier *seins nus* ('naked breasts'), is almost bound to recall for the reader the sexual connotations of the earlier conversation, whether or not it reminds her/him of the actual words previously used. The magnolia has become the symbol for something sexual, for Chauvin's desire, which has never been explicitly articulated. Chauvin's sexual desire is a fantasy of the reader's, an inference, unstated. The magnolia refers to it as something which has been kept silent, whose articulation is absent, left 'blank'. The same process is at work with

17 ibid, pp 79–80.

the wine, which can be read as a symbol for Anne's (sexual) desire, having potentially acquired this meaning (to add to the ancient bacchanalian symbolism that it carries amongst others) in the preceding chapters. And in this case, the symbolic value of the wine is confirmed. Reinforcing the impression of the presence of Anne's desire, the reader is then told that other women besides Anne 'likewise raise arms which are naked, delectable, irreprochable, but are those of wives'. The 'but' marks them out as different from, even inferior to, Anne. Anne is also a wife, the reader might remember but straight after these words comes a reference to the man on the beach and the 'quayside café'. Although this sentence brings a complete break with the last in terms of the place and person it refers to, because it is in the same paragraph it appears to be linked to what precedes it and the reader assumes the connexion.

At this point the reader, if s/he is going to be able to 'make sense' out of what is being recounted, must almost inevitably infer that the man is Chauvin, that Anne's desire has something to do with him and their meetings in the café, that that desire is sexual in some way and that it makes her different from the other women, because it is for a man who is not her husband. None of this is stated instead it is left 'blank', to be more or less unconsciously assumed by the reader.

The other notable 'blank' to be found in this passage is around the use of *on* ('one'). In the preceding part of the chapter, *on* recurs, excusing Anne for lateness.[18] In the passage cited above, *on* has noticed Anne fingering the magnolia and becomes the source of a look and an opinion. *On* has become someone specific. This is, of course, inference on the part of myself as reader, but it is an inference which nothing contradicts and which everything suggests. Later, at the end of the chapter, *on* will look into the child's room and see Anne lying on the floor. *On* here takes the form of *une ombre* ('a shadow').[19] It would be almost perverse not to assume that *on* is Anne's husband but he is never mentioned by name. He is without any explicit existence in the text other than as *on* (and when Chauvin refers to him) but because the reader can infer him as the referent of *on*, he is constructed as a man to whom reference has been avoided, evaded, or perhaps suppressed. He has become a 'blank'.

In *Moderato cantabile*, 'blanks' may be produced by means of the juxtaposition of sentences which then seem to be connected, as above and, as I have indicated earlier, in dialogue. Alternatively, they may be produced by the use of symbolism, as in the case of the magnolia or the wine, where the signifiers *magnolia* and *vin* both become loaded

18   ibid, p 93.
19   ibid, p 103.

with resonances, so that their significance seems to the reader to exceed the possibility of its articulation and so becomes constructed as inarticulable. The 'blanks' are thus those elements of the reader's fantasy which the text produces by means other than explicit articulation. They are created through the operations of the reader's desire to 'make sense' of the text. The reader can only embark upon such an enterprise if s/he assumes that there is a sense to make, that is, if s/he assumes the presence of an effort of coherent representation, a desire on the part of the author to mean something by the text,[20] in terms of which the elements s/he is given do 'go together'.

Of course, most, if not all works of fiction require some work of inference on the part of the reader. For example, in the passage from *Un barrage contre le Pacifique*, the reader's inference is required to produce the irony of the narrator; and other authors besides Duras have used simliar techniques to create an effect of 'blanks'. A notable example of such an effect can be seen in Alain Robbe-Grillet's *Le Voyeur*, in which the reader is invited to understand that the central character, Mathias, has committed a murder which is not actually recounted. Like *Moderato cantabile*, this is a third person narration. However, it is entirely in free indirect style, which gives the reader/narratee insight into Mathias's thought processes throughout. This allows the reader to explain the 'blank' in terms of Mathias's psychology: he has suppressed the murder and the text can be read as an attempt to render his confused, disavowing thought processes.

In *Moderato cantabile*, the reader might be able to understand the 'blanks' in dialogue in psychological terms but the narration itself is too impersonal and detached to make its 'blanks' appear effects of a personalised narrator's suppression of things s/he does not want to describe, or think about. However, the reader's confidence that the elements of the narrative do 'make sense' is aided by apparently transparent reference to the 'real world'. And the story is clearly not out of control; on the contrary, it is fixed and finished in the past historic, seen through the eyes of this impartial narrator, told in the most apparently impersonal of language. Because of the apparent impartiality of the narration, and thus its authority as source of objective knowledge, the reader is not led to infer that the 'blanks' are the result of any deliberate omission of information. The narration appears simply to record what there is to tell, rather than having been 'edited down' from some fuller original version. The result is

---

20 Something which Jean Mistler seems unsure about. 'Critics are with their rights to ask why this second attempt; for it cannot be anything other than an attempt, with the aim of creating a finished work later on.' (*Moderato cantabile*, p 162)

that where things are left unsaid, it seems that they are in some sense unsayable.

★   ★   ★

Le Ravissement de Lol V. Stein is a first person narration, narrated by someone who turns out, on page 74, to be Jacques Hold, lover of Tatiana Karl and eventually of Lol. Here, the most obvious 'blank' is Lol herself, and this is explicitly stated: 'To know nothing about Lol was already to know her. One could, it seemed to me, know still less, less and less about Lol V. Stein.'[21] And this is the narrator's aim:

> Like one parched, I long to drink the misty and insipid milk of the words that come from Lol V. Stein's mouth, to be part of the thing lied by her. Let her carry me off, let the affair at last turn out differently from now on, let her grind me up with the rest, I shall be servile, let hope lie in being ground up with the rest, being servile.[22]

The story the narrator tells is of his desire for Lol and his attempt, doomed ultimately to failure, to achieve the end described above. Lol is constructed as the focal point of the text because the questions the text asks are: who is Lol? and what does she want? These questions, as is clear from the beginning, are unanswerable. The narrator makes constant reference to the unknowable nature of Lol V. Stein, 'her burnt up being...her ravaged nature'.[23] She herself is largely silent. In areas where she might be expected to manifest personality, or desires, such as in the organisation of her house and garden, the only evidence of individuality is in her extreme desire to conform:

> A strict order reigned in Lol's house at U. Bridge [...] The arrangement of the bedrooms, of the sitting-room, was a faithful reproduction of that seen in shop windows; the layout of the garden, which Lol took care of, reproduced that of the other gardens in U. Bridge. Lol was copying, but whom? the others, all the others, the greatest possible number of other people.[24]

Jacques Hold begins her story with a 'false version that Tatiana Karl tells and that which I have invented about the night of the Casino at T. Beach. Starting from these, I shall tell my story of Lol

21 *Le Ravissement de Lol V. Stein*, Paris, Gallimard, Folio series, 1964, p 81.
22 ibid, p 106.
23 ibid, p 113.
24 ibid, pp 33–4.

V. Stein'.[25] The authority of a large part of the text is then in doubt. Those parts that appear authoritative are those which recount things that happen in the presence of the narrator. These are written in the present tense, which gives them a certain immediacy and presence, and thus authority. The narrator is not lying or inventing, he is describing. However, his knowledge is limited to what he can see; the rest is supposition. For example, when he and Lol are talking about Tatiana in the tea rooms in Green Town:

> I can see that a dream has almost been reached. Flesh is tearing, bleeding, awakening. She is trying to listen to an inner tumult, she does not succeed, she is overcome by the realization, albeit incomplete, of her desire. She blinks rapidly under the effects of light which is too strong. I stop looking at her for the time that the very long ending of this moment lasts.[26]

What is 'happening', what is of interest to the narrator, is invisible, as it is to the reader, whose desire for knowledge, at least when s/he adopts the place of the narratee in an unselfconscious reading, is hooked into that of the narrator as it is constructed by the text. It is Lol's 'inner tumult', which remains always beyond the narrator's grasp because he cannot see it.

A kind of voyeurism pervades *Le Ravissement de Lol V. Stein*, and the voyeur can never see all, is never participant in the action, does not even want to be. Jacques Hold watches Lol but she is unknowable, even her appearance is 'bland' (*fade*), somehow indefinite. Lol in her turn watches Michael Richardson and Anne-Marie Stretter, or Jacques Hold and Tatiana Karl but she loses sight of the first couple when they leave the casino at T. Beach, and all she sees of the second is what is visible from the field behind the hotel. Even then, what she wants to see is herself being forgotten, herself as an absence, a 'blank'.

Like Anne and Chauvin, Lol is trying to reconstruct a lost event, that of the ball at T. Beach. But when she and Jacques Hold visit the T. Beach casino, nothing happens. For the reader/narratee, the moment is constructed as lost forever yet its effects are still present in Lol. It is present and not, produced as an abscence, an unattainable knowledge, because it is present only as a memory.

Whereas, in *Moderato cantabile*, the writing itself seems to leave gaps where the reader must infer connexions, the narration of *Le Ravissement de Lol V. Stein* makes the necessary connexions in the sequence of events and provides a certain amount of 'psychology'.

25 ibid, p 14.
26 ibid, p 131.

Jean Bedford is 'easy to reassure',[27] Jacques Hold interprets the thoughts and feelings of Lol and Tatiana during a conversation between the three of them:

'You frighten me Lol.'

Lol is surprised. Her surprise strikes exactly the fear that Tatiana is not admitting to. She has uncovered the lie. It's done. She asks gravely:

'What are you frightened of Tatiana?'

Suddenly Tatiana is no longer hiding anything. But without admitting the real meaning of her fear.

'I don't know.'

Lol looks around the sitting-room once more and explains to Tatiana a different thing from the one Tatiana would have liked to know. She returns, Tatiana is caught in her own trap, to the happiness of Lol V. Stein.

'But I didn't want anything, you understand, Tatiana, I didn't want any of what there is, of what happens. Nothing stays.'

'And if you had wanted it, wouldn't it be the same now?'

Lol considers and her air of reflection, her forgetful pretence has the perfection of artistry. I know she is saying the first thing that comes into her head:

'It's the same. On the first day it was the same as it is now. For me.'[28]

Jacques Hold tells the reader what he knows, but because he is a figure in the text, his knowledge is constructed as limited and lacking the automatic authority of the third person narration. Even before he introduces himself, the first person narration is full of uncertainty although, because the identity of the narrator is in doubt (it could even be the implied author), the limits of the narrator's knowledge and authority are less clearly defined. Jacques Hold interprets, but he is fallible. With Tatiana Karl, Pierre Beugner, or Jean Bedford, he seems to be able to fill in the psychological details, interpreting their words and giving the reader insights into their hidden meanings. With Lol, on the other hand, his insights are always into the limitations of the possibility of insight. For example:

She snuggles against me again, shuts her eyes, keeps silent, attentively. Her contentment breathes deeply at my side. No sign of her difference under my hand, in my sight. And yet, and yet. Who is there at this moment, so near and so far, what prowling ideas keep coming to visit her, by night, by day, in all lights? at this very

27   ibid, p 34.
28   ibid, pp 49–50.

moment? At this moment when I might believe her to be in this train, next to me, as other women would be?[29]

Lol is different from 'other women', 'Tatiana Karl, for example'.[30] For her difference to be felt, for her to be produced as a 'blank', the rest of the text must be comparatively 'full'. And so it is. Some details the reader might wish to speculate on are absent, such as the names of Lol's children, for example, but, like the number of Lady Macbeth's children, such information is not constructed as missing. The reader does not need to know such things and is in no way encouraged to ponder on them. In *Moderato cantabile* the psychology and the connections between descriptions implicitly produced by the realist narrative are perceived as 'missing' or 'suppressed', because otherwise the narration seems so authoritative and unproblematically transparent. Here, however, the psychology and connexions are present, just as might be expected in a realist text, narrated in the first person by a narrator closely involved with the other figures. Jacques Hold even has insights into Lol's psyche, and describes it as having a certain coherence. That coherence, however, is the coherence of absence, for the reader is told that what is absent in Lol suffering is and the meaningfulness of 'personality'. It is the absence which is Lol which is the object of the narrator's interest and the answer to the questions posed by the text, which thus appears to be constructed around a 'blank'.

★   ★   ★

Le Vice-consul, like *Le Ravissement de Lol V. Stein*, is apparently constructed around absence personified. This time it is in three different figures: the beggar-woman, Anne-Marie Stretter and the eponymous hero. The interplay of points of view from which this novel is narrated is more complex than that of those texts I have discussed so far for although the narration is primarily in the third person, the narrator of the story of the beggar-woman is Peter Morgan, who is writing his version of her life. This novel also resembles *Moderato cantabile* and *Le Ravissement de Lol V. Stein* in the great importance it gives to events which occur before the chronological point where the narration begins, these events being the actions of the vice-consul at Lahore and the journey of the beggar-woman from Battambang to Calcutta. As in the other two novels, much of the text is taken up by the attempts of figures such as Peter Morgan and Charles Rossett to reconstruct what happened.

29 ibid, p 168.
30 ibid.

The narration progresses to a large extent through dialogue, particularly during the reception at the French embassy, where there is much discussion of and interest in the vice-consul and/or Anne-Marie Stretter, often on the part of those simply designated as *on*. As in *Le Ravissement de Lol V. Stein*, the effect of 'blanks' is produced through the interest shown by some figures in the text in others about whom nothing can ultimately be known. Nothing can be known about the beggar-woman because she is mad; her memory is 'obliterated', she does not speak any recognisable language, but merely sings in what may or may not be the language of Savannakhet, Laos, and repeats the vocable 'Battambang'. She cannot be questioned, she can only be invented and this is Peter Morgan's project.

The vice-consul can and does speak, but he cannot explain himself. This is made clear fairly early on in the text, when Charles Rossett reads the vice-consul's letter to the ambassador, in which he says:

> I cannot explain myself, either concerning what I did at Lahore, or as to the why of this refusal. No outside authority, nor those of our administration, could really be interested, I think, in what I would say. The administration should not see in this refusal either mistrust or disdain with regard to anybody. But I shall simply limit myself here to stating that I find it impossible to give a comprehensible account of what happened at Lahore.[31]

The mystery is established, never to be resolved, at least, not explicitly. Moreover, the vice-consul's actions, his random shooting of lepers in the gardens of Shalimar, are often referred to simply by the name of the place where he perpetrated the act, Lahore. In this way, the name Lahore comes to act both as a symbol for the vice-consul's inexplicable psychological state – 'One thinks: He had to see Lahore to be sure of Lahore? Ah! In this town he used a cruel language.'[32] – and also as a euphemism for his actions, which are thus constructed as too awful, or impossible, to name, as in the following dialogue between Charles Rossett and the vice-consul:

> 'What do people say? That the worst is what?'
> 'Lahore.'
> 'It's so repellent, Lahore, that nothing else can be found to compare it with?'
> 'People can't help themselves...I'm sorry to say this to you, but one cannot understand Lahore, however, hard one tries.
> 'That's true', said the vice-consul.[33]

31 *Le Vice-consul*, Paris, Gallimard, 1966, p 39.
32 ibid, p 137.
33 ibid, p 104–5

The vice-consul himself, like those of his actions which are designated by the name Lahore, is constructed as repellent and incomprehensible. When he walks in the gardens in front of the ambassador's
office, 'Other people come out and walk through the gardens. It is mid-
day. No one comes up to him.'[34] The ambassador tells Charles Rossett:
'We have staying with us at the moment a charming young English
friend who cannot stand the sight of the vice-consul of Lahore...It's
not fear exactly, it's a sort of uneasiness... People avoid him, yes, I
admit it...I avoid him a little.'[35] The vice-consul makes a hole in
the social scene wherever he goes. At the reception at the embassy
he talks to Charles Rossett, the ambassador and the Spanish vice-
consul's wife, but all with apparently little enthusiasm and with
total incomprehension on the part of his interlocutors. The sole
exception to this lack of interest and understanding comes in his
conversation with Anne-Marie Stretter. He has already declared to
Clarles Rossett that he loves her and waits all evening to dance with
her. When finally he does so, she seems to understand him as no one
else has; but what she understands is unclear:

'I would like you to say that you see the inevitable side of
Lahore. Answer me.'
She does not reply.
'It is very important that you should see it, even for a very short
moment.'
She backs away slightly, startled. She thinks she ought to smile.
He does not smile. She is also trembling now.
'I don't know how to say...On your file there is the word
impossible. Is that the word this time?'
He remains silent. She asks again:
'Is that the word? Answer me...'
'I don't know myself, I'm trying to find it with you.'
'Perhaps there is another word?'
'That is no longer the problem.'
'I can see the inevitable side of Lahore', she says. 'I could
already see it yesterday, but I didn't know it.'
'That is all'.[36]

Because Anne-Marie Stretter seems able to see what the vice-
consul means, the reader can assume that he does in fact mean
something. However, that something is 'blank', inexpressible in
words, but understandable in other ways, at least by certain people
such as Anne-Marie Stretter. In order to 'make sense' of what is

34 ibid, p 45.
35 ibid.
36 ibid, pp 127–8.

going on, the reader will try to understand the inexpressible also, following the clues that s/he is given in the text such as the vice-consul's interest in leprosy, the *bonheur gai* ('joyful happiness') he experienced at Montfort, or any of the other details to be gleaned about the vice-consul, either from the latter's speeches or from the suppositions of others.

At the same time, Anne-Marie Stretter becomes constructed as being in touch with this inexpressible. Like the vice-consul, she has already been the object of a certain amount of speculation. At the beginning of the account of the reception at the embassy, we are told:

> The woman from Calcutta intrigues people. No one really knows how she occupies her time, she mainly receives people here, very little at home, in her residence which dates from the days of the first trading-posts, on the banks of the Ganges. Nevertheless, she occupies herself somehow. Is it by eliminating the other possible occupations that one decides that she reads? Yes. After the time spent playing tennis, and the time for walking, what else would she do, shut up at home?[37]

What indeed? The reader's speculation is invited and the missing answer is thus constructed as a 'blank'. Later, when they are dancing together, Anne-Marie Stretter affirms her understanding of and allegiance to the vice-consul:

> 'I know who you are', she says. 'We do not need to know each other any better. Do not be mistaken.'
> 'I am not mistaken.'
> 'I take life lightly', her hand tries to withdraw itself, 'that's what I do, everyone is right, for me, everyone is completely, profoundly right.'
> 'Don't try to go back on what you have said, there's no longer any point.'
> 'That's true.'
> 'You are with me.'
> 'Yes.'
> 'At this moment', he pleads, 'be with me. What did you say?'
> 'Nothing important.'
> 'We are going to part.'
> 'I am with you.'
> 'Yes.'

37   ibid, pp 93–4.

'I am with you here completely, as with no one else, here this evening, in India.'[38]

Here are two people who seem to understand one another. Anne-Marie Stretter knows 'who the vice-consul is' and does so by knowing very little about him, other than what he did at Lahore. The reader is invited to infer that her knowledge is unformulated and primarily sympathetic, a supposition made stronger when she says to him 'I am with you'. Later, in answer to the question, 'In fact, who was the vice-consul from Lahore like?' Anne-Marie Stretter replies, 'Me'.[39] Her dancing with the vice-consul and her affirmation that she understands and is sympathetic to him, sets Anne-Marie Stretter apart from the other figures, who do not understand him at all and mostly avoid him when possible. She is in the same category as he, different from the rest, linked by a bond of tacit, 'blank' understanding. She is also singled out by all the male figures, except for the director of the European Circle, as an object of sexual interest. But the reader is given little direct insight into her psyche. She does not speak much and when she does, other than to the vice-consul, she appears distant and barely involved in the conversation. She spends a lot of time asleep. Michael Richard explains her attraction for men in the following terms: 'And what if the vice-consul from Lahore was just that, one of those men who seek out this woman, in whose presence they believe oblivion will come?[40] This is reminiscent of Lol V. Stein, whose attraction for Jacques Hold lay in her ungraspable 'blandness', in which everything is 'ground up'. Like Lol, Anne-Marie Stretter is 'bland' and distant. She is unknowable and ungraspable.

In *Moderato cantabile* and *Le Ravissement de Lol V. Stein*, the narration seemed to be 'uttered' from fixed points: in the former, it was the all-seeing eye of the narrator, who could, however, only know what was visible; in the latter it was Jacques Hold, who observed or invented the story of Lol V. Stein. In *Le Vice-consul*, the point from which the text is narrated shifts and is not always easily defined. For example, in the following extract from the account of the reception at the embassy, much of the information is conveyed in free indirect style by the undefined *on*, or by one of the guests. *On dit* can be translated variously into English as 'they say', 'people say', 'it is said', 'someone says', or 'one says', and, as none of these will do for all the instances of *on* in this passage, I have had to translate it in two different ways, 'someone' and 'one', which alters the effect of the original French.

38 ibid, pp 143–4.
39 ibid, p 204.
40 ibid, p 159.

On dit: Tiens, le voilà, voilà Michael Richard...vous ne savez pas?

Michael Richard a dans les trente ans. Son élégance dès qu'il entre attire l'attention. Il cherche des yeux Anne-Marie Stretter, la trouve, lui sourit.

On dit: Vous ne savez pas que depuis deux ans...tout Calcutta est au courant.

Près de Charles Rossett la voix sifflante: il vient de l'autre bout du buffet, un verre de champagne à la main.

– Vous avez l'air bien absorbé.

On dit: Il reste encore, le vice-consul, regardez comme il reste tard.

On pense: Il lui fallait voir Lahore pour être sûr de Lahore? Ah! il tenait à cette ville un langage cruel

Ne rien lui dire, pense Charles Rossett, rester sur ses gardes. Il n'a sans doute pas encore vu Michael Richard, d'ailleurs, quelle importance? Que voit-il? Elle, on dirait, elle seulement.

J'ai envie de champagne, dit Charles Rossett, depuis que je suis ici je bois trop...

On pense à lui en termes d'interrogatoire. Cette bicyclette de femme, celle de Mme Stretter, comment se présente-t-elle à vos yeux?

On entend la réponse: Je n'ai rien à dire sur les raisons...

On songe: Et quand il a été confirmé dans ce qu'il croyait qu'était Lahore avant de la voir il a appelé la mort sur Lahore.

Une femme: Le prêtre dit que Dieu fournit l'explication si on le prie. Quelqu'un se moque.

– Vous verrez, dit le vice-consul à Charles Rossett, ici l'ivresse est toujours pareille.

Ils boivent. Anne-Marie Stretter se trouve dans le salon à côté avec George Crawn, Michael Richard et un jeune Anglais qui est arrivé avec lui. Charles Rossett saura où elle se trouve jusqu'à la fin de la nuit.[41]

Someone says: Look, there he is, there's Michael Richard... don't you know?

Michael Richard is in his thirties. His elegance draws people's attention as soon as he comes in. He looks around for Anne-Marie Stretter, finds her, smiles at her.

Someone says: Don't you know that for two years...all Calcutta knows about it.

Near Charles Rossett the whistling voice: he has come from the other end of the buffet, a glass of champagne in his hand.

'You look very preoccupied.'

41 ibid, pp 137–8.

Someone says: He's still here, the vice-consul, look how late he's staying.

Someone thinks: So he had to see Lahore to be sure of Lahore? Ah! In this town he used a cruel language.

Don't say anything to him, thinks Charles Rossett, stay on the alert. No doubt he has not yet seen Michael Richard, anyway, what does it matter? What does he see? Her, you would think, only her.

'I want some champagne,' says Charles Rossett, 'since I've been here I've been drinking too much...'

One thinks of him in interogatory terms. That woman's bicycle, Anne-Marie Stretter's, how does it appear to you?

One hears the reply: I have nothing to say about the reasons...

One muses: And when he was confirmed in the belief he had held before seeing Lahore as to what Lahore was, he called death down upon Lahore.

A woman: The priest says that God provides the explanation if one prays to him. Someone laughs.

'You'll see,' says the vice-consul to Charles Rossett, 'here drunkeness is always the same.'

They drink. Anne-Marie Stretter is in the salon next door with George Crawn, Michael Richard and a young Englishman who came in with him. Charles Rossett will know where she is until the end of the night.

In this passage, the inferred origin of the words jumps around from *on* to Charles Rossett, to the vice-consul, to the narrator. The first three instances of *on*, where *on* speaks, could be inferred by the reader to be remarks made by unspecified guests at the reception watching the proceedings, who are not intimate friends of the Stretters. However, the reader/narratee will be drawn to the assumption that the *on* who 'thinks', 'hears', or 'muses' is someone who has spoken with the vice-consul, who knows his story and is interested in it; someone fairly specific. S/he may well be led to speculate who it might be. Could it be Charles Rossett, who has seen the vice-consul with Anne-Marie Stretter's bicycle? Perhaps so, as the third person narration often seems privy to his thoughts, as it is to those of Peter Morgan. Too specific to be impersonal, *on* must be a person with a name; but that name is missing. It has become a 'blank'.

As well as the identity of *on*, the reader might speculate as to the meaning of the words attributed to 'a woman'. Following the 'pertinence principle', s/he might well assume that they are of relevance to the previous thoughts attributed to *on*, which are about the vice-consul. However, no clues are given here. If the reader infers that there is a link, it is left unstated by the detached narration, and thus constructed as 'suppressed', unsayable or 'blank'.

Le Vice-consul is a third person narration, but it does not hold the figures it portrays at equal distance. Like *Le Ravissement de Lol V. Stein*, it constructs certain figures such as the beggar-woman, Anne-Marie Stretter, the vice-consul, as objects of interest of others', for Peter Morgan, Charles Rossett, and *on*. The first three are all linked with each other in various ways throughout the text and also with India, to which they appear to have a special relation. The beggar-woman walks and walks until she comes to Calcutta, where suddenly, 'she stays'.[42] She becomes associated with the lepers: 'Right next to her sleeping body are those of the lepers',[43] and it is she whom Peter Morgan follows and writes about as part of his attempt to 'grasp the suffering of Calcutta, to throw himself into it, so that it might be done and his ignorance cease with the grasping of suffering'.[44]

The beggar-woman is constructed as quite different and separate from the British and French colonisers. Her story is told separately from that of the white figures, and when she does appear in the rest of the text, she is mad, her speech means nothing, she owns nothing to give her an identity the Europeans can understand. The latter react to her in different ways. Peter Morgan apparently copes with her by trying to reconstruct her story, Charles Rossett, when he meets her on the island of the Prince of Wales Hotel, is horrified and scuttles back into the enclosure where only whites are allowed. Both are affected by her strangeness and incomprehensibility, but neither can just accept it. They either flee or try to rationalise it.

Anne-Marie Stretter also seems interested in her, but differently so. It is she who identifies the language of the beggar-woman's song as perhaps that of Savannakhet, from where they both have come, down the Mekong and thence to Calcutta. Anne-Marie Stretter leaves water out for the lepers and the beggar-woman during the monsoon and the latter follows her to the islands. In Peter Morgan's book both of them will figure. They seem to coexist peacefully, to their mutual benefit.

The vice-consul is linked to India and to Anne-Marie Stretter by his actions in Lahore. In his conversation with the 'Director' of the European Circle, who repeats everything he tells him, he says of his youth at Neuilly:

The thing was, Director, I was waiting for India, I was waiting for you, I did not yet know it. Whilst waiting, at Neuilly, I was

42 ibid, p 71.
43 ibid, p 29.
44 ibid.

clumsy. I broke lamps. Say: the lamps broke and fell. I heard them smash in the emtpy corridors. You can say: already, at Neuilly, you understand?[45]

Already, in Neuilly, the vice-consul apparently felt things that were to crystallise in Lahore. His breaking of lamps is a forerunner to his smashing mirrors in Lahore; in his youth he is destined for India.

The other thing he does in Lahore is to shoot lepers. Leprosy seems to be a preoccupation amongst Calcutta's white inhabitants (we never hear about the rest). One woman has to be sent back to Europe because she is afraid she has leprosy, and lepers are discussed at the reception. For example, 'Did you know that lepers burst when hit like sacks full of dust?[46] The vice-consul describes to Anne-Marie Stretter the impossibility of explaining his actions at Lahore in terms of leprosy:

'Why do you speak to me of leprosy?'
'Because I have the impression that if I tried to tell you what I would like to be able to tell you, everything would dissolve into dust...'[47]

Later he says to the Spanish vice-consul's wife: 'I want leprosy, rather than being frightened of it.'[48] Through constant reference to it, leprosy acquires symbolic value as a kind of dreadful absolute, to which differnt relations are possible. Most of white society avoids it and fear of it is usual amongst new arrivals. However, the vice-consul desires it, Anne-Marie Stretter and the begger-woman coexist with it. Indeed, the beggar-woman has gone beyond its reach: 'Nothing more can happen to her, leprosy itself...'[49]

Apart from the story of the beggar-woman, the heat and leprosy are the most salient features of India mentioned in the text. Like leprosy, India is beyond the grasp of the whites, who find comfort in recreating 'France in India'.[50]

Since neither the beggar-woman nor Anne-Marie Stretter are afraid of leprosy in the way that most of white society is, they appear to have a different relation to India as well. Peter Morgan wants to grasp 'India's suffering' by writing, whereas the beggar-woman, with her terrible life, is past all suffering; Anne-Marie

45   ibid, p 88.
46   ibid, p 114.
47   ibid, p 125.
48   ibid, p 131.
49   ibid, p 157.
50   ibid, p 100.

Stretter accepts it and sleeps; the vice-consul has plunged himself into it. Each of these three characters is built around what is constructed as an impossibility of articulation, the 'blank' of suffering India, and through them India itself becomes a vast 'blank', which Europeans, in the shapes of Peter Morgan and Charles Rossett, can struggle to render intelligible and articulate, but which must always elude them: 'Boredom, here, is a feeling of colossal abandonment, of a size with India itself, the country sets the tone[51] and 'You know, India is a bottomless pit of indifference, in which everything is swallowed up.'[52]

So *Le Vice-consul* presents the reader with at least two different figures attempting to reconstruct what is essentially the same vast 'blank' around India, and personified in different ways by the beggar-woman, the vice-consul and Anne-Marie Stretter. Third person narration is kept to a minimum. It does not describe India but through the unanswered, and apparently unanswerable questions posed in the text, makes it appear as the unknowable which has caught the beggar-woman, Anne-Marie Stretter and the vice-consul and rendered them incomprehensible as well.

*   *   *

The last of the texts I want to discuss in detail in relation to 'blanks' is *Détruire, dit-elle*. This is in some ways the most explicit, but in others the most obscure of the five. The style is similar to that of *Le Vice-consul* inasmuch as the text is basically a third person narrative, of which most is taken up with direct speech. Those parts which are not in direct speech are composed of short, simple sentences describing the figures' actions, or aspects of their surroundings. These read like the stage directions for a play – in fact there is a *note pour les représentations* ('note for performances') at the end – and *Détruire, dit-elle* also became a film of the same name. The sparseness of the text is perhaps what led Maurice Blanchot to ask, 'is it "a book"? "a film"? something between the two?'[53] However, I want to discuss it here in its manifestation as a novel.

The obscurity of *Détruire, dit-elle* lies in what might be described as the minimalism of the construction of the figures, Alissa, Stein, Max Thor, Elizabeth Alione, and the hotel in which they are staying. The descriptions of these figures and their hotel is in Duras's

51   ibid, p 116.
52   ibid, p 117.
53   Maurice Blanchot, 'Détruire', in *Marguerite Duras*, Paris, Albatros, Ça Cinéma series, 1979, p 139.

familiar style of very short sentences describing primarily what is visible. The text opens:

> Cloudy weather.
> The picture windows are closed.
> From the dining room side, where he is, the grounds cannot be seen.
> She though, yes, she can see, she is looking. Her table is touching the window-ledge.
> Because of the bright light, she is screwing up her eyes. Her eyes move one way, then the other. Other clients are also watching these tennis matches that he himself cannot see.[54]

There are no detailed descriptions of the hotel. Max Thor, the 'he' watching Elizabeth Alione here, will never be described at all, although she will be. The narration gives just enough information to set a scene, and all is done in this clipped, simple style, without contradiction or complication. The language seems impersonally transparent, the information it gives perfectly clear it is just that there is not very much of it. Blanchot reassures the anxious: 'Characters? Yes, they are in the positions of characters', 'Certainly, what is happening there happens in a place that we can put a name to: a hotel, the grounds, and, beyond, a forest', 'Where do they come from? Who are they? Certainly they are beings like ourselves: there are no others in this world'[55]. However, in *Détruire, dit-elle*, Duras eschews many of the conventions of realist fiction which she has maintained until now, stripping the figures of all 'character' while their behaviour does not follow conventional rules. For example, here is the first conversation between Alissa and Stein, who have never met before:

> 'Alissa', he calls at last. 'It's Stein.'
> 'Stein.'
> 'Yes. I'm here.'
> She does not move. Stein slips to the ground, places his head on Alissa's knees.
> 'I don't know you, Alissa', says Stein.
> 'He has stopped loving me in a certain way perhaps?'
> 'It's here that he realised that he could no longer imagine his life without you.'
> They are silent. He places his hands on Alissa's body.

---

54 *Détruire, dit-elle*, Paris, Minuit, 1969, p 9.
55 Blanchot, op cit, p 140.

'You are part of me, Alissa. Your fragile body is part of my body. And I don't know you'.[56]

This is clearly not realist dialogue in the sense that all the preliminary formalities and introductory conversations that one might expect to take place when two people first meet are absent. However, if the reader takes the place of the narratee and enters into the terms of the text, then this conversation is getting down to the 'essentials' of what *Détruire, dit-elle* is about, what it stages: madness, despair and the workings of desire.

Alissa and Stein's conversation is representative of the rest of the novel in style and tone. Most of the dialogues concern the immediate events described, with the exception of those in which Elizabeth Alione talks about her pregnancy, the young doctor and her stillborn child. The action is entirely confined to the hotel and to the interaction between Max Thor, Stein, Alissa, Elizabeth Alione and, at the end, Bernard Alione. Passing references are made to the existence of other guests at the hotel, but they do not encroach in any way upon the events or conversations described. The text creates a world which seems hermetically sealed, where everything that goes to make everyday life as it is usually described is absent. Within this world, Max Thor, Stein and Alissa pursue Elizabeth Alione. But to what end? This is intimated, rather than articulated. Whilst Alissa and Elizabeth Alione are talking, Stein and Max Thor are watching: Stein says 'Capital destruction will first take place at the hands of Alissa'.[57] Elizabeth Alione seems to be the target for this destruction, but she avoids it by going home with her husband. Alissa, who is to bring the destruction about, is, like the beggar-woman of *Le Vice-consul*, mad. Like Lol V. Stein, who at the time of her marriage to Jean Bedford, 'was looking younger. She might have been taken for a fifteen year-old',[58] and who 'still looked unhealthily young' when Jacques Hold meets her, Alissa is very young – young enough to be her husband's daughter. Furthermore, she never grows any older:

'How old is Alissa?'
'Eighteen.'
'And when you met her?'
'Eighteen.'[59]

---

56   *Détruire, dit-elle*, pp 49–50.
57   ibid, p 59.
58   *Le Ravissement de Lol V. Stein*, p 29.
59   *Détruire*, dit-elle, p 134.

Like the Anne-Marie Stretter of *India Song* (and by inference, she of *Le Vice-consul*), or 'the woman' of *L'Amour*, Alissa *est à celui qui la veut* ('is any man's who wants her).[60] She is a 'blank' inasmuch as it seems there is nothing to know about her; she has no 'personality', nor, apparently, a history, for she never gets any older. Stein and Max Thor are almost as 'blank'. Max Thor is a teacher, but what he teaches is 'history...of the future'. '"There's nothing any more", says Max Thor. "So I don't speak. My pupils sleep."'[61] About Stein, the reader is told nothing other than that he is Jewish. Alissa says to Elizabeth Alione, 'I can't talk about Stein'[62] and this stated impossibility fuels the production of a 'blank' around him.

In *Détruire, dit-elle*, an important event has once more occurred before the chronological beginning of the narration. This is Elizabeth Alione's relationship with the young doctor. What happened between them is not clear, but apparently it has made her interesting to Stein, Max Thor and Alissa:

'I realized,' says Elizabeth Alione softly, 'that you were interested in me because of...that alone. And that perhaps you were right.'
'That what?'
Elizabeth gestures, she does not know. Alissa takes Elizabeth Alione by the shoulders.
Elizabeth turns. They are both caught in a mirror.
'Who reminds you of that man?' asks Alissa in the mirror, 'of that young doctors?'
'Stein, perhaps.'
'Look,' says Alissa.
Silence. Their heads have drawn close together.
'We are like each other', says Alissa: 'we would love Stein if it were possible to love.'[63]

Exactly what it is that interests the three in Elizabeth Alione is never stated, but merely designated as 'that', the inexpressible. However, the reader/narratee is led to understand that she is ripe for 'capital destruction'; which is perhaps what Alissa is attempting when she expresses disgust at the story of how Elizabeth Alione showed the young doctor's letter to her husband:

Elizabeth shouts.
'Do you want to reduce me to despair?'

60 ibid, p 131.
61 ibid, p 122.
62 ibid, p 78.
63 ibid, p 99.

Alissa smiles at her.

'Yes, stop talking.'[64]

It is up to the reader to infer what might come of Elizabeth's despair but it seems possible to conclude, from this dialogue, that her experience with the young doctor has brought her closer to Alissa, Stein and Max Thor, and has begun the process of destruction. This process seems to be one she is too frightened to continue, but which would, if she let it to go on, render her the same as the others, described by Blanchot as 'radically ravaged beings'.[65] Nothing can be known about such beings, because they lack the trappings of identity such as those that Lol V. Stein built, if unconvincingly, for herself at U. Bridge. The only things that give them individual identities are their names, the descriptions of both men as Jewish and a brief reference to the past of Max Thor and Alissa. Their names, the suggestion of race or history and the lack of any indications to the contrary lead the reader/narratee to understand that these are indeed 'beings like ourselves', that is, that the text is portraying, or intending to portray, 'human beings' in a world purporting to bear some relation to the extra-textual 'real world'. But the lack of any further information with which s/he can construct some more complex form of identity for these figures, information which more traditional works of fiction would normally provide, means that they appear 'ravaged'.

The text uses Duras's familiar realist technique of simple description of the visible, the hotel windows, certain actions on the part of the figures. But the information supplied is scant, and must of it concerns what cannot be known – a kind of anti-information; its chief role seems to be to indicate what cannot be told or known: a vast 'blank' in life.

So, in Duras's later novels, the 'blanks' appear as points where the inexpressible erupts into the narration, where linguistic meaning breaks down. It might indeed be possible to draw, as Marini and others have done, analogies between Duras's 'blanks' and silences or blockings of sense in the speech of analysands. However, rather than seeing Duras's 'blanks' as manifestations of a 'feminine libidinal organization', expressing itself through her writing, I would suggest that they are produced by the internal workings of the texts. My survey of five of Duras's novels has revealed recurrent features which are productive of 'blanks', and I have identified these as follows.

---

64 ibid, p 98.
65 Blanchot, op cit, p 141. I have translated *détruire* and *êtres détruits* here as 'to ravage' and 'ravaged beings' respectively, but have rendered *destruction* as 'destruction'.

THE LOST MOMENT

Realist novels tend to begin with or just before the occurrence of the first major event which sets the unfolding of the plot in motion: *War and Peace* begins with Pierre's coming into his inheritance, the start of the wars between Russia and France under Napoleon and Nicolay's and Sonya's vows, all of which are the conditions which make various strands of the plot possible; Albert Camus' novel *La Peste* begins with Rieux's discovery of the first dead rat; *Un barrage contre le Pacifique* begins with the death of the horse and the decision taken by Suzanne, Joseph and their mother to go into Ram, where they meet M. Jo.

In contrast to these, in the more experimental novels I have discussed, the major catalyst, the event which is constructed as setting the text in motion, occurs 'beyond the scope' of the narration. In *Moderato cantabile*, the shooting occurs outside the room where the 'eye' of the narration is recording Anne Desbaresdes's child's piano lesson, whilst in the others the event, the Lahore shooting, the ball at S. Thala, or Elizabeth Alione's relationsip with the young doctor, occurs before the chronological beginning of the text. This is a very common feature of Duras's work, and such an event plays a part in most, if not all of her texts. Even in *Un barrage contre le Pacifique*, the dam of the title was built and destroyed before the death of the horse which opens the novel. However, the story of the dam is recounted by the narrator as a flashback. The reader is told what happened. Furthermore, the part it plays in the text is structurally different from that of, for example, the Lahore shooting. It is not set up as a problem which the text is trying (and failing) to solve in the same way.

Beginning with Duras's next published work, *Le Marin de Gibraltar*, the 'lost event' is no longer simply recounted by the narration, but is reconstructed by figures in the text. The structure of a novel can be seen in terms of a movement towards the answer, revealed at the end, to a question or questions posed at the beginning. In Duras's novels, the movement towards reconstruction of the lost event provides one of the motor forces behind the structure of the text, although arguably it is more important in some (*L'Amante anglaise, Moderato cantabile*) than in others (*Dix heures et demie du soir en été, Détruire, dit-elle*). However, the figures are portrayed as unable to describe the event or its effects and, in those novels where the third person narration might, with its authoritative voice, explain to the reader exactly what happened and what s/he should understand by it, as happens, for example, in *Un barrage contre le Pacifique*, the event always occurs 'off stage', beyond the scope of a highly reliable, but limited (for example, to what is visible from a particular place) narrator. In this way the reconstruction is rendered impossible, although the effects of the lost event reverberate through the text and constant reference is made to it. The reader/narratee thus feels a lack of knowledge of 'what really happened' though s/he knows that something did, because its effects are still felt. The absent event, or more particularly, its meaning, the reason why it causes certain effects, thus appears as a 'blank', which can never be filled in, because it is always 'off limits'. The answers to questions relating to this event are thus constructed as definitively absent.

THE WITHERING AWAY OF CHARACTER

Even in her earliest works, Duras does not go into very great detail in the creation of 'character'. The reader is not given detailed descriptions of the figures in the novels: their histories, idiosyncrasies of speech, the colour of their eyes, etc. Nevertheless, until *Moderato cantabile*, the information given appears adequate in terms of the conventions of psychological realism, which is a category into which the novels fit with relative ease. The characters are constructed as 'real people', who could be assumed to exist outside the text, and, like 'real people' portrayed through discourses other than those of realist fiction, such as those of biography, history or contemporary journalism, they have desires which can be, and are, articulated. They then act in accordance with those desires, like, for instance, Suzanne who wants to leave the plain, is bored by M. Jo and thinks a great deal of her mother and brother. Her actions in *Un barrage contre le Pacifique* are comprehensible in these terms.

With *Moderato cantabile* there is a change. The reader/narratee is still presented with figures whom s/he reads as being 'real' in the way that other figures in texts of realist fiction might be said to be read as being 'real', that is, the reader can imagine them as potentially existing beyond and being described by, rather than produced by, the text. Most of Duras's figures have names which are, with the exception of Jean-Marc de H..., the vice-consul, given in full and often repeated. This naming of the characters fixes them in terms of a social being and status[66] and also contributes to the reader's imagining them as 'real people', designated, but not fully defined by their name. The name makes the figure present as an individual,

---

66 In this context, the truncation of the vice-consul's name fits into the tradition of realist fiction where characters are often designated in such a way 'to protect their reputations', since the text is constructing them as 'real people.'

but in doing so constructs that figure as someone about whom more could be known. This effect is heightened by Duras's use, in many cases, of the full name of a figure (Anne Desbaresdes, Lol V. Stein, Anne-Marie Stretter) where the frequent appearance of that figure might be expected to lead to a shortened form of the name being used in the text. The repeated use of the full name gives an impression of formality to the narration, as if the narrator were not intimate with the figure thus named; the latter is thus produced as more distant and unknowable, and at the same time more imposing, than if a shorter form were used.

The reader/narratee imagines the figures as being subjects of desire ('real people') and so reads their actions as manifestations of the presence of their desires and their fears. However, the nature of their desires is never articulated although its presence is strongly suggested. In *Moderato cantabile*, the meetings of Anne Desbaresdes and Chauvin make up the main body of the text but exactly *why* they meet is never stated. Their desire is constructed as both what, in one strand of the narration, the text is 'about' and that which goes unexplained. In the years that follow *Moderato cantabile*, Duras produces sparser and sparser texts in the same vein, where the desire of the figures portrayed is constructed as both the *raison d'être* of the text and as that which cannot be spoken.

The figures are portrayed for the most part outside a precise social context. This may be due to a temporary escape in the form of a holiday (*Dix heures et demie du soir en été, Détruire, dit-elle*), or to the age of the figures concerned (*L'Après-midi de M. Andesmas*); it may be that one of the most important figures is mad, and thus to some extent 'outside' society (*L'Amour, L'Amante anglaise, Le Vice-consul*); often one of the key figures portrayed is a woman married to a wealthy man, who therefore has time on her hands and is able to follow the dictates of her desires (Lol V. Stein, Anne Desbaresdes, Anne-Marie Stretter). In some later texts (*L'Amour, La Maladie de la mort, L'Homme assis dans le couloir*), the figures have neither names nor history; indeed, these texts appear more as fantasies which may be of relevance to 'reality', but do not attempt to portray it, almost all the conventions and devices which realist fiction uses to produce an impression of imitating 'reality' having been abandoned.

As the figures become less and less 'filled out', and the texts become more and more confined to the manifestation of their (ill-defined) desires as opposed to portraying their 'characters', so their desires become less and less clearly articulated and the importance of *oubli* ('oblivion') and of the individual figures' attaining of a state in which they are 'ravaged' grows. In this way, the reader is led to concentrate on attempts to reach, and manifestations of, a state about which nothing can be said, whilst any other details about the figures are, with each successive text, pared away further and further. This trend continues into Duras's film-making, and is finally reversed with the publication of *L'Amant* (1984) and *La Douleur* (1985).

SYMBOLISM

In many of Duras's texts, certain signifiers acquire resonances which make them appear as symbols for something which remains undefined. This is the case in *Moderato cantabile* with *la fleur de magnolia*, or *la vedette*; in *Le Vice-consul* with *la lèpre*, or *Lahore*, in *Détruire, dit-elle* with *la forêt*, and there are many other instances. These signifiers appear to be elevated to the status of symbols through their repeated occurrence in certain contexts although in fact, they cannot be said to be symbols in the true sense of the term, since they do not stand in the place of something precise. I have already discussed this in relation to the *fleur de magnolia, la lèpre*, and *Lahore* in the context of the novels in which they occur. In every case the reader is invited to infer the desire, fear, or horror of the figures in the text in relation to these signifiers, but is never told exactly what the cause of these emotions is. In this way, these and other signifiers appear as symbols for something which exists but is unnamable, or else become symbols for an emotion. Their use thus produces 'blanks' arising because a signifier such as *la fleur de magnolia* carries with it all the resonances of all the unstated but inferred meanings which accrue to it as the text progresses.

'SEAMLESS' DISCOURSE

It is at those points of the text where, in order for the reader to continue reading it as a coherent whole, with a movement carrying it from beginning to end, s/he has to infer links between things that are not explicitly connected, or assume meanings that are not given in the text itself, that the 'blanks' are produced. The reader's inference takes the place of the information that the text does not provide.

The 'blanks' appear as an impossibility of articulation, rather than as information which could have been included and which has simply been ommitted through some whim or lack of knowledge on the part of the narrator. The reader/narratee does not 'fill in' the 'blanks' whilst reading, at least not consciously, although s/he might

want to do so after reading. The text itself gives clues, but not answers, and the 'blank's remain 'blanks' although critics and editors
of annotated editions might have given their own versions of how to
fill them in.

In her work after and including *Moderato cantabile*, Duras
achieves this effect by reducing the 'scope' of the narration. These
texts do not construct an omniscient narrator, or even a narrator
whose knowledge is limited but who interprets events, understands
the motivations of the figures portrayed and suggests readings to the
reader from a spatial and/or temporal 'vantage point', as happens
in *Un barrage contre le Pacifique*. Instead, the place of the narrator,
and the knowledge available to her/him are restricted. In *Un barrage
contre le Pacifique*, the omniscient narrator is produced as having a
'point of view' at points of contradiction in the discourse of the text.
The reader/narratee infers a desire on the part of a personalised
narrator, which produces these contradictions and must be interpreted, in order for sense to be made of the narration. The narrator
is produced in this text as having an ironic overview of what is recounted from a position 'outside' the text. S/he is the mediator,
through whom the reader's understanding must pass, and has
opinions on what s/he narrates, which the reader is aware of, if
dimly.

With *Moderato cantabile*, this type of narrator disappears. The
text is in the past historic, thus narrated from a position temporally
'outside' the text. However, the narrator is constructed as not having
an opinion or a point of view on what s/he is narrating, but as merely
recording what s/he saw. In fact, the narrator is not produced as a
distinctive 'voice' at all, but seems to disappear into the impersonal
discourse of the text. This is the case in other third person narra-
tions, such as *Le Vice-consul, Détruire, dit-elle* and *L'Amour*, where
again, the narrator appears to be recording simply what is visible;
except that in the case of these three texts, the narration is in the present tense, thus rendering more strongly the immediacy of the visible,
whilst also preventing the construction of the narrator as 'outside'
what is happening.

The 'disappearance' of the narrator is facilitated by lack of disturbance in the discourse of the text. The narration does not contradict
itself, nor, for the most part, does it require much interpretative work
on the part of the reader to discover – or invent – the pertinence of the
words. Sentences are kept as simple as possible and apparently
describe only what might be seen from a particular vantage point:
for example, in the café in *Moderato cantabile*, or in the hotel in
Détruire, dit-elle, with as little use of any rhetorical devices as possible. There are occasions where the narration seems uncertain, as,

for example, in *Moderato cantabile* when it is said of the child,[67] 'he appeared to be thinking, took his time, and perhaps he was lying.' Yet whilst it might be said that this uncertainty temporarily breaks the 'transparency' of the text and produces an uncertain narrator, the uncertainty reinforces the narrator's role as that of faithfully recording just what is visible, lacking knowledge and refusing to interpret anything else.[68]

In the case of *Le Ravissement de Lol V. Stein*, the text is not a third person narration. Jacques Hold, the first person narrator, apparently 'invents' much of the story, infers motives for behaviour on the part of the other figures, and interprets their actions. However, his account of Lol is largely in terms of what he can see, even if what he sees is not what one might expect to be put into the category of the visible: 'I see everything. I see love itself'.[69] Such divergence from the conventions of what is and is not visible can be understood by the reader in terms of Jacques Hold's specific vision, he being the subject who 'utters' the narration. Furthermore, his narration uses, for the most part, a style which is only a little less sparse than that of the third person narration of *Moderato cantabile* or *Le Vice-consul*, and where the reader infers a simple recording of events without rhetorical embellishments. Jacques Hold is not, it seems, fond of simile, metaphor, synechdoche, or any other figure of speech which might possibly trouble the apparent transparency of his language. The discourse of *Le Ravissement de Lol V. Stein* is seldom, if ever, disturbed by conflicting meanings or inconsistencies which might bring its veracity into doubt, and any peculiarities of style can be put down to momentary wanderings on the part of Jacques Hold's desire.

It is perhaps significant that the narration of Duras's texts is so often, with the exception of *L'Amante anglaise*, the narration of the visible. The scopic drive, according to Lacan, 'is the one which most completely avoids the limit of castration',[70] allowing the subject the greatest sense of identification, both in relation to, and with the object. Moreover, much of his theory of the role of the phallus rests on the importance of the sight of the penis. 'Seeing is believing', as they say. The undisturbed discourse of the visible in Duras' texts

---

67 *Moderato cantabile*, p 66.
68 In the light of my use of the word 'recording', it is interesting to note that in *L'Amante anglaise*, where there is no narrator as such, the text being composed of a series of dialogues, it is stated at the beginning, *tout ce qui est dit ici est enregistré* ('everything that is said here is a recording') (*L'Amante anglaise*, London, Heinmann, 1972, p 23). It is as if here Duras were experimenting with a different sense, with the ear of the tape-recorder, rather than the eye of the camera. Like the eye, the ear does not interpret or judge, but merely records what it hears, faithfully and impartially.
69 *Le Ravissement de Lol V. Stein*, p. 105.
70 Lacan, *Les Quatre Concepts fondamentaux de la psychanalyse*, p 74.

gives the reader an authoritative and apparently objective account of 'what happened', avoiding any disturbing eruptions of the unconscious into the process of reading. Linear time is observed throughout unless, as in *Le Ravissement de Lol V. Stein*, flashbacks are sanctioned by the presence of a first person narrator, constructed as a man with faculties of memory and imagination. Thus Duras constructs a kind of ultra-clear, hyper-realist discourse with meticulous precision.

At this point it seems apposite to look at Duras's and Gauthier's suggestions that the former's texts exhibit a 'a reworking of usual grammatical sense', or a 'violent rejection of syntax'. Both these ideas would run contrary to the view that I am putting forward, that Duras uses language in such a way as to produce an impression of almost complete expressivity, at least in the strictly narrative parts of her texts. The phrase from *L'Amour* that Gauthier quotes comes from the following passage:

> *Quelqu'un marche, près.*
> *L'homme qui regardait passe entre la femme aux yeux fermés et l'autre au loin, celui qui va, qui vient, prisonnier. On entend le martèlement de son pas sur la piste de planches qui longent la mer. Ce pas-ci est irrégulier, incertain.*
> *Le triangle se défait, se résorbe. Il vient de se défaire: en effet, l'homme passe, on le voit, on l'entend.*
> *On entend: le pas s'espace. L'homme doit regarder la femme aux yeux fermés posée sur son chemin.*
> *Oui. Le pas s'arrête. Il la regarde.*
> *L'homme qui marche le long de la mer, et seulement lui, conserve son mouvement initial. Il marche toujours de son pas infini de prisonnier.*
> *La femme est regardée.*
> *Elle se tient les jambes allongées. Elle est dans la lumière obscure, encastrée dans le mur. Yeux fermés.*
> *Ne ressent pas être vue. Ne sait pas être regardée.*
> *Se tient face à la mer. Visage blanc. Mains à moitié enfouies dans le sable, immobiles comme le corps. Force arrêtée, déplacée vers l'absence. Arrêtée dans son mouvement de fuite. L'ignorant, s'ignorant.*[71]

Someone is walking, nearby.
The man who was watching passes between the woman with closed eyes and the other in the distance, he who is coming, going, a prisoner. The pounding of his footsteps can be heard on the wooden promenade that runs along the shore. The footsteps are irregular, uncertain.

---

71 *L'Amour*, Paris, Gallimard, 1971, pp 9–10.

The triangle loses shape, breaks up. It has just lost its shape: in fact, the man is passing, one can see him, one can hear him.

One can hear: the gap between the footsteps grows. The man must be looking at the woman with closed eyes who is placed in his path.

Yes. The footsteps stop. He is looking at her.

The man who is walking along by the sea, and only he, maintains his initial movement. He is still walking with the infinite step of a prisoner.

The woman is being looked at.

She has her legs stretched out. She is in dark light, embedded in the wall. Eyes shut.

Does not feel herself being seen. Does not know she is looked at.

Stays facing the sea. Face white. Hands half buried in the sand, immobile like the body. Force stopped, displaced towards absence. Stopped in her movement of flight. Not knowing this. Not knowing herself.

Whilst it seems clear that this passage reveals some unusual use of language, I do not think that it really breaks any grammatical rules, except by omission of, for example the subject *elle* ('she') of *ne sait pas être regardée* ('does not know she is being looked at'); and the subject is not strictly speaking necessary here, since the feminine agreement of the past participle shows that the subject of the verb must be feminine, and that feminine subject could be none other than *elle, la femme* ('the woman'). Similarly, in the last paragraph, the reader/narratee can easily infer, and if necessary supply, those subjects or verbs which have been omitted: *(Son) visage (est) blanc* ('(Her) face (is) white').

This does not appear to me to constitute either a 'reworking of usual grammatical sense', or a 'violent rejection of syntax'. On the contrary, it relies on the reader being able to situate the words s/he reads within a syntactic structure in the context of which they can have meaning. The ability of the narration to signify depends upon the resilience of syntax to the omission of subjects and verbs, on the linguistic competence which enables the reader to 'make sense' of this particular performance. I will return to the question of the effects of exactly what has been omitted, the subjects and verbs in the description of the woman, or the feminine subject of the passive verbs, when I come to discuss Duras's construction of the women figures in her novels later on. Suffice it to say here that it is precisely because the reader knows what is grammatically required that s/he not only notices that certain elements are missing (something funny has happened to the syntax), but is also able to read despite their absence.

In this passage there are no contradictions, no problems of interpretation arising from conflicts within the discourse. The narrator
describes, as if s/he were present at the scene and in the present
tense, what s/he hears and sees. Even those verbs which have *elle*
as subject and require an insight into the psychic workings of 'the
woman', such as *Ne ressent pas être vue* ('Does not feel herself being
seen'), or *L'ignorant, s'ignorant* ('Not knowing this, not knowing
herself'), seem, to me at least, in the light of the rest of the passage,
to be attributable to one who observes and infers, rather than to
a narrator who 'knows' what 'the woman' is thinking. What does
occur in this passage, and in many other places in Duras's texts,
is a kind of extreme precision and fixing of what is being described.
Here it can be seen in the two expressions of the man watching the
woman: *il la regarde* ('he looks at her') and then, a few lines later,
la femme est regardée ('the woman is looked at'). Here the effect is
almost one of the cinematic technique of shot-reverse shot; first the
reader is given the subject of the look to focus on, and then the object.
Or perhaps in 'he looks at her' what the reader fantasises is the look,
which disappears into its object in 'the woman is looked at'. Either
way, the vantage point offered to the reader by the narration is not
disturbed.

Duras often creates an effect of hyper-precision in a temporal
sense, by use of tenses. In *Moderato cantabile*, for example:

> *Anne Desbaresdes attendit cette minute, puis elle essays de se relever
> de sa chaise. Elle y arriva, se releva. Chauvin regardait ailleurs. Les
> hommes évitèrent encore de porter leurs yeux sur cette femme adultère.
> Elle fut levée.*[72]

Anne Desbaresdes waited for that minute, then she tried to get
up from her chair. She succeeded, got up. Chauvin was looking
away. The men still avoided resting their eyes on the adulteress.
She was up.

Here we have the movement from an action, *se releva* ('got up'), to
a state, *Elle fut levée* ('She was up'). The narration gives the reader
not only the process, but also its goal, the end of that process, which
the verb in the past historic alone does not convey with sufficient
precision.

So this hyper-realism facilitates the production of 'blanks' by
giving extremely precise and clear information about the visible, but
about very little else, other than that which can be inferred from
what is visible, as in the passage from *L'Amour* cited above. The
psychological motivations for the figures' actions are not recorded

and must be inferred by the reader/narratee. Furthermore, much of
what is recorded is dialogue, in which the figures who, in the words of
Henri Hell, 'only exist, in fact, through their speech', make manifest
the presence of their desires, but never state what those desires are.
Jacques Hold invents, Michael Richard suggests, but their inven-
tions and suggestions reveal the desire for silence – oblivion – whilst
the voice of the third person narration is unable even to articulate
as much as that. At the same time, the clarity and precision with
which the texts are narrated do everything to facilitate the reader's
imagined idea of 'what is happening', and do not confuse by presenting more than one angle from which to view events and figures.
This single position from which the 'visible' is narrated gives an air
of objectivity and truth to the narration. There is no interpretation
here, it implies, merely a recording. Let the reader make of it what
s/he will.

In the light of this insistence on the visible in her writing, it is
interesting to consider how Duras uses a visual medium, that of
film, to create 'blanks' similar to those produced by her texts. In
films such as *India Song*, or *Aurélia Steiner, dit Aurélia Melbourne*, she
manages to undermine the power of the immediate presence of the
visible by the relation of soundtrack to image. In both of these films,
the soundtrack tells a story. In *India Song* one voice questions
another about a story which is more or less that of *Le Vice-consul*,
whilst on the screen, a handful of actors represent, rather than
portray the protagonists in a way which is linked to the story that
unfolds, but which is obviously not meant to be an accurate depiction of that story. In *Aurélia Steiner, dit Aurélia Melbourne*, the
images are of Paris seem from the Seine and have no direct link to the
soundtrack, which tells the story of a seduction.

The effect of disconnexion between soundtrack and image in both
cases is, in a sense, one of interference. The person watching the film
cannot simply imagine what is happening on the basis of the soundtrack, because the images are there, partially occupying the place of
imaginary images to go with the words. At the same time, the power
of the images themselves, the meaning they might have if seen in
isolation, is undermined by the soundtrack, which imposes different
meanings upon them in a way which is not fixed. The ultimate effect,
particularly, I think, in *India Song*, where the relation of image to
sound is all the more fluid because there is a link of content between
them, is one of uncertainty. The person watching is offered a story
which is not quite within reach, nothing is present, the images may
refer to the story, but they do not tell it, the story itself is a reconstruction of something in the past, the protagonists are dead. As in
the novels, there is a sense that knowledge is unattainable, because
the information offered is not definite, or not enough, suggested

rather than present. Instead there is an impossibility of visual representation where that knowledge might be, a 'blank'.

Words have an infinite capacity to produce meanings. Within the
conventions of realism, they have an endless capacity to name and
to describe. In her writing, Duras restricts the productive, and
apparent descriptive capacity of her words to the visible. She uses
words to create images – which lack the Imaginary plenitude of
actual images, since they are only images evoked by words. However, as fantasies of the visible, they carry the traces of Imaginary
wholeness and monolithc certainty, and this certainty in the fantasy
enables Duras to create 'blanks' where knowledge is understood to
be missing, whilst also avoiding the potential plentitude of actual
images. In her films, on the other hand, she undercuts the plenitude
of the real image by using the power of words to create images which
do not coincide with those on the screen, or to suggest ways of understanding the image which are not instantly apparent. In both cases,
both films and writing, it is the interaction of Symbolic and Imaginary, the interplay of certainties and lack of knowledge, that Duras
uses to create the 'blanks'.

But does this make her work feminine, or the 'blanks' the place of
the woman? To the extent that they are produced from inferences
and resonances, it is perhaps possible to see the 'blanks' as points
of 'non-sense', where too many different menings cluster around
a particular signifier so that it can no longer mean and becomes
opaque; or as points where a doubling, or a plurality of meanings
are produced, in the manner of Irigaray's 'woman-speak'. In this
light it might be possible to view the 'blank' symbolised by *la fleur de
magnolia* in *Moderato cantabile*, for example, as a manifestation of
Montrelay's 'feminine' effects within language although, it would
not be true to say that 'everything is manifest, nothing is hidden' in
the case of this, or any other of the blanks.

However, as I have explained in my discussion of the Lacanian
analysts, I do not think such a way of using language can be called
specifically 'feminine' in itself; for it works in the same way as
innuendo or jokes, by controlling and using the power of unconscious
links between signifiers, and I do not see why or how such universally
found phenomena can be gendered. Furthermore, I do not think it
is possible to see them as disrupting the rules by which (masculine)
language or literature work. Rather, they are dependent upon the
resilience of the rules to omissions. Duras's 'blanks' may require that
the reader assume meanings on an unconscious, or pre-conscious
level, but they do not break meaning down. The power of her writing
comes from understatement and interpretation, rather than the
eruption of the unconscious into the conscious process of reading with
untameable excesses of meaning.

CHAPTER 5
What Does the Reader Want?

So, I hope to have shown, in order to read Duras's texts, certainly from *Moderato cantabile* onwards, the reader has to be prepared to put in a certain amount of work, inferring links and connexions. Of course, as many literary critics and theorists have pointed out, reading always involves a process of inference and reconstruction; any novel invites its readers to bring their own understandings of the world to bear on the information on the page, and each one requires different types of interpretations. Part of the pleasure of reading many novels lies in the tension they set up between what is said and the interpretation the reader is invited to put upon it, generating, for example, irony, humour, or suspense. I discussed an example of the workings of such a process in relation to the extract from *Un barrage contre le Pacifique* cited above, where interpretation and reconstruction is required to 'make sense' of the ironic description of M. Jo's father.

In Duras's later writing the reader still has to be prepared to infer many unstated connexions between phrases and motivations for actions. However, these are constructed as present, but impossible to articulate or to understand intellectually because the impersonal language of the text cannot express them, rather than because of the idiosyncracies of any figure.

These are the points where the 'blanks' appear. In order to read any text, one must believe that it is producing meaning, and Duras's work, after and including *Moderato cantabile*, no doubt requires more preparedness on the part of the reader to believe that what s/he is reading has been written with skill and control by an author who wanted to mean something by it than, for example, *Un barrage contre le Pacifique*, where there is a storyline to follow, told by a narrator who offers a certain amount of interpretation, and the questions posed by the text are ultimately also answered by it. The pleasure to be had from reading Duras's later work does not come from find-ing out what happened in the end, nor from having 'understood the irony', 'got the joke', or felt the suspense. It comes, if it comes, from experiencing the 'blanks' and the process of anihilation that Montre-lay describes. To enjoy reading these texts, the reader must accept that there will be 'blanks', that all will not be revealed. S/he must accept the position of narratee and read as the text demands.

Not all readers do so; neither the critic Jean Mistler, quoted in the 10/18 edition of *Moderato cantabile*, nor my mother, somewhat mystified by her of reading the same text, seem to have been satisfied with the information presented to them. It works on some, but not on others. So what is it about Duras's work that makes some readers settle happily into the place of the narratee, whilst others do not, and indeed are not even sure that such a place is available to them? Why do some readers become interested, even fascinated, where others turn away? In the previous chapter I tried to indicate some of the different processes by which Duras creates 'blanks' in her writing. In this chapter, I want to look at what the texts offer the reader, to make her/him want to read, and to accept the place of narratee.

THE AUTHOR'S DESIRE

Reading always implies a certain passivity on the part of the reader; it is a reactive rather than an active process. I want to use a Lacanian framework to look at what is involved in reading more closely, as I think it is useful as a means to understanding the process.

In Lacanian terms, language is Other, it is that in which the subject identifies him/herself in the order of the Symbolic and from which s/he is also separated at the same time. Complete identification is impossible as it would mean the eradication of the unconscious, either by completely blocking off the 'chain of the signifier', or by the subject's total dissolution into it. So there is always a gap between the subject and the Other and this gap is desire as it is manifested in language. According to Lacan, desire is the desire of/for the Other; it is the desire of the subject to identify with(in) the Other as completely as possible, by meeting the Other's desire, just as the child wanted to be the phallus for the mother.

As I suggested above, from a Lacanian point of view, a novel (or any utterance) signifies the presence of desire on the part of the utterer. It is a demand articulated to an other (who partially occupies the place of the Other). If the utterance takes the form of a novel, it is the reader's desire which is at stake: the narrative demands a narratee, the one who will understand it. The reader wants to read to the extent that her/his desire is called up for the desire that manifests itself in the existence of the text. This fantasised desire is a conflation of the desire of the Other, which is an effect of using language, and the desire of the implied author, as the source of this particular novel. The reader can attempt to meet that desire by 'understanding what the author meant', thus adopting the position of narratee and producing a fantasy in relation to the signifiers on the page. Her/his role is passive to the extent that her/his desire is a response to an already extant manifestation of desire. A novel is to some extent a discrete object, and, unless s/he decides to make up her/his own story, the reader's fantasy must ultimately be limited to what the text relates, suggests and finally completes.

Until s/he reaches the end, and can see the novel as a finite object, s/he will be unable to grasp its meaning as a separate (conglomeration of) signifier(s). It is only at the end that the meaning 'behind' it will become clear. This is, I think, what Julia Kristeva is getting at when she says, 'a signified (or a process of telling) must be concealed in order to trigger off a novelistic rhetoric'.[1] Looking at the process in this way, it is a the uncovering, or perhaps more accurately, the production of this signified, the desire behind the text, which is on one level what the reader desires.

But whose desire is it that the existence of the text signifies? Is it the implied author's or the narrator's or that of both? The last answer seems the most likely to apply in most cases, although the degree to which the two are seen as separate will vary from text to text. In *Le Ravissement de Lol V. Stein*, or *Le Marin de Gibraltar*, the subject who utters the text is, apparently, the man who is the first person narrator. As there is nothing to suggest that the implied author disagrees in any way with what he is saying, it seems likely that, during the immediate process of reading, unless the reader is reading in a highly self-conscious manner, or does not find the narrator credible, s/he will attribute the desire behind the text to him even though s/he knows the book was written by a woman, Duras.

In *Un barrage contre le Pacifique*, a narrator with a 'personality' is again produced, but this time unnamed and narrating without otherwise participating in the action. The identity of this narrator is thus undefined and might well be more or less consciously conflated by the reader with the implied author.

In those of Duras's texts narrated in the style that I have called 'hyper-realism', the narrator is not produced as a 'personality' at

---

1 Julia Kristeva, *Le Texte du roman*, Berlin, Federal Republic of Germany, Mouton/de Gruyter, 1976, p 217.

all, but primarily as the subject of a look. S/he also hears things. Here again, the reader might conflate narrator and implied author, since the narrator is unnamed; except that the narrator's desire has been whittled down to what appears to the reader/narratee as an almost purely scopic manifestation. Furthermore, the narrator exhibits uncertainties and a lack of knowledge which one would not immediately associate with an author who, the reader might tend to assume, has a fairly intimate knowledge of the actual events described in a text, since s/he invented them; the reader might expect the author to know 'what happened', even if s/he may also find significance in the text which the author as a person (what Booth would call the flesh-and-blood author) was unaware of and did not consciously intend. On the level of the plot, uncertainties and the restriction of knowledge of figures and events to that which can be described in visual terms are not consonant with the role of the implied author of a work of fiction as opposed to the narrator, and in Duras's later novels there is a dissociation of narrator and implied author.

The fact that these texts can all be classified under such a heading as 'Duras's novels' is indicative of the importance generally ascribed to the author as prime source of the desire whose existence they manifest. The reader constructs an idea of Marguerite Duras, career author and public myth, and makes her the ultimate authority in her novels. Certainly, Mistler, my mother and others have addressed their complaints of incomprehension in her direction, not in that of the narrator of *Moderato cantabile*. In fact, I would suggest that Duras's texts, chronologically starting with *Moderato cantabile* make the reader sense the discrepancy between author and narrator more than texts where the narration is less sparse, thereby potentially fostering the reader's desire for the seemingly unattainable desire of the author in all her manifestations, the ultimate one who knows. But Duras's desire, though sensed and interpreted, is constructed largely as 'blank'. In my experience, this either seems to cause frustration in readers, and the abandoning of further attempts to read work by Duras, or else compels them to read further texts by Duras in search of illumination, or confirmation of their assumptions as to the form that desire takes. The latter being my case.

In the hyper-realist third person narratives and one first person narrative Duras published between 1958 and 1971, there are always gaps in the narrator's knowledge, made perceptible to the reader. A lack is constructed and where there is lack, says Lacan, there is desire. Certainly in Duras's texts, this principle seems to hold good, so long as the reader is prepared to accept the gaps and keep on reading. The reader has to desire the desire of the author enough to make her/him infer and fantasise the links and connexions that enable her/him to produce a coherent fantasy out of the information available. The guarantee in the mind of the reader that coherent 'sense' is there to be made, over and above the ease or difficulty s/he may find with the texts, is the author's name on the cover. The reader can assume that, even if the narrator does not appear to be able, or want, to give an interpretation of the significance of what the novel relates, the author has her reasons, be they conscious or unconscious, for producing the text and that everything in it has significance in relation to the whole. This assumption is supported by the fact of its publication, and also by the general context of favourable reviews and critical work. But Duras herself does not give a great deal away, at least directly. Instead the reader finds 'blanks'.

The ostensibly autobiographical *L'Amant*, which readers might have expected who lead to a greater understanding of what 'lies behind' Duras's writing, does not really do so. Instead it encourages the reader to produce a fantasy of Duras as an (unattainable) object of desire, by constructing a view of her as she was in her youth, the object of a man's overwhelming and undying passion. She describes herself, often in the third person, in her careful, controlled way, making of 'the child of fifteen' a work of art. This depiction of the youthful Duras is flanked by more recent manifestations of herself as object of desire. The opening paragraphs describe how the image of a man's more recent (but chronologically undetermined) homage to her beauty, 'I think you are more beautiful now than when you were young, I liked your young woman's face less than the one you have now, ravaged' is 'the one of myself which I like the most of all, the one in which I recognise myself, in which I delight'.[2] The text ends with the return of the man from Cholon: 'And then he had told her. He had told her that it was the same as before, that he still loved her, that he could never stop loving her, that he would love her until death.'[3]

The publication of *L'Amant* and *La Douleur*, with their autobiographical references, have perhaps added further weight to the importance of the reader's fantasy of Duras's desire as the organising force of her texts, of Duras as the source of meaning, but even without these two texts, the self-referentiality of her work is conducive to such a fantasy. The most obvious form this self-referentiality takes is in what I would call the 'Lol V. Stein cycle'. There are several texts and films which fit into this 'cycle': *Le Ravissement de Lol V. Stein, Le Vice-consul* and *L'Amour, India Song, La Femme du Gange*

2 *L'Amant*, Paris, Minuit, 1984, p 9.
3 ibid, p 142,

and *Son nom de Venise dans Calcutta désert*. There are discrepancies between them and they cannot be regarded as episodes in a unified 'story', although they are very closely linked. *Le Ravissement de Lol V. Stein* recounts the ball at S. Tahla, where Anne-Marie Stretter and Michael Richardson meet and go off together; *Le Vice-consul* recounts events in which the French ambassador's wife, who is called Anne-Marie Stretter, and one Michael Richard, who first met her in Calcutta, both figure, as they do in *India Song*; in *L'Amour*, the identity of the three figures is uncertain, but 'the traveller' and 'the woman' attempt a similar reconstruction of a ball at S. Thala to that attempted by Lol and Jacques at S. Tahla, and I am tempted to identify 'the traveller' as Michael Richard(son), 'the woman' as Lol V. Stein and 'the madman' as Jacques Hold. This identification is not strictly speaking necessary, and each of these works can be taken in isolation, although I suspect that each gains by association with the others.

Besides these connexions there are a million and one echoes and repetitions in Duras's work. I do not intend to list them all as there really are too many. However, I do want to mention the ones that have struck me the most forcefully. Firstly, there is the recurrence of references, direct and indirect, to anti-semitism and the persecution of the Jews in Nazi Germany. Many of Duras's figures are identified as Jews, beginning with Stein and Max Thor in *Détruire, dit-elle*. Then there are recurrent settings for events – often hotels and tennis courts. In many of Duras's works events take place somewhere very hot and the sea is often close by. Events themselves, such as murders or suicides for love, recur from text to text, as do phrases, or variations on phrases: *elle est à qui la veut*,[4] or *elle est à qui veut d'elle* ('she is anyone's who wants her').[5]

Finally there are the constant features to be found in most novels in some form and combination, but which appear in Duras's work in a more exposed form than is common, the grand themes of death, desire and oblivion, of madness and memory, which each work restages so that each can be taken as an investigation of the same problems, but from a slightly different angle. All this contributes to the construction of a kind of 'Durassian universe', in which the author, who, as is only right, moves in mysterious ways, is the creator and source of meaning.

The indirect, but very powerful presence of the implied Duras in her texts has no doubt contributed to the way in which her work has been received by readers and critics, which seems to be polarised into

4 Said of the woman in *L'Amour*.
5 Said of Alissa in *Détruire, dit-elle*.

the very enthusiastic and the uncomprehending. In the '*Moderato cantabile* file' printed in the 10/18 edition, opinions are split along these lines and such a division appears to have continued ever since. However, as one might expect, most criticism of Duras's work fits into the former category. The reader reading her/his first Duras text, even in translation, is fairly likely to be aware of the author's reputation, particularly since the success of *L'Amant*. This will inevitably affect her/his attitude and degree of interest s/he has in adopting the place of the narratee and 'understanding' the text (although the effect may vary from individual to individual). If the reader has heard of Duras as an interesting and innovative writer, and wants to see in what ways this might be the case, her/his desire in relation to Duras the author has already been called up by what s/he has heard and s/he is more likely to make the necessary efforts of reading to try to find out 'what Duras is doing' in her writing, what her desire is, than if she were reading a text by a complete unknown, even though such an effect may be totally unconscious.

However, it is abundantly clear that reputation, self-referentiality and a perceptible split between impersonal narrator and implied author have not always been enough to hook the reader's desire into the text. Robert Poulet's comment on *Moderato cantabile* seems to sum up objections I have come across: 'The reader has to strain her/his thoughts to such an extent in order to understand where the scene is taking place, who is present, what is happening, that no novelistic enchantment can possibly keep a hold over them.[6] Here is a man who could not find the place of the narratee. I suspect that those who react like this do so because they are looking for something that is not there in the text and because their imagination – their desire – has simply not been caught by what is.

The reading of Duras's work after and including *Moderato cantabile* requires a passivity on the part of the reader which is, I think, greater than that required by many other texts, where more information is given. This may seem paradoxical, given the intense effort of concentration described by Poulet, although it seems to be a view shared by Montrelay in relation to *Le Ravissement de Lol V. Stein*, in the article I have quoted above and to which Marini took such exception. What Poulet is complaining of is, I suspect, that an immense conscious effort of reading produces very little that is definite. How true. But it seems to me that attempts to read Duras in such a way are largely doomed to failure. If, on the other hand, the reader accepts that there will be 'blanks', and even that these are

6 Robert Poulet, 'La Règle du jeu transgressée', in *Moderato cantabile*, p 153.

part of the 'point', then s/he has more chance of a satisfactory encounter with the text. Such a reading, however, requires a willingness to enter meekly into the 'Durassian universe' and to accept the laws by which it operates and which govern the connexions and inferences the reader must make in order to read the text.

The laws of the 'Durassian universe' are not exclusive to it, any more than the discourse Duras uses are entirely her own invention. If they were, her texts would be unintelligible. On the contrary, in order for the reader to 'understand' texts which are so sparsely written, it is necessary that the links s/he is required to make do not appear totally extraordinary, in fact, that they should be familiar, or obvious, as I have discussed above in relation to grammatical omissions in the passage from *L'Amour*. Furthermore, the reader's desire must be captured sufficiently that s/he wants to read. The text must provide her/him with the possibility of a fantasy which will be in some way pleasurable. These considerations apply of course in relation to any text. However, the more 'full' the text, the more things it tells the reader, the more the reader can pick and choose what to accept as the basis for fantasy and what to reject as boring, unlikely etc. and thus the more flexible the relationship between reader and text. Similarly, if the text tells a story from a point of view in the sense of 'attitude', the reader can adopt the place of the narratee in relation to the plot, whilst being critical of the point of view from which it is narrated, and can in turn interpret that narration from a different point of view. I might, for example, read *L'Etranger* by Albert Camus putting myself in the place of an Arab, a possible candidate for Meursault's arbitrary shooting, in which case my views on the 'absurdity' of the protagonist's trial and subsequent death might differ from what Camus intended.

In Duras's texts, from *Moderato cantabile* until *L'Amant*, such a critical reading is more difficult. Firstly, with the exception of *Le Ravissement de Lol V. Stein*, there is no obvious point of view from which the story is being told and which can either be accepted or criticised. Secondly, the interest lies not so much in the answers to questions posed in the text, but rather in the generation of the questions, much of which requires a lot of sympathic imagination on the part of the reader, as opposed to intellectual analysis. Some readers apparently find this frustrating, others do not and indeed they find it quite the opposite of frustrating. I suggest that this is because Duras's later novels set up a relation of text to reader/narratee similar to a structure which psychoanalysis defined long ago as an escape route from frustration and fear of castration: that of fetishism.

THE TEXT AS FETISH

Freud's theory of fetishism as a sexual practice holds that the little boy, horrified by his first sight of a woman's genital's – probably his mother's – 'refused to take cognizance of the fact of his having percieved that a woman does not possess a penis. No, that could not be true: for if a woman had been castrated, then his own possession of a penis was in danger'.[7] The boy's response, says Freud, is to disavow his knowledge. However,

> it is not true that, after the child has made his observation of the woman, he has preserved unaltered his belief that women have a phallus. He has retained that belief, but he has also given it up. In the conflict between the weight of the unwelcome perception and the force of his counter-wish, a compromise has been reached, as is only possible under the dominance of the unconscious laws of thought – the primary processes. Yes, in his mind the woman *has* got a penis, in spite of everything; but this penis is no longer the same as it was before. Something else has taken its place, has been appointed its substitute, as it were, and now inherits the interest which was formerly directed to its predecessor.[8]

So, according to Freud, the fetish is a substitute for the woman's missing penis. It comes to stand in the place of unwelcome knowledge.

When Freud looks at fetishism, his concern is to explain why certain men adopt 'inappropriate' objects for their sexual desire, but the basic structure he describes can be seen in operation beyond this particular area of interest. In Freud's description, the fetish is cathected as a kind of screen erected between the (male) subject and unwelcome knowledge. However, that knowledge is implicit in the very fact of the cathexis of the fetish, which only occupies the position it does in order that the lack of the original object might be disavowed. The cathexis of the fetish necessitates simultaneous disavowal and recognition of the woman's missing penis which, were it present, would obviate the need for fetishism. So the fetish allows for presence and absence of knowledge at the same time. The fetishist's contiguous acceptance and disavowal of knowledge remain unconscious; although the desire for the fetish arises from their conflict.

To put this in Lacanian terms, for the child of both sexes the absence of a penis in the mother signifies the impossibility of satisfaction of the total demand for love – for plenitude – which the child

7 Freud, 'Fetishism', p 153.
8 ibid, p 154.

makes to her. The absent penis signifies lack in the mother and the existence of her desire, which the child wants to fulfil – by being the phallus for her – but cannot. In Lacan's paradigm, it is at this point that the maternal phallus is transferred, in the fantasy of the child, to the mother's object of desire, the father. The phallus is then repressed, becoming the repressed signifier of impossible *jouissance*, whilst the Name-of-the-Father takes on the position of signifier of the impossibility of *jouissance* and the institution of the Law.

From here the two sexes follow different paths. The little boy, in the Lacanian model, grows up to identify himself in the father's place, although it is impossible for him to occupy that position completely, since the position of the father as ultimate authority and source of the Law is a product of the child's fantasy, rather than the father's actual attributes. Women and their genitals are instated for him in the position of objects of desire by the somewhat circuitous route of the father's phallus, representing by their castration the potential (but never the actual) guarantors of the man's possession of that phallus.

The Lacanian fetishist, however, does not quite follow this route. Instead he cathects an object which signifies both presence and absence of the phallus in the mother, both the possibility and the impossibility of *jouissance*. In this way, the fetishist changes the form of repression that the phallus undergoes. By cathecting a part of the body other than the genitals, such as the foot, or an article of clothing, he avoids confronting castration and sexual difference, and spares himself the necessity of a firm identification in relation to these, maintaining a possibility of *jouissance*. He must, however, keep the fetish in its place as cathected object of the sexual aim in order for the fantasy of possible *jouissance* to hold good.

In these accounts of fetishism, the fetishist is a man. However, I think the structure of fetishism is one which can be seen in the psychic workings of both sexes. This structure is one in which a knowledge which requires the end of one attitude and a shift of position on the part of the subject is avoided or disavowed, by means of the substitution in the place of that knowledge of an object which screens or blocks it, thereby allowing the subject to retain an ambiguous position and obviating the need for the unwelcome shift. I would argue that in her later work Duras writes in such a way as to make of her texts fetishes which signify both the presence and absence of knowledge, both the reader's possibility and impossibility of understanding – and meeting – her desire as manifested by the text.

For the fetishist as described above, the fetish signifies both the possibility and impossibility of sexual pleasure, or *jouissance*, primarily in relation to the mother. That *jouissance* would be the plenitude of fusion with the mOther, which, in the child's fantasy, is rendered impossible by the mother's desire for something the child cannot be – the phallus. If *jouissance* is the plenitude which would be achieved in total identification with the (m)Other, then when a text stands in the place of the Other – or rather, as I suggested above, as the manifestation of the desire of the Other – then *jouissance* would be the identification of the reader with the inferred Other of the text.

Both these forms of *jouissance* are impossible but, just as the fetishist avoids the problem by screening out the visual proof of the woman's castration, so Duras, in her later novels and texts, avoids the problem of the finitude of a text in which problems are solved and questions answered, and hence, also, the necessity for the reader of being constituted as a unified, separate subject in order to understand the finite knowledge constructed by the text. For the knowledge is never attained, and so the possibility of the *jouissance* of identification with the Other of the text (Duras?) is never totally excluded for the reader who adopts the position of the narratee from which to read. Hence, I suggest, the fascination readers have described.

It is the production of 'blanks' which makes this effect possible. For the reader whose imagination and desire gets caught up by Duras's later novels is not given a knowledge, but a framework from which s/he can infer the presence of something which cannot be described directly. The reader does not, as I have said before, 'fill in' the gaps; but s/he perceives them and assumes the presence of something indefinable, which cannot be put into words. The reader who reads this way is thus, like the fetishist, spared the 'castration' of a finite knowledge, spared the detachment and splitting of subject from text and from him/herself, which is required by understanding a certainty, spared the feeling of 'is that all?' The text appears as in some way not finite (infinite?), since it does not produce a certainty, so much as a state of fascination. Duras leaves 'blanks', particularly where desires should be, in which both the possibility and impossibility of *jouissance* in relation to the text are suspended in conflict. The reader has to read from the position of the narratee in order to understand at all but s/he never knows if s/he has 'got it right', nor is s/he encouraged to ask that particular question. What s/he is left with is a feeling of something that has not, and cannot, be said, but which can be felt. S/he is offered the fascination of uncertainty and ambiguity and the pleasure of the possibility of unseparated identification with the implied Duras and the knowledge she can only express in 'blanks'. Like the fetish, Duras's later novels avoid certainties that could be disappointing – psychoanalytically 'castrating' – for the reader, and keep her/him on the brink, at least for as long as s/he is prepared to allow the process to work and to maintain the text in the position of fetish.

So the novels offer the presence of Duras's unnamable desire, buried in simple tales told in simple language. But some people are not interested in Duras's desire, presumably because they are not interested in the stories she has to tell. Perhaps they do not feel personally concerned, their desires travel along different channels. So what does Duras's work offer the reader besides simply the mysteries of the author's desire? In relation to which already extant and culturally pre-determined assumptions and objects of desire does she invite her readers to construct their fantasies? Which simple and familiar narrative structures does she pepper with her 'blanks'?

As many people have pointed out, much of Duras's work tells stories which, told in another way, would appear quite conventional and banal. Many of her texts share various elements with works of popular, and particularly 'romantic' fiction which, though they may lack the artistic merit of Duras's own work may also be far more widely read. I doubt that Duras shares a great many of her readers with the writers of romantic fiction, although clearly her readership has widened since the publication of *L'Amant*. However, I think it is important to note the similarities, which are not irrelevant to an understanding of the power that Duras's writing can exert. To note them is not necessarily to find fault with Duras's work; after all, there are many different ways of telling stories which have similar features. As Flaubert said, style is everything.

THE RETURN OF THE FAMILIAR

Lives apart

With certain exceptions Duras's work is not concerned with the material details of everyday life. The figures she portrays have other worries. The exceptions to this rule (notably *Un barrage contre le Pacifique*, but also to varying degrees *Des journées entières dans les arbres, Madame Dodin* and *Le Square* and *L'Amant*) were almost all written before 1955 and the shift that comes with *Moderato cantabile* and the arrival of the 'blanks', while *L'Amant'* is written in a different style again, more 'filled-out' and with a different relation to 'the real world', since it is ostensibly Duras's portrayal of herself at fifteen. In most of the novels, however, concerns such as working and making money, even making food, are absent. Most of the figures who are given explicit social status are wealthy: Anne Desbaresdes is married to a rich man, she lives in a large house with a magnolia tree in the grounds, they give sumptuous dinner parties, prepared without any participation on the part of Anne, and during the day she has the time to take her child for long walks. Meanwhile Chauvin, whom she goes to visit in the dingy café, is a rather romanticised variant on the worker at play. Although he says he works in the town, he apparently has every afternoon free (and enough money) to sit and drink with Anne. If he has material worries, they are not enough to impinge upon his obsession with her.

In *Le Ravissement de Lol V. Stein*, the reader is presented with a similar world of ease and large houses, with servants to look after the children. It is a world of ballrooms and casinos, of days in which Lol has nothing to do but walk about S. Tahla. In *Le Vice-consul* all figures who speak for themselves, the Europeans, are members of the diplomatic corps, or at least move in those circles and are part of the upper echelons of society.

The central figure of *L'Amante anglaise*, Claire Lannes, is not a wealthy woman. However, she is mad, and her madness sets her apart, as much as wealth would do. Madness is also the distancing factor for the figures in *L'Amour*, whilst others, such as the figures in *Détruire, dit-elle* or *Dix heures et demie du soir en été* are staying in hotels, distanced from life's worries.

Far away places with strange-sounding names

Many of Duras's novels are located in exotic, or at least foreign, places. In *Le Ravissement de Lol V. Stein*, S. Tahla is an unplaceable town on the coast, but which coast? Certainly it is not the French: 'Tatiana asks Lol where she is going to spend her holidays. "In France", says Lol.'[9] Possibly it could be in the United States, as the appellation Lol V. Stein, like John F. Kennedy, or Cecil B. DeMille might suggest. Such a location would be reinforced by the presence of names such as Green Town and S. Tahla, but what are Pierre Beugner and Jacques Hold doing here? And if the anglophone reader can make 'South' out of the 'S.' of S. Tahla, what of the 'U.' of U. Bridge? What emerges is a fantasy land somewhere outside Europe and there is no need for the reader to puzzle over the exact geographical location; although the names of the places and figures have a vaguely exotic ring which provides a pleasurable stimulus to the imagination.

In *Le Vice-consul*, the reader is again presented with wealthy figures in exotic surroundings, surroundings even more exotic, this time, for those who have no personal connexion with India. The

9 *Le Ravissement de Lol V. Stein*, p 142.

period is indeterminate, but the apparent luxury and distance from the Indians of the lives of the European figures would suggest that the events described took place whilst India was under British rule. This impression is strengthened by the film *India Song*, which seems to be telling the same tale about people long dead. To the pleasure of the gracious life-style of the inhabitants into which the reader is plunged can be added nostalgia, a past forever lost, which is good material for fantasy, as the popularity of historical novels demonstrates. The lepers and the figure of the beggar-woman do of course represent another side of life in India, but this is the other side of the same colonial coin. On the one hand, there is the life of the rich, European rulers, fainting with the heat, their social life centering around European clubs and balls given in one or other of the residences of the eminent; on the other, the 'starving millions', nameless, like the beggar-woman, a prey to disease and the over-production of children. Such images are unlikely to shock or surprise the European reader, since they do not jar with other, similar views which abound in films and in literature. Nor do they detract from the pleasure to be had from imagining the lives of the white rulers.

The absence of material worries means that Duras's figures are left free to concern themselves with two fundamental problems of human life: love and death. And this they do.

Eros and Thanatos

Most love stories, or stories about death, murder stories for example, tell a tale of disruption ending with a final resolution. However, in Duras's work this is often not the case. Her texts constantly restage problems of sexual desire, its relation to identity and to death, and they invite the reader to fantasise the desires of the figures portrayed, which are always constructed as very great, sometimes overwhelming and leading to 'destruction' – madness or death. However, at the end there may be no clear resolution and order is not necessarily either restored or undermined. Chauvin and Anne Desbaresdes brush their lips together and no more, although the latter's response to Chauvin's expression of his desire for her to be dead, '*C'est fait*' ('It is done'), seems to indicate that some sort of resolution has been achieved. Lol's story ends with her lying in the field behind the Hôtel des Bois whilst Jacques Hold and Tatiana Karl spend their last hours together. The vice-consul is not allowed to stay with Anne-Marie Stretter after the reception and Elizabeth Alione goes off with her husband, to be followed to Leucate by Alissa and friends. (Sexual) desire provides the central problem of the texts, but the questions posed, around which the narratives are built, are not answered. The hidden signified is not uncovered, but hinted at instead. It is there by inference, in the 'blanks'.

Cherchez la femme

I ended the last chapter by saying that I did not see why Duras's writing style should in itself be called 'feminine', any more than any other way of using language to generate resonances and inuendos should be so called. However, if we look at the points around which the 'blanks' are constructed, rather than simply the way in which they are produced, then it does make sense to see them as being in some way feminine, or 'the place of the woman'. For, whilst the reader's reconstruction of the text and its 'blanks' is fostered by the elements I have discussed so far in this chapter, and the pleasurable or compelling fantasies they offer, the 'blanks' themselves are most often generated around the central woman figure, and particularly around her desire – what she wants. So I now want to look at Duras's portrayal of women in more detail to see what kind of construction of women and women's desire results.

CHAPTER 6
Was will das Weib?

THE WOMAN FIGURES

In all of Duras's works the figure of a woman occupies a central place. However, the form this centrality takes undergoes a marked transformation between Duras's earlier and her later work. There is a world of difference between the position given to Françou in *La Vie tranquille* and that of Anne Desbaresdes in *Moderato cantabile*, and again between the latter and the place of Alissa in *Détruire, dit-elle*. Finally, the perspective shifts again with Duras's depiction of herself at fifteen in *L'Amant*. In this section, I want to discuss each of the texts in chronological order, looking at the effects of this transformation on the relationship of the reader/narratee to the woman figure and the change in role that the woman figures undergo in relation to the meanings generated within the texts. I shall therefore go through the novels in chronological order, looking at each in turn.

In *La Vie tranquille*, Françou is the first person narrator. She is thus produced as the subject whose desire is the source of the narrative insofar as she is constructed as uttering it. Furthermore, the events she narrates are often set in motion because she wishes them to occur. It is, as she describes it, her desire which makes things happen. She brings about Nicolas's murder of Jérôme by telling him about Jérôme's affair with his wife Clémence, and in her relationship with Tiène it is her desire which brings his into being. Before Jérôme's death Françou describes Tiène as 'without desire'.[1] But if Françou's desire is the overwhelming force behind the events related by *La Vie tranquille*, the other figure whose desire is a mighty force to be reckoned with is Luce Barragues. Nothing will stop Luce, says Françou, in her desire for Tiène: 'A thousand mountains could not stop her. If it killed her mare, if she grew old in the process, if she

---

1 *La Vie tranquille*, Paris, Gallimard, Folio series, 1944, p 156.

grew old only in order to succeed. Nothing could stop her but me.'[2]

Next to Françou and Luce Barragues and the strength of their desires, the other figures seem pale and wan. If Tiène is 'without desire', Nicolas comes across as a weak creature, slavishly devoted to Luce and unable to rekindle her interest in him, humiliated by her and finally driven to suicide by her rejection of him. His desire is impotent and he can only turn it destructively against himself. The desire of Françou or Luce is turned outwards and acts upon the world, whilst the men who are apparently objects of their desire are comparatively powerless as agents and tend to react to the actions of Françou and Luce, rather than initiating anything themselves.

Duras was to publish two more texts narrated in the first person by a woman figure before *L'Amant: Le Boa* and *Madame Dodin*, both of which are short stories. In both of these texts the unnamed narrator is primarily an observer, but whilst in *Madame Dodin* the narrator's role is to describe the rituals observed by the *concierge*, *Le Boa* tells how the juxtaposition of two different spectacles, the devouring of a chicken by a boa constrictor at the zoo and the seventy-five-year-old body of Mlle Barbet, who runs the narrator's boarding school, affect the narrator's view of sexuality. This latter story describes the process by which the narrator's desire is channelled in certain directions and how she comes to see it as vital that a woman's body be looked at by a man. The narrator's own narcissism and her fantasies of being looked at are thus recounted and the reader is offered identification with the position of the adolescent girl, as seen through the eyes of the adult woman narrator.

The role of the narrator of *Le Boa* is different from that of Françou in *La Vie tranquille*. Françou is active, her desire leads her to action, whilst the former is much more passive, reacting to the sight of the snake and the old woman. Her resulting fantasies are ones of being looked at, or of going to a brothel where 'one gave oneself up to men' and which 'was like a sort of swimming pool and one went there *to have oneself* washed, *to have oneself* cleansed of one's virginity, *to have the solitude lifted* from one's body'.[3] Whereas Françou's desire goes out to Tiène, Nicolas, even perhaps to Luce Barragues, in *Le Boa* the adolescent's desire is for herself, or for the desire of others for her. She is the object as well as the subject of her desire. As the adult woman narrating the text in the past historic, she is subject and source of knowledge about this finished epoch of her life, which was important in structuring her desire in the position of a woman. The story can thus be read as a narcissistic reconstruc-

2   ibid, p 210.
3   *Le Boa*, in *Des journées entières dans les arbres*, Paris, Gallimard, 1954, p 113. My emphasis.

tion of the narrator's adolescent narcissistic self. Her desire is constructed as a potent force, even though it is directed back to herself.

In *Madame Dodin*, the woman narrator is much less apparent as a distinct figure in the text. She plays very little part in the events she relates and the reader only knows she is a woman because of the gender agreement of past participles in French. She simply observes the workings of other people's desires and her own desire is constructed as not exceeding the bounds of the narration of events. She certainly does not occupy a central place as a figure in the story, that place is given to Madame Dodin.

Madame Dodin talks all the way through the story about her hatred of tenants, the dustbins, or about Gaston. The text presents her as full of desires which far exceed her existence as a *concierge* and which lead her to steal parcels from the tenants in her charge and to develop an intense, if unusual, relationship with Gaston. Like the mother in *Des journées entières dans les arbres*, she is old. Her children have grown up and she has become somewhat obsessional in her idiosyncrasies but nevertheless, her place in the text is that of a subject of desire, a producer of fantasies and an instigator of events, even if those events tend to repeat themselves. She speaks for herself, irrepressibly, one of the last of Duras's woman figures to do so, until at last the author speaks as herself – or a version of herself – in *L'Amant*.

The last short story in the same collection, *Les Chantiers*, gives an indication of the direction Duras's texts will take in their portrayal of women, men and relations between the sexes. It is the story of a man staying, like many of Duras's other figures, in a hotel somewhere unspecified. There, whilst out one day, he meets by chance a fellow resident of the hotel, a woman with whom he becomes fascinated and whom he watches during the following days. The narrative describes the short period leading up to what the reader/narratee is led to assume is the consummation of their mutual sexual desire. Of course this is not the first time that sexual desire between man and a woman appears in Duras's work, but it is the first of Duras's texts to concentrate entirely on a story of growing sexual desire. In previous texts, other social relations, such as those of work, or within the family, are also explored, involving the portrayal of a larger number of figures in some detail. Another difference visible for the first time in *Les Chantiers* is the shift in the structural place of the woman figure in the narrative. From the position of a subject in the text, either as narrator, the one to whom problems are posed and whose role is to find a resolution of those problems, or a figure such as Madame Dodin, who is portrayed as a subject of desires which manifest themselves in words and actions throughout the text, she

has moved to the position of object of desire and occupies the role of
the problem to be solved. Rather than being the motivating force
asking the questions the story poses, her desire becomes the answer,
that which must be drawn out and investigated.

These differences are apparent from the very beginning of the
texts, where the reader is introduced, if not to the main problems
posed by the narrative, at least to the context in which those problems arise and the manner in which they are to be presented. The
opening lines of *La Vie tranquille* introduce the first person narrator
as a woman telling her story in the conversational perfect tense
which, even though her role as instigator of events is not immediately
apparent, sets her up as the subject of the text inasmuch as she is
constructed as the source of the desire signified by the existence of the
text. It also gives her an immediate presence; firstly in relation to the
reader, since reading creates the effect of a narration of things past
which is itself happening in the present; and secondly in the text,
since, unlike the past historic, the perfect does not create the impression of completed action related by a detached observer, but instead
gives the impression of a more immediate link between narrator and
event because it is the tense of personal anecdotes and of stories told
from a subjective viewpoint. It does not have the apparent distanced
objectivity of narratives in the past historic.

> *Jérôme est parti cassé en deux vers les Bugues. J'ai rejoint Nicolas qui,
> tout de suite aprés la bataille, s'était affalé sur le talus du chemin de
> fer. Je me suis assise à côté de lui, mais je crois qu'il ne s'en est même pas
> aperçu.*[4]

Jérôme, bent double, set off towards Les Bugues. I went over to
Nicolas who, immediately after the fight, had collapsed on the
railway embankment. I sat down next to him, but I don't think he
even noticed.

The men here would seem to be posing problems for the woman
narrator and for each other, although it is unclear from these
opening lines, and indeed it continues to be unclear for some time,
exactly what has happened. Such lack of clarity disappears from
Duras's later writing. *Un barrage contre le Pacifique* opens with a
financial venture: the buying of the horse by Suzanne, Joseph and
their mother.

> It has seemed to all three of them that it was a good idea to buy
> this horse. Even if it would only pay for Joseph's cigarettes. In the
> first place, it was an idea, it proved that they could still have

4 *La Vie tranquille*, p 11.

ideas. And then, they felt less isolated, linked by this horse to the outside world, still capable of extracting something from that world, even if it was not much, even if it was a pittance, to extract something which had not been theirs until that point, and to bring it over to their corner of the plain, all saturated with salt, over to the three of them, all saturated with boredom and bitterness.[5]

Here the basic problems facing the protagonists, and with which the novel is concerned, poverty, boredom, bitterness and a hostile environment, are all outlined, along with the three's desire to extract something from the world. This then provides the context to M. Jo's attempts to woo Suzanne, which occur in the following section. The areas touched on in these opening lines are very wide and concern social and psychological relations of various kinds. Whereas, in *La Vie tranquille*, the areas of concern of the novel are not made immediately clear by its opening, in *Un barrage contre le Pacifique* the reader is plunged straight into the story of three people doing battle with the world.

Social relations are again an area of concern in *Madame Dodin*, where the reader is at once introduced to the eponymous heroine as a working woman and source of desires.

Every morning, Mme Dodin, our *concierge*, puts her dustbin out. She drags it from the little courtyard in the middle of the block of flats out to the road – with all her might, taking no precautions – on the contrary – in the hope of making us jump in our beds, and that our sleep will be disturbed as hers is, every morning.[6]

The desire to wake the tenants is directly related to Mme Dodin's feelings about her job as *concierge* and the nature of those feelings is made clear in these lines, as is her resistance to menial work.

In contrast, *Les Chantiers* opens with another description of a woman's actions, but to very different effect.

She had come into the avenue, walking in the direction of the man, and had come past him. Then, retracing her steps, she had come back again close by him, she had walked down the avenue in the opposite direction and she had gone into the wood. The avenue disappeared into this wood.

It was late, a little before dinner. The man himself was lying on a deckchair in the avenue, halfway between the gate of the hotel gardens and the building site, and he had seen the girl come out of the wood. Automatically, his gaze had followed her.[7]

5 *Un barrage contre le Pacifique*, p 13.
6 *Des journées entières dans les arbres*, p 119.
7 ibid, p 187.

Here what is portrayed is a woman, about whom nothing more is known that that she is a woman, and whose actions are unexplained, being watched by a man. In the other opening passages I have discussed, the reader is invited to become interested in a problem, or perhaps more accurately a conflict, between Nicolas and Jérôme, between the mother, Suzanne and Joseph and their miserable situation and between Mme Dodin and her job. Here there is no problem, no conflict, nor is there any reference to work, family, psychological state, or anything else which might contextualise the actions described. All that is offered is a woman, or perhaps, more specifically, since the reader is aware of his presence almost immediately, a woman being looked at by a man. She has taken the place of the problem.

The use of the pluperfect tense here creates an effect of remembering, a restaging of the woman's actions prior to some development resulting from them and yet to be revealed. It is as though the woman's actions are being recalled for closer scrutiny, implying that, although unexplained, or perhaps because unexplained, they are worthy of interest. The reader is invited to be interested and offered another, if as yet not very, then at least potentially interested figure from whose place to watch the young woman pass. This is quite different from the introduction to the actions of Mme Dodin, which are explained in terms of her social status and her wish to wake the tenants. Mme Dodin's character and presence is excessive – she overflows out of her role as *concierge* – where the nameless 'she' of *Les Chantiers* is mysterious.

It is the portrayal of women as objects for investigation which Duras continues in most of her work following *Des journées entières dans les arbres*. There are, of course, exceptions; Anna in *Le Marin de Gibraltar* can certainly be seen as a precursor of the mysterious woman, whilst the position occupied by Maria in *Dix heures et demie du soir en été* is in some ways closer to that of Françou than to that of the woman in *Les chantiers*, as is that of the woman figure in *Le Square*. The autobiographical narrator of *La Douleur* and *Monsieur X. dit ici Pierre Rabier* and Thérèse in *Albert des capitales* and *Ter le milicien* are also subjects of desires and actions rather than objects. However, although the collection in which they appear was published in 1985, the texts were originally written much earlier, according to Duras, and for this reason I do not think that they mark a reversal of the clear overall trend.

The first step in the production of the enigmatic woman figure in Duras's work is the separation of the narrator and the woman. Duras's first person narrators are not constructed as enigmas, although on consideration one might find them rather mysterious.

Still, although we may not know much about them, we know what we need to know. They are constructed as the desiring subjects ordering the texts and there are no effects of 'blanks' in relation to them. In *Un barrage contre le Pacifique* and *Les Petits Cheveaux de Tarquinia*, Duras shifts to third person narration, with the result that the reader is distanced to varying degrees from all the figures, since the text is constructed as being produced from somewhere 'beyond' the events narrated. However, in each of these novels free indirect speech is used in relation to one figure, Suzanne and Sara respectively, so that the reader/narratee appears to have privileged insight into their thoughts, and is offered identification with them, although that identification is always somewhat uncertain, since free indirect speech produces an ambiguity around the question of who exactly is speaking.

However, if anything, and in spite of its ambiguities, free indirect speech has the opposite effect from that of producing an enigma. In *Un barrage contre le Pacifique*, Suzanne's feelings and motivations are made clear by this means, as, for example, in relation to M. Jo:

> He asked for nothing. He was happy just to look at Suzanne with troubled eyes, to look at her still more, to augment his look with an extra look, as you do when you are suffocated by passion. And when Suzanne found herself falling asleep with the tiredness and boredom of being looked at in this way, he was still there when she awoke, still looking at her with eyes brimming over still further. And there was really no end to it. And if, at the beginning of their relationship, it had not displeased Suzanne to arouse such feelings in M. Jo, she had soon, alas, seen all their variations.[8]

Here Suzanne's attitude is articulated, from her point of view, if not in words she might be expected to use, in terms of 'boredom' and 'tiredness'. In relation to her brother Joseph, Suzanne's feelings are left unspecified, but since she is shown constantly thinking about him as an object of admiration, his presence and opinion on events being of the utmost importance to her, the reader can infer her admiration, her desire, as, for example, when M. Jo brings the gramophone and she immediately thinks of Joseph: 'The packet could only be opened in front of Joseph. The gramophone could only appear, come out of the unknown, in Joseph's presence. But it was as impossible for her to explain this to M. Jo as it was to explain to him who Joseph was.[9] To explain 'who Joseph was' is constructed as impossible, either for Suzanne alone or with the indirect assistance of the nar-

8 *Un barrage contre le Pacifique*, p 69.
9 ibid, p 76.

rator; but the reader does not need an exact definition of Suzanne's feelings for her brother in order to make sense of the narrative. That the 'unsaid' of those feelings might be related to the incest taboo is a possible area of speculation which the reader may choose or not to ignore as s/he will. S/he is not bound to acknowlege a 'blank' here; and whilst one might choose to do so, and thus to argue that the inarticulate presence of Suzanne's incestuous desire for Joseph is constitutive of the former as in some way an enigmatic presence, a 'blank', I think that in fact it is not so much Suzanne the desiring subject who is thus constituted as mysterious, but rather Joseph, the object of her desire, who is seen throughout the text as taciturn and distant, only revealing much of his thoughts and feelings when he tells the story of his meeting with the woman in the city.

In the other third person narration I mentioned above, *Les Petits Chevaux de Tarquinia*, the reader is given Sara's point of view in free indirect speech. As in the case of Suzanne, there seem to be gaps in the articulation of Sara's feelings: her love for her child is made clear, but her attitude to 'the man' is not. However, if Sara is apparently unable to articulate her feelings, there is a man on hand who has the means of understanding and expression. Ludi's are the words used to explain Sara's incapacity to take 'the man' as her lover:

> Then she saw both of them from behind. One of them she would know forever. The other, no, she would never know him any better. The other was becoming a man that she would never know. One can't live all possible lives at the same time, said Ludi. Knowing the one was not compatible with knowing the other.[10]

Later, towards the end of the novel, Ludi explains to Sara that which she has not apparently been able to articulate for herself: 'You can't have a holiday from love, he said, it doesn't exist. Love is something you have to live totally, with its boredom and everything, you can't have a holiday from that.'[11] Thus any mystery arising from Sara's actions is interpreted for the reader and she is produced, not as enigmatic, but more as intuitive, in contrast to Ludi's more analytical presence. The experience is given to a woman, but the understanding and articulation of that experience is given to a man.

In this Duras follows the traditional classification of women and men as 'intuitive' and 'rational' respectively. However, it should be noted that, although *Les Petits chevaux de Tarquinia* portrays no particularly intuitive men, and whilst Gina is constructed as capricious, irrational and demanding, again traditional attributes of

10 *Les Petits Chevaux de Tarquinia*, Paris, Gallimard, Folio series, 1953, p 176.
11 ibid, p 219.

women, Diana, the third major woman figure is, like Ludi, analytical in her approach to the world. She is also the only woman figure portrayed as not involved in a sexual relationship with a man. Indexal she is a woman who 'has never stayed with a man for three days in a row'.[12] Such a woman is rare indeed in Duras's work, given her insistence on the importance of sexual desire in the lives of woman, and I think it is significant that Diana is portrayed as to a certain extent asexual, as well as an analytical thinker. It seems that Duras can only portray 'intuitive' women in the context of (hetero)sexual relationships.

Chronologically speaking, *Les Petits Chevaux de Tarquinia* follows a work in which this structure is more clearly perceptible: *Le Marin de Gibraltar*. The latter novel is narrated in the first person by a man who becomes the lover of Anna, the main, and almost the only, woman figure. This produces quite a different effect from the third person narratives discussed above, where free indirect speech gives 'insights' into the thoughts of women figures. Anna is seen only through the eyes of the narrator, or through direct speech. Before he sees her for the first time, the narrator has been told that she is rich and beautiful. In the context of a culture which has an underlying assumption of heterosexuality (although we know he is heterosexual anyway), and where the desiring subject is presumed male unless proved otherwise, with the beautiful woman as an object of his desire, Anna is immediately constructed, like the woman in *Les Chantiers*, as a potential object of desire for the narrator. His first sight of her confirms her position and his relation to her: he sees her without her seeing him and he does not know what she is thinking. She is constructed as the object and not the subject of a look. The description is entirely restricted to her physical state.

> I was looking at the woman. She, though, had not seen us. She was lying down, with her head on her hand. Her other hand lay still between her breasts. She lay, with her legs drawn up a little, abandoned, as in sleep. One would have thought that the heat of the sun did not bother her at all.[13]

As the narrative continues, Anna's desire for the sailor from Gibraltar is articulated, but through her speech rather than insight into her thoughts. By questioning her, the narrator slowly extracts the story of her life and quest. The object of Anna's desire, the sailor from Gibraltar, is quite possibly unfindable, perhaps imaginary, and so her search is possibly interminable. Insofar as the sailor is

12   ibid, p 88.
13   *Le Marin de Gibraltar*, p 100.

not found and she goes on searching, there is some part of her that remains unfathomable, unlike the narrator's previous girlfriend, Jacqueline, the optimist who is happy with her lot – or wants to be – and it is in the uncertainty of the ultimate satisfaction of Anna's desire that her enigma lies. This enigma remains unsolved. However, throughout the novel the narrator expresses a certain conscious effort to preserve the mystery, which he, if not Anna herself, might potentially be able to elucidate:

> Her gaze strayed a little, as if she were inviting me to contemplate this mystery, and were expecting me to enlighten her in turn.
> So, you're living out a great love just like that, all alone on the sea?
> I swore to myself at that moment not to enlighten her in any way if – you never know – one day, if such a day could be, I had more insight than she into this strange story.[14]

This decision on the narrator's part provides, in a sense, the guarantee of Anna's role as an enigmatic woman, for it is a decision never to articulate his understanding of her desire. However, the problem around which the novel is constructed is that of the nature of the narrator's desires. The plot is the story of their exploration, firstly in relation to Jacqueline and then to Anna, and the story of the Kudu provides a certain resolution. The mystery has been fathomed but it can only be spoken of indirectly or allegorically, or the charm – perhaps Anna's charm, that of the unknown – will fade. As the novel progresses, the narrator makes Anna speak, tell him her story and reveal the nature of her desire, after which he then 'plays it back' to her in an altered form, allusively rather than analytically, colluding rather than explaining. So the mystery remains, perhaps a little artificially, intact. Anna's desire is still, in part at least, inarticulately directed elsewhere, and they can all go off happily to Cuba to look for the sailor from Gibraltar.

The effect of the novel is to construct the narrator in a position of power and control in relation to Anna, since he apparently 'understands' her, and this offsets what might otherwise, perhaps, be the threatening aspects of a woman whose desire is directed elsewhere, and who is therefore all the less interested in him. For the reader/narratee, Anna is constructed as enigmatic, but containedly so. Her desire is ultimately within the grasp of the narrator, both in terms of the plot, since he reveals with his Kudu allegory that he does in fact understand more than she does in this strange story, and in terms of the framework around which the novel is built, beginning as it does

14   ibid, p 152.

with the narrator realising that he cannot go on with either his job or Jacqueline, and ending with his apparent understanding of the nature of love and the establishment of the possibility that he and Anna can, indeed must, continue their relationship in the shadow of the sailor. Anna is only a facilitator of his understanding, albeit a crucial one, and the novel is his story, not hers.

So in these three early novels, a certain distance is established in relation to the central woman figure but all three women, Suzanne, Anna and Sara, are constructed as more or less active and independent subjects of desire. Their desire is usually articulated either in free indirect speech, or by another (male) figure in the text, occasionally by themselves, or through a combination of these. The desires of the men figures are also investigated in these novels and, since each novel portrays more than one permutation of the heterosexual couple, a variety of possible positions are shown within the general relation of 'love' as it is staged and characterised by the novels. *Un barrage contre le Pacifique* raises problems in many different areas besides those specifically to do with love, whilst *Le Marin de Gibraltar* and *Les Petits Chevaux de Tarquinia* both seem to be concerned with the illustration, via the experiences of individuals, of generalisations about love which are more or less explicitly ennunciated in the text itself: the allegory of the Kudu, or Ludi's 'You can't have a holiday from love'. To this extent, the novels are in some sense vehicles for more or less explicit 'messages'. The woman figure has a role to play in the exploration of the problem, but she is not herself the problem around which the novel is constructed.

In the period following the publication of *Les Petits Chevaux de Tarquinia* and ending with that of *Le Ravissement de Lol V. Stein*, Duras's work shows some variation, both in the areas she explores and the forms she uses. Following the collection *Des journées entières dans les arbres*, appeared *Le Square* which is almost entirely made up of dialogue in the context of a third person narration. The dialogue is between two figures: a travelling salesman and a maid. Because there is so little third person narration, the text reads more like a play than the *roman* it calls itself on the front cover, and the reader is offered the possibility of identification with both figures. Here the man figure, the salesman, is shown as lacking in desire, unable to want things, to change himself, or to imagine the possibility of a better life. He says: 'I want to be clean and well fed every day, and then I also want to sleep, and then again I also want to be decently dressed. So where would I find the time to want more?'[15] All his fantasies centre around his journey to a town in another country,

15 *Le Square*, Paris, Gallimard, 1955, p 16.

now long past, and which he looks back to as his time of happiness, now gone. The maid, on the other hand, hates her job and refuses to accept her situation. She is determined to change her life. She is portrayed as somewhat directionless, since she knows clearly what she does not want, but finds it difficult to imagine anything else.

I can't even begin to start thinking about anything, not even in terms of details. Nothing has begun for me, apart from the fact that I'm alive. And if sometimes, when it's a beautiful day in summer, for example, I feel that perhaps that's it, that perhaps the thing is beginning without seeming to, I'm frightened, yes, I'm frightened of letting myself go with the beautiful weather and of forgetting, even for a moment, what I want, of losing myself in the details, of forgetting the essentials. If I'm already considering the details, in my existence, I'm lost.[16]

Both are stuck, the one in the details of daily life and a memory of a vision of happiness, the other in a refusal of the present so absolute that she cannot move from it. However, there are differences: the salesman, with his despairing acceptance of life, is a pale figure beside the maid and her absolute, albeit masochistic, refusal of her situation. Furthermore, the maid expresses herself with force and vigour, in comparison with the salesman's rather less energetic utterances. This woman is not an enigmatic object presented to the reader through the desire of another but a woman who speaks for herself as a desiring subject, her desire contagious enough to encourage the salesman to contemplate going dancing with her the following Saturday. She is resolved to overcome all odds and to improve her life by sheer strength of will.

But then, with *Moderato cantabile*, comes a very different figure, Anne Desbaresdes. As I have discussed above, *Moderato cantabile* is a third person narration, written, with as few figures of speech as possible, in a manner which appears at first sight to be purely denotative, insofar as explicit comment, interpretation and general intrusion on the part of the narrator are kept to a minimum, and things are described in terms of that which might be seen and heard by an observer, who restricts her/himself to recording just that and no more. A film transcribed. But, just as in a film shots are planned, conventions followed and particular objects and people filmed in particular ways, all without the viewer necessarily thinking about these processes, so with *Moderato cantabile*, the narrator is selective in what s/he sees and how s/he records it. I have already discussed the creation of 'blanks' in the narrative of *Moderato cantabile* which,

16   ibid, p 42.

I have suggested, rely for their production upon the unobtrusiveness of this selective process, which is not obvious to the reader who adopts the position of the narratee. It is around and in relation to Anne Desbaresdes that these 'blanks' are clustered.

The reader is first introduced to Anne during the course of her son's piano lesson, as 'a woman, sitting three yards away',[17] but after this she is always named by the narrator as 'Anne Desbaresdes', by other figures (Mlle Giraud and Chauvin) as 'Madame Desbaresdes' and only by the *on* of the seventh part as 'Anne'. As I have already suggested, the formal use of the full name has the effect of a constant distancing of the narrator, and thus the narratee, from the figure so named. Furthermore, the constant, almost incantatory repetition of the name colours the presentation of she whom it designates: no ordinary woman this, whose full name is repeated so often like a spell.

This distancing effect is, however, accompanied by close and constant scrutiny of Anne. There are many references to her reactions to what Chauvin says to her: 'Anne Desbaresdes moaned',[18] 'She started, but only very slightly',[19] 'Anne Desbaresdes withdrew into herself, her face turned hypocritically downward, but grown pale',[20] 'She turned her attention to clutching the glass tightly, grew slow in her gestures and speech'.[21] Anne is thus constructed as the object of a look that concentrates on her feelings, on what cannot be seen, but only hinted at by the text and inferred by the reader. The importance of her internal state is reinforced by constant, if oblique, references to it of the type cited above. A much less allusive type of description of emotional states is used for the child and Mlle Giraud during the piano lesson:

> The sonatina. This pretty little sonatina by Diabelli, off you go. What tempo is it in, this pretty little sonatina? Tell me.
>
> At the sound of this voice, immediately, the child drew back. He seemed to be thinking, took his time, and perhaps he was lying.
>
> 'Moderate and singing', he said.
>
> Mademoiselle Giraud folded her arms, sighed as she looked at him.
>
> 'He does it deliberately. There's no other explanation.'
>
> The child did not move a muscle. With his two little fists resting on his knees, he was waiting for the consummation of his

---

17 *Moderato cantabile*, p 9.
18 ibid, p 33.
19 ibid, p 27.
20 ibid, p 84.
21 ibid, p 80.

torture, but satisfied with the ineluctability, wrought by him, of its repetition.[22]

The child's feelings are explained for the reader, with thus no air of mystery surrounding them. Mlle Giraud's attitude to the child is also made plain, here and elsewhere during the description of the lesson.

Again of a different type from the way in which Anne is described are references to Chauvin, which are mainly in terms of his actions or gestures: 'He picked up his glass abruptly, finished it in one go, did not reply, turned his eyes away from her',[23] 'He ordered some wine, took another step towards her'.[24] There are occasions when the description is simply of an emotional state; as when Anne first returns to the café, 'he had also turned pale',[25] and towards the end of their encounters he puts his head in his hands – but explains his motive for the gesture: 'I am tired'.[26] Otherwise the text pays far more attention to indications of Anne's emotional fluctuations than to his.

During the course of their conversations, the emotions, mainly Anne's must be inferred by the reader from the outer appearances given by the text. This makes Anne more mysterious a figure than Chauvin, since the references to her which indicate emotion require more effort of interpretation on the part of the reader, effort which must be made if s/he is to 'make sense' of the text. Furthermore, Chauvin, who is usually described as doing something to or with something or someone else, is not constructed as the object of a contemplative look in the same way that Anne is. It is Chauvin's actions that are observed, as opposed to Anne's person.

However, it is their dialogue which firmly establishes Anne and her desire as the problem of the novel. As I have already discussed, the impression created by the dialogues in *Moderato cantabile* is one of complicity between Anne and Chauvin; somehow they understand one another without passing through language, or rather, by means of the 'blanks' in what they say to each other, this impression being created at the points where the reader has to assume that the utterances of the protagonists have some pertinence in relation to each other. However, it would be more accurate to say that Chauvin appears to understand Anne and Anne to understand his understanding of her. For, although in may ways he is as unknown a

22 ibid, p 66.
23 ibid, p 33.
24 ibid, p 26.
25 ibid, p 38.
26 ibid, p 109.

figure as Anne, he does not appear to excite the same interest in her as she does in him. Indeed, Chauvin's main role in *Moderato cantabile* seems to be that of providing the words which suggest Anne's secret desires. Whereas he appears fascinated by her, she seems fascinated almost exclusively by herself; or perhaps by the description of someone who could be herself, which Chauvin gives her.

Chauvin's utterances are almost all either descriptions of Anne's house and life within it, or episodes in the story of the lovers, leading up to the killing of the woman by the man whereas Anne either talks about herself, or asks him questions about the lovers. The reader can infer Chauvin's desire for Anne from various passages, such as the one cited above in which he describes how he saw her at the reception wearing a magnolia flower. He is a man, he seems very interested in her, the assumption needs little prompting and is fostered by the text. The object of Anne's desire is, however, less clear. That she feels something, that she wants something, this the reader is greatly encouraged to infer from her reaction to the things Chauvin says to her. The question is what? The asking of this question is not really fostered by the text in relation to Chauvin, for Anne in no way returns his interest in her, he is never the object of investigation and interest for anyone, and the text does not construct him as a problem, as Anne is, but more as a facilitator. So *Moderato cantabile* shows a man and a woman exploring the same enigma, and that enigma is the woman, or rather, the nature of her desire.

Following *Moderato cantabile* in chronological order of publication, *Hiroshima mon amour* reveals a similar structure as the actress explores her own past and her own desires through the medium of her Japanese lover. The film explores the actress's fantasies and desires. It is her the suffering that is set up as a parallel to that of Hiroshima. To this extent, the woman is again the object of investigation. However, the actress retrieves her past, that is to say, there is something fixed to retrieve and she recognises it. She remembers through the Japanese man, but she carries out the reconstruction herself, and what she remembers are her old desire for the German soldier, her old suffering in Nevers, herself as a subject. This has a very different effect from the portrayal of Anne in *Moderato cantabile*, Anne who hears everything from the lips of Chauvin and who allows him to carry her with him on a wave of desire, dependent upon him for the articulation of the fantasy – the story of the lovers – which brings her desire into being.

Like *Hiroshima mon amour*, Duras's next published novel after *Moderato cantabile*, *Dix heures et demie du soir en été*, has a central woman figure whose role is one of subject of desire. However, like

Diana of *Les Petits Chevaux de Tarquinia*, she is the object of nobody's desire (other than, possibly, her daughter's) – a rare phenomenon in Duras's work, at least as far as young women are concerned. Nobody, including Maria herself, wants to explore her desire. Like Anne, Maria drinks, but she drinks alone and the desire which catches her attention is not that of a lover for her, but that of her husband for their companion, Claire, or, in a more negative form, that of Rodrigo Paestra for his wife. Maria acts. She saves Rodrigo Paestra and pronounces the end of her relationship with Pierre, knowing, unlike him, that it is finished. The novel is a third person narration, but it follows Maria, using free indirect speech. Maria is not mysterious, nor lacking in self-knowledge, at any point in the narrative. In spite of her drunkenness, her understanding is clear and her actions are planned. Rescuing Rodrigo Paestra is a way of preventing the consummation of Claire and Pierre's mutual desire. Her plan fails because Rodrigo Paestra shoots himself, but not for want of her trying.

If there is an enigmatic figure in *Dix heures et demie du soir en été*, it is Rodrigo Paestra himself who, like Anne Desbaresdes, is almost always referred to by his full name and whom everyone is talking about and looking for. Not that his act is portrayed as inexplicable: murders motivated by sexual jealousy are traditional fare in literature and every so often in the newspapers. But insofar as he is spoken of far more than he speaks, he appears as a slightly mysterious figure. However, he is not constructed as the central figure of the novel, being overshadowed in importance by Maria, whose situation is similar to his own but whose reaction is different. Paestra refuses to accept his wife's adultery and kills all those involved, including himself. Maria tries to prevent Pierre and Claire from acting upon their mutual attraction, but, failing, actively accepts it and declares her relationship with Pierre over. She is a woman who takes her destiny into her own hands, as did Rodrigo Paestra, but without the latter's inability to move beyond his own refusal.

L'Après-midi de Monsieur Andesmas tells a tale analogous in some ways to that of *Dix heures et demie du soir en été*, but with a shift of emphasis. Because the latter novel is written in the third person, Maria is to some extent produced as an object of investigation for the narration, but the use of free indirect speech also allows the reader/narratee partially to adopt her position in relation to the events described. She is thus established as an object of investigation insofar as the narrative describes her actions, and a subject of investigation in relation to Pierre, Claire and Rodrigo Paestra. Subject and object at once, she looms larger than any other figure in the novel, none of whom are given anything like the same amount of attention.

In *L'Après-midi de Monsieur Andesmas* however, the figure of the young woman, Valérie, is given much more importance than Claire, who has an analogous role as the young adulteress.

Like *Dix heures et demie du soir en été*, *L'Après-midi de Monsieur Andesmas* tells of the end of one set of relations, as a new couple is formed and old ties are broken. Both M, Andesmas and Mme Arc are in an analogous position to that of Maria, being left behind as Valérie and Michel Arc come together. But whereas Claire, in the former novel, is a rather sketchy figure, saying nothing extraordinary and seen by Maria mainly as the addressee of Pierre's desire, very little as an entity on her own, Valérie appears constantly as an object of desire: for her father, M. Andesmas, for Mme Arc, whose first sight of Valérie has marked her very deeply, and for Valérie herself, whose relationship, putative or otherwise, with Michel Arc represents her coming to desire herself as an object of desire for a man.

The text is a third person narration, with free indirect speech used in relation to M. Andesmas. The three female figures, the little girl, Mme Arc and Valérie, are all seen largely, if indirectly, through his eyes, and each of them is produced as in some way enigmatic. The little girl forgets things all the time, she wanders off to the pool to do we know not what, her thoughts and desires remain a mystery, and insofar as her actions puzzle M. Andesmas, the reader is invited to be puzzled too. Mme Arc is, at first, somewhat enigmatic in that she sits with M. Andesmas 'keeping interminably silent' (*en se taisant interminablement*) and arousing an 'avid curiosity' in him.[27] However, once she begins to speak, she ceases to be incomprehensible, and by the end of the novel M. Andesmas no longer wants to hear what she has to say.

However, neither of these two figures compare in charismatic stature with Valérie. The narrator never describes Valérie, she exists only insofar as M. Andesmas thinks of her, or Mme Arc speaks of her. Her car alone is visible. She thus appears only in terms of the desire she calls up in others. It is only through her importance for them that she is present in the novel. Thus she is always primarily an object of desire. Furthermore, with the exception of Michel Arc, she is the only figure who occupies such a position in relation to the other figures. Abandoned by her, M. Andesmas is of interest to no one – not even, apparently, to his prospective employee Michel Arc – presumably because of his advanced age, whilst Mme Arc has lost her husband to Valérie and the little girl fails to become M. Andesmas's substitute for Valérie. All are failures as objects of

27 *L'Après-midi de Monsieur Andesmas*, Paris, Gallimard, 1962, p 75.

desire whilst, although Michel Arc fits the category to some extent, since M. Andesmas is waiting for him and Mme Arc regrets losing him, his role is most important as that of the man who desires Valérie and so brings her to fruition as an object of desire – who awakens her narcissism in relation to her appearance.

So it is in relation to Valérie that all the other figures are constructed, but for the reader, Valérie is produced only through the desires and fantasies of those other figures. In this ways, the novel becomes the vehicle for the construction of Valérie as an object of desire and fantasy, but as nothing else. She comes to occupy a central position in the novel, without ever appearing in it directly. Her position as object of desire is never threatened by her actual appearance, which might, by its portrayal of her as an individual, detract from her role as the fantasy of Young and Beautiful Woman.

However, powerful figure though she might be, Valérie's role as object of desire does not leave much room for her own desires to be investigated and indeed, they are not. The reader knows that Valérie wanted the house and has it, that her narcissistic desire to have herself seen as beautiful is just coming into being, but beyond that, her desires are not explored. Instead, the novel is concerned with the desire of others, particularly her father, for her, and it is the point when he realises that he has lost her to the desire of others that the novel describes. Like *Dix heures et demie du soir en été*, one can read *L'Après-midi de Monsieur Andesmas* as a restaging of the moment of separation from an object of desire and as an investigation of the pain and desire produced in that event. But whereas the former novel concentrates more on the process of separation than on the figure representing the lost object (who would, in that case, by Pierre), here far more importance is placed upon the object of desire, Valérie, who, because she is portrayed entirely through the desire of others for her and never appears directly to disturb the image, is fetishised and offered to the reader's desire as an object having great power over those whose destinies and feelings are so affected by her beauty;

Like Valérie, the eponymous heroine of *Le Ravissement of Lol V. Stein* is constructed primarily as an object of somebody's desire but she is also a subject of desire, in the manner of Anna of *Le Marin de Gibraltar*. A similar structure can be seen here as in the latter and in *Moderato cantabile*: a woman, Lol, and a man, Jacques Hold, are both fascinated by the same enigma, Lol's desire. Here, however, the man is the first person narrator. This means that the reader is invited to witness the exchange between them from the place of one of the participants, Jacques Hold, with the result that he 'disappears' from the narration as an object of scrutiny, at least in an unselfconscious reading, and becomes simply the scrutiniser, whilst Lol is always the scrutinised. This is also the structure of *Le Marin de Gibraltar*, except that in the latter the narrator also scrutinises himself and his ultimate concern is love itself, as is shown in his Kudu allegory, and not the idiosyncratic Anna's desires.

In *Le Ravissement de Lol V. Stein*, it is Lol in all her peculiarity who is the object of investigatio, and any general observations are left to the reader. However, the reader/narratee is given no 'direct' access to Lol's thoughts. Everything comes via Jacques Hold, who makes it up where necessary – *j'invente*[28] – and whose testimony is a victim to the filtering and embellishments of his desire for Lol: 'I kown Lol V. Stein in the only way that I can, through love'.[29]

Valérie is also constructed in this way, with the important distinction that Lol and the nature of her desire appear in the novel as the problem around which it is constructed. In *L'Après-midi de Monsieur Andesmas*, Valérie is an object of fascination and desire for the other figures, but they are also investigated by the novel. It is their desire that the narrative explores, not Valérie's, and the reader is invited to see their feelings of pain and loss as its central concern. In *Le Ravissement de Lol V Stein*, the emphasis has shifted right away from the problem of moving through a process to that of refinding a state; it has moved from the problem of the pain of separation to that of the enigmatic woman, who is constructed as a personification of absence, being somehow a 'blank', with her psyche locked into a desire to restage and refix a process of separation into a state of 'rapture'.

Although Lol is portrayed as exceeding Jacques Hold's understanding insofar as she is a 'blank', she only exists in the text as the object of his desire. She herself is the subject of certain desires as well, but because the novel is narrated in the first person by a man who is fascinated by her, beginning with his 'invention' of her life prior to their meeting and ending with the last of his rendez-vous with Tatiana in the Hôtel des Bois and so possibly the end of his affair with Lol, her desires are constructed as being of interest to the reader entirely through the medium of his. Lol is produced as a problematic object of a man's desire and her own desire is perceptible only insofar as he perceives it. She is enigmatic insofar as she eludes his understanding but he is the only point of reference. The nature of Jacques Hold's desire is not constructed as a poblem. He says of Lol, 'I love her', and this is apparently self-explanatory, although their relationship is certainly unconventional. But, he

28   *Le Ravissement de Lol V. Stein*, p 14.
29   ibid, p 46.

is not under scrutiny here. Montrelay may well ask, 'What does this man want?; as she continues, 'the question remains entirely unanswered...'[30]

In *Le Vice-consul*, Anne-Marie Stretter, another woman figure who is constructed primarily as an object of desire, appears on the scene once more, after her cameo role in *Le Ravissement de Lol V. Stein*. Readers of the former who have read the latter may remember the description of her (or is it another Anne-Marie Stretter?) and the mainly unanswered questions surrounding her.

> Who was she? People found out later: Anne-Marie Stretter. Was she beautiful? How old was she? What was it that she had known and that the others had not? By which mysterious path had she reached what appeared as a joyful, sparkling pessimism, a smiling indolence, light as a nuance, or a cinder? Profound audacity alone, it seemed, was all that kept her on her feet. But how gracious this other woman was, in the same way as she. Their prairie gait carried them both equally wherever they went. Wherever? No more could happen to that woman, thought Tatiana, nothing, nothing. But her end, she thought.[31]

Anne-Marie Stretter's brief but devastating appearance in *Le Ravissement de Lol V. Stein* sets her up as a woman of immense and mysterious power, an object of desire par excellence. This will obviously affect the expectations of those who have read the novel on discovering a figure of the same name in *Le Vice-consul*, or in *India Song*. However, the Anne-Marie Stretter of *Le Ravissment de Lol V. Stein* is scarcely more than a symbol, the third term in the triangle formed by Lol, Michael Richardson and herself, about whom nothing needs to be known other than that it is within her power to capture the attention of Michael Richardson so utterly that he forgets Lol completely and irreversably. She only appears at the beginning of the novel, in the scene at the ball in S. Tahla, and although she is constructed as an enigmatic figure, the questions raised in relation to her do not need to be answered by the reader in order to make sense of the narrative. It is not until *Le Vice-consul* that she becomes a more complex figure. I have already discussed the portrayal of Anne-Marie Stretter as a 'blank', so I shall not repeat my account of how this effect is produced. However, what I do wish to discuss here is how she is constructed in relation to (sexual) desire, her own, or anybody else's.

Anne-Marie Stretter first appears in *Le Vice-consul* when she is

30 Montrelay, op cit, p 21.
31 *Le ravissement de Lol V. Stein*, p 16.

seen by the eponymous hero: 'Anne-Marie Stretter is in fact just crossing the grounds around the embassy and he sees her'.[32] There follows a description of what she does until the vice-consul goes on his way, a description which is thus in some way dependent upon the vice-consul's presence, although it is not explicitly written as a description of what he sees. After this, we see her watched by Charles Rossett as she leaves the embassy in the company of an Englishman. Free indirect speech gives Charles Rossett's thoughts. 'So what people say about her is doubtless true.'[33]

The reader may infer that 'what people say' is that Anne-Marie Stretter has a lover, or perhaps several; particularly since rumours concerning ladies of leisure traditionally concentrate on their illicit sexual adventures. She is portrayed as someone who is talked abut, and that in relation to (sexual) desire. Following this comes Charles Rossett's sight of the vice-consul doing something with Anne-Marie Stretter's bicycle and later we learn of the vice-consul's fascination with and love for her when he talks to the director of the European Circle. She is apparently the only woman this rather mysterious man has ever desired, which implies that there is something unusual about her. Later, we find that many men, in particular George Crawn, Michael Richard, Peter Morgan and Charles Rossett, are fascinated by her.

Anne-Marie Stretter herself says very little and spends part of the time she appears with the above-mentioned men asleep. Apart from giving orders that food and water be put out for the lepers and beggars, and inviting the vice-consul to the reception at the embassy, she does not do very much at all. She is a woman apparently without desires, or with very few. The vice-consul says of her, 'she is a woman who has no preferences' – this in relation to the men she takes as lovers – and indeed, it is that which draws him to her.[34] When Charles Rossett or Michael Richard kiss her, she seems indifferent, neither rejecting nor particularly interested in their embraces. Even in relation to the vice-consul, for whom she does show a certain preference – 'I am here with you completely, as with no one else, here this evening, in India' – she is completely passive, responding but initiating nothing and making no attempt to have him stay with her after the reception. She is always being watched, often by Charles Rossett in particular, and the reader is made privy to his imagining her in other situations, such as reading with her daughters, or during her previous life in Venice or Savannakhet, but the narrator never

---

32 *Le Vice-consul*, p 36.
33 ibid, p 48.
34 ibid, p 171.

describes her when she is alone, without a male onlooker. She is always shown in relation to someone else's desire, usually a man's, although we are once told that the other white women of Calcutta discuss her too.

So the text constructs Anne-Marie Stretter as a mysterious object of men's desire, spoken of far more than she speaks, looked at, but seldom looking, or at least not without her look being an object of scrutiny rather than an act in itself. Her desires appear to be almost non-existent and rather than a desiring subject, she is 'that woman in whose presence [men] believe oblivion will come', indefinable and mysterious, the enigmatic flame to many male moths. The reader is invited to see in her the solution to problems posed by the novel. She lives in harmony with India, she holds the key to the vice-consul's psyche and to his, and many other men's desires. Yet she always remains ungraspable, seen only through the eyes of her uncomprehending admirers.

There are of course two central women figures in *Le Vice-consul:* Anne-Marie Stretter and the beggar-woman. The latter is constructed as being in some ways the antithesis to the former, an 'anti'-object of desire. Far from being an ambassador's wife, hostess to the highest society, the beggar-woman is a total outcast. She understands nothing at all except 'indirectly', in Peter Morgan's 'fictitious' account of her travels from her mother's house to Calcutta, and her appearances in the novel outside the context of this narrative are few and far between. Unlike Anne-Marie Stretter, she is the object of nobody's sexual desire, and Peter Morgan's desire in relation to her is in fact to grasp, through his understanding of her, 'the suffering of India'. Arguably, the vice-consul is also trying to come to terms with 'the suffering of India', and it is this that stimulates his interest in Anne-Marie Stretter; but with the big difference that he expresses his interest as love.

As a subject of desire, the beggar-woman is only given existence in parenthesis between sections of the main body of the novel, in Peter Morgan's writings. Furthermore, the authoritative status of these is dubious since Peter Morgan actually knows nothing of her life. Otherwise, she is seen as a subject even less than Anne-Marie Stretter, and even more than the latter represents the point where meaning disappears and 'oblivion' takes over, to the point of madness. She repels the men who are drawn to Anne-Marie Stretter. She is produced as neither object nor subject of desire, but as a point of nonsense, an unintelligible manifestation of 'the suffering of India', with which the figures in the novel, and through them the reader/narratee, are grappling.

In Duras's next published novel, *L'Amante anglaise*, it is Claire

Lannes the murderess whose desire is under scrutiny. After Anne-Marie Stretter and the beggar-woman, whose primary role is that of facilitating the desires of others, blank figures inviting the inscription of the onlooker's fantasy, Claire Lannes looms comparatively large as a subject, the strength of whose desire leads her to an act of major proportions: the murder, dismembering and disposal of her unfortunate cousin Marie-Thérèse Bousquet. Nevertheless, her position in the text is that of the object of investigation. The investigator first interviews Robert Lamy and Pierre Lannes to 'set the scene'; but his declared interest is in Claire: 'I am trying to find out who this woman Claire Lannes is, and why she says he committed this crime.'[35] He then asks Claire herself to talk and the reader is given her words, through the medium of a tape-recorded interveiw. So Claire is allowed to speak for herself, but always in response to the investigator's questions. When his interest wanes, the novel ends, in spite of Claire's plea, 'listen to me'.[36] In this way, Claire is constructed in the role of object of investigation and desire for the reader, but only insofar as she is such an object for a figure in the novel, a figure who is, furthermore, a man, as are all the other figures who talk about Claire. As in previous novels, the reader's access to the central woman figure is therefore entirely mediated through a man's desire.

Like Lol V. Stein and Anne-Marie Stretter, Claire remains ultimately unknowable. She is insane, her desire is bound up with a past long gone, when she had a love affair with the policeman from Cahors and, like Lol V. Stein, she has lived as an automaton since he left her. However, unlike Jacques Hold, who has a function in the re-establishment of the triangular scenario which provides the condition necessary for the reappearance of Lol's desire, the investigator of *L'Amante anglaise* arrives when 'it's all over'.[37] Claire's desire has made an albeit negative reappearance in the murder, and has to all intents and purposes returned to its previous low ebb. She is unable to say why she killed Marie-Thérèse Bousquet. The one thing she could tell, which comes to appear more and more important in the eyes of the investigator, is what she did with the head, but this she refuses to reveal.

Maybe I don't know anymore where I put it; I've forgotten the exact place?
'An indication, even a vague one, would be enough. One word. Forest. Embankment.'
'But why?'

---

35 *L'Amante anglaise*, p 52.
36 ibid, p 129.
37 ibid, p 103.

'Out of curiosity.'

'So it's only that word that counts amongst all the rest? And you think I'm going to let that word be got out of me? So that all the others can be buried alive and me with them in the asylum?'

No, no, you'll have to spend a lot of time with me, you and other people, before that word leaves my lips.[38]

The word which would reveal the whereabouts of the head comes to represent the key to Claire, at least as she is seen by the investigator, as if it were her essence. He is not interested in all the rest, if it does not lead to this particular revelation. Because she refuses to disclose her one last secret and to reveal herself, the investigator loses interest in her. She is only visible, or more accurately, audible, whilst the investigator will has the possibility of grasping 'who this woman is'. But he decides what will constitute 'who she is', and when he realises he is not going to gain that specific knowledge, he stops listening. In this way, the text only gives the reader that which is articulated within the confines of the investigator's desire. Claire says that if she utters the word, she will be buried alive in the asylum, losing herself as a living subject when she loses the word which names her desire for the investigator. So whatever she does, she is doomed to disappear, and disappear she duly does, still asking to be listened to.

So Claire is explicitly constructed as the problem of the novel, with her desire being under investigation by a man figure, who exists only as the asker of questions and about whom we know and need to know nothing other than his desire to find out 'who this woman is'. And, as in so many of Duras's works that question remains unanswered – the problem of the novel is not solved and Claire retains her secret.

In *Détruire, dit-elle*, Duras's next published novel, the woman under scrutiny is Elizabeth Alione. Set in a hotel, this novel begins, like *Les Chantiers*, with a woman unknowingly being watched by a man. This at once sets up the positions of subject and object of desire, and offers the reader the position of the man subject watching the woman object. However, unique in Duras's work apart from *L'Amant*, *Détruire, dit-elle* also portrays a woman figure who desires Elizabeth Alione, Alissa.

As I have already discussed, Alissa is constructed as a 'blank' without a history, sexually available to Stein as to Max Thor, without apparent preference. It is through her that the 'capital destruction' of Elizabeth Alione is to be wrought, but Alissa, eternally eighteen years old and with her 'child's mouth', is to be the

38　ibid, p 127.

agent, not the mastermined of this process. When she begins her assault on Elizabeth Alione, Stein and Max Thor look on, commenting on an deciding about what will happen:

> 'Shall we let her go into the forest with Alissa?' asks Max Thor. 'No', says Stein, 'no'.[39]

Both Max Thor and Stein and Alissa's lovers, but they are not each other's. Apart from Alissa's expressions of confusion and unhappiness on discovering that Max Thor has become interested in someone else, nobody seems to feel much desire for any of the men, although Alissa does say to Elizabeth Alione, 'We would love Stein if it were possible to love'.

For both men Alissa is an object of desire, as is Elizabeth Alione for Max Thor. Again the woman figures are presented as objects of interest for the reader through their positions in relation to the two men, as opposed to being presented without the guarantee of male desire. Although Alissa's desire for Elizabeth Alione is mentioned, this happens only once,[40] and her fascination with Elizabeth seems a reflection of Max Thor's, rather than being generated spontaneously and independently. Alissa is presented as a kind of vessel for free-floating desire, not so much a subject as a point of intersection of the desires of others. She is portrayed as a kind of innocent magician, acting at the behest of Max Thor and Stein, who have ultimate control.

Elizabeth Alione is not childlike, she is a grown woman, a mother. However, she is constructed as completely passive. Watched, usually unawares, rather than watching, never initiating anything, her final response to Alissa, Max Thor and Stein seems to be passive resistance rather than a positive choice for life with her husband. Even her relationship with the young doctor seems to have been one in which she remained totally passive, receiving his love but not actually explicitly reciprocating. She is portrayed as apparently without desire herself, sleeping a 'light sleep, almost childlike'.[41] She is nearly 'ravaged' – but not quite, for she still retains a certain degree of subjecthood. She is, for example, afraid of the 'capital destruction' offered her, which would suggest that she has something to lose.

In *Détruire, dit-elle*, 'capital destruction' seems to have quite a different effect on women from the one it has on men. In women it seems to produce a kind of vacancy – Alissa's 'blue gaze',[42] bottomless and conveying nothing – or the capacity to sleep endlessly. Both

39 *Détruire, dit-elle*, p 65.
40 ibid, p 101.
41 ibid, p 51.
42 ibid, p 42.

Elizabeth Alione and Alissa spend a proportion of their appearances in the text asleep, as does Anne-Marie Stretter in *Le Vice-consul*, and whilst they sleep, the men watch them. The final scene of *Détruire, dit-elle* epitomises this situation and encapsulates the relations between women and men figures in the novel, with the women as powerful, intuitive, but ultimately dependent, and the men as the observers, who do not act, but who decide what action should be taken. Stein and Max Thor talk whilst Alissa sleeps – 'their sleep'[43] – discussing her and the pursuit of Elizabeth Alione. Meanwhile, strange music is heard from nowhere and Alissa, in her sleep, pronounces the words 'it's the music on the name of Stein',[44] with which the text ends. The men are the sources of action, whilst Alissa, with her childlike innocence, is the source of intuitive knowledge. In this last passage, the reader is offered the place of the men talking from which to view Alissa who, asleep, cannot provide a position from which to interpret or understand events. When she finally speaks, it is to proffer a short and cryptic phrase. This is preceded by a physical description of her, something never used in relation to the men: 'In her sleep, Alissa stretches her child's mouth with an absolute laugh.'[45] In this way, when she speaks, uttering mysterious phrases informed by unconscious knowledge, the reader is reminded of her physical presence as the object of a look. She is a 'blank' (as the other woman figure, Elizabeth Alione would be, if she would let herself be 'ravaged'). On the other hand, the men remain present as subjects, discussing the two silent women figures: the one who is absent and the one who is alseep.

Abahn Sabana David, which follows *Détruire, dit-elle*, continues the theme of 'destruction' and the portrayal of Jews as 'ravaged beings', after the fashion of Stein and Max Thor. The novel portrays such beings as those who threaten the order and unity of society, a threat which is seen as a positive force. *Abahn Sabana David* is more explicitly about politics and the role of political parties than other work by Duras, apart perhaps from the film *Le Camion*. Unlike her other work, the place given to relations of sexual desire here is comparatively small, and the main concern is ostensibly the killing or escape of 'the Jew'. It is the latter, his namesake Abahn and his potential killer David who are the most important figures, whilst the woman figure Sabana appears more as a facilitator of the action than as a focus of attention, unlike the women figures in

43 ibid, p 133.
44 ibid, p 137.
45 ibid.

the novels discussed above. However, it is worth mentioning that Sabana is described only as 'David's woman',[46] that is, in relation to David, whereas the men figures are either described as Jews (Abahn and 'the Jew'), or worker (David is a mason). The other woman figure, Jeanne is also 'David's woman' and, as it later becomes apparent, 'Gringo's woman'.[47] Sabana appears forceful and an initiator at the beginning of the novel:

> It is the woman who walks up to front door first. The young man follows her.
> It is the woman who goes into the house first. The young man follows her.
> It is she who shuts the door.
> At the other end of the room, the tall, thin man with greying temples watches them come in.
> It is the woman who speaks.[48]

but she is already on the way to being 'ravaged', as the following exchange with Abahn would indicate:

> They look at each other. He asks:
> 'Who are you?'
> She stares at him, her gaze is immense, questioning.
> 'I don't know', she says.[49]

She changes sides with little problem and then disappears from proceedings for the climax, when David is led to give up his fearful allegiance to Gringo and join the Jews. In the final section, Sabana tells Jeanne that she is leaving with David, whilst Jeanne, though obviously sympathetic, says that she has to stay behind because she is 'Gringo's woman'. It seems fair to say that *Abahn Sabana David* ultimately reinforces Duras's previous protrayals of women as rather passive creatures in relation to men, who are the initiators and, more often than not, the agents of action.

In the last of Duras's texts to be called a 'novel'. *L'Amour*, we return to a scenario by now familiar, with a central (mad) woman figure and two men. The novel begins in a familiar way, with a man watching a woman who is unaware that she is being watched,

---

46 *Abahn Sabana David*, Paris, Gallimard, 1970, p 147. *La Femme de David* would normally translate as 'David's wife', but since Jeanne is also both *la femme de David* and *la femme de Gringo*, it seemed better to leave marriage out of the translation.
47 ibid, p 149.
48 ibid, pp 77–8.
49 ibid, pp 27–8.

although here the man watching is also watching another man. There is a difference, however, between the presentation of the woman being watched and the man; the woman is 'a woman with her eyes closed. Sitting down', whilst the man is walking and his eyes are open, although '[he] isn't looking, not at anything, anything but the sand in front of him'. He is active, albeit in a seemingly mechanical way: 'his step is incessant, regular, distant',[50] whilst she remains completely still.

This passivity of the woman, her place as object rather than subject of a look, is reinforced in the passage I have already discussed, in which certain parts of speech are missing. As Xavière Gauthier points out in *Les Parleuses*, many of the verbs of which the woman figure is subject in this passage are in the passive voice and in the negative: *Ne sait pas être regardée* (Doesn't know she's being looked at). Furthermore, in the last part of the passage it is the subject of the verb, *elle* (she), or *la femme* (the woman) which has been omitted from the text, sometimes the auxiliary to the verb as well, as, for example, in [*Elle a été*] *Arrêtée dans son mouvement de fuite* [She has been] Stopped in her movement of flight).[51] The subject here disappears into the part of the verb – the past participle – which describes the action done to it. The subject *elle* is implied but does not exist independently of that action. The woman figure is established as a passive subject and indeed, barely a subject at all. This is in contrast to the active men, who are either walking or providing the look in terms of which the text is constructed.

As in other of Duras's novels, the third person narration follows a particular figure, 'the traveller', and it appears to be narrated from a point of view very close to his, seeing what he sees and never relating anything where he is not present. He is constructed as the subject behind the action. The woman figure and 'the man who is walking' appear locked into a timeless round of waking and sleeping, the woman periodically giving birth to children, whom she then abandons. But there is a difference in the way the narration describes their timeless existence: the man walks ceaselessly 'at the eternal pace of a prisoner',[52] 'in his unfathomable waiting',[53] whilst the woman, typically, sleeps. Whilst he, like a prisoner, is waiting for something and therefore in some sense a creature of history, she is unaffected by events. Even after visiting S. Thala with 'the traveller', she still says; 'I no longer know the town, S. Thala, I have never gone back there'.[54] She follows

50 *L'Amour*, p. 8.
51 ibid, p 10.
52 ibid.
53 ibid, p 134.
54 ibid, p 137.

'the man' or 'the traveller', but otherwise she remains still, asleep, or
sometimes watching the sea, apparently totally without desires, mad.
She is described as a 'dead dog of thought' harking back to the appearance of the dead dog in *Le Ravissement de Lol V. Stein*, 'the dead dog
on the beach at high noon, that hole of flesh'.[55] The equation of woman
and dead dog makes of the woman in *L'Amour* a hole in thought, a
point of non-sense of the type Montrelay describes. As the woman
whom 'the traveller' visits in S. Thala says, 'Wherever she goes,
everything disintegrates'.[56] She is a woman figure in the tradition of
Lol V. Stein, Anne-Marie Stretter and Alissa, but of all of these she is
the most 'ravaged', the most passive, the most apparently desireless,
but in some ways the most powerful in terms of the narrative, since it
is because of her, it seems, implicitly if not explicitly, that the man
sets fire to S. Thala. She is the object of both men's desire, she it is
who prevents 'the traveller' from killing himself and for whom he
gives up everything, it is to her that 'the man' always returns:

> – *Objet de désir absolu, dit-il, sommeil de nuit, vers cette heure-ci en*
> *général où qu'elle soit, ouverte à tous les vents – il s'arrête, il reprend –*
> *objet de désir, elle est à qui veut d'elle, elle le porte et l'embarque, objet*
> *de l'absolu désir.*[57]

'Absolute object of desire,' he says, 'sleep of the night, usually
around this time, wherever it is, open to the wind', he stops, he
begins again, 'object of desire, it is his who wants it, it carries him
and takes him off, object of absolute desire.'

Here he is almost certainly talking about the sea, but the speech
could equally well apply to the woman, since both she and the sea
can be referred to as 'elle' in French. All possibility of action or story
stems from the men's desires: the novel is set into motion by 'the
traveller's first sight of the woman and man; it builds up to the
return to S. Thala, the scene of the ball and the impossibility of
bringing the past into the present; it ends with the two men sitting,
talking about and watching the woman, as Stein and Max Thor
watch and talk about Alissa in the final part of *Détruire, dit-elle*,
while S. Thala, the unfaithful representative of the past, burns.
The men watch the woman act in her habihral way, which is repeated with each recurring dawn, a mad woman forever locked in
an unattainable past, always fascinating, but, or perhaps because,
always absent. Nothing more can happen to her, like the Anne-

---

55 *Le Ravissement de Lol V. Stein*, p 48.
56 *L'Amour*, p 81.
57 ibid, p 50.

Marie Stretter of *Le Ravissement de Lol V. Stein*,[58] or the beggar-woman of *Le Vice-consul*,[59] but unlike her predecessors, she cannot even die.[60] She remains outside the workings of such dynamics as those of history and desire. She is both above and below the realm of the human and the words *Dieu...ce truc...*('God...that thing...')[61] might well apply to her.

The woman provides motivation for the men's actions and, as long as the men have actions they can perform, a story is possible. But once they have done them, with no effect on the woman, they are left with her alone, the end of history and meaning, the 'dead dog of thought'; and so the novel must end.

What we have seen in the course of this discussion is the transformation of the woman figure from subject and initiator (as, for example, Françou), through a variety of novels where the women figures' desire presents the problem which they themselves investigate with the aid of a man or men (for example, Sara, or Anne Desbaresdes, even Lol V. Stein), to a series of texts which are constructed in such a way as to have a central 'blank', embodied by a woman figure who, more or less without desire herself, provides a catalyst for the desires of men (Anne-Marie Stretter, Alissa and 'the woman' of *L'Amour* taking on this role). The relation of the reader/narratee to the central woman figure undergoes a shift from that of possible identification in the earliest novels, where s/he is offered the place of the woman from which to view events, to a point where the woman figure is constructed as different, other, the object to be watched, but never understood or identified with. In these later writings, the only place from which to view the woman is that of those men for whom her existence provides a precondition for their desires.

This effect is achieved by abandoning any 'psychological' insights which, in earlier novels, were provided by the third person narration. In later novels, the narration apparently records the man or men figures watching and desiring the woman figure. The reader knows about their desire because they express it more or less explicitly. The men figures' actions are portrayed as arising from their fascination with the woman. Alternatively, as in *Le Ravissement de Lol V. Stein*, the third person narrator is replaced by a first person narrator and 'psychological insights' are given, but these are lacking in authority in comparison with those provided by a third person narrator, and

---

58 *Le Ravissement de Lol V. Stein*, p 16.
59 *Le Vice-consul*, p 157.
60 *L'Amour*, p 104.
61 ibid, p 143.

are always arrived at and given within the context of the narrator's desire ('since I love her').[62]

In novels following *Moderato cantabile* (with the exception of *Dix heures et demie du soir en été* and the inclusion of *Le Marin de Gibraltar*), the woman figures are portrayed to the reader as being already objects of desire for another figure in the novel, from whose place the reader is then invited to see them. The reader's desire is channelled along the lines of the desire of Jacques Hold, Charles Rossett, etc., towards the far distant object. In earlier texts with this structure (*Les Chantiers*, *Le Marin de Gibraltar*, or *Moderato cantabile*, the woman's desire is investigated by the man figure and, as it is brought out, there is a progression of events towards a form of consummation or completion. The woman acts upon her desire and this provides part of the motivation for the progression of events. By the time of *L'Après-midi de M. Andesmas*, the problem has shifted from one of bringing out and understanding the woman's desire, to that of the power of her narcissistic desire for herself, which requires that she be the object of some suitable man's desire, and the pain of separation experienced by those who no longer fulfil the requirements of the object's narcissism and fall by the wayside. It is not the woman's (Valérie's) desire that is being examined here, for that particular narcissism is a given. Instead it is the effects of this narcissistic desire on other figures that is investigated.

This problem of separation is again explored in *Le Ravissement de Lol V. Stein*, but rather than portraying figures in the moment of transition, this latter text fixes that moment in the person of Lol herself, whose desire is entirely bound up in the night of the ball at T. Beach, scene of her abandonment and total separation from the couple formed by Michael Richardson and Anne-Marie Stretter. It is forever fixed, beyond the grasp of Jacques Hold, or of anyone else. In a sense, *Le Ravissement de Lol V. Stein* represents a point of intersection, or a watershed between texts preceeding and following it. In terms of narrative structure, it is an investigation of a woman's desire by a man who desires her and which moves towards a kind of completion. At the same time, Lol's desire is established from the beginning as being locked into the triangular situation of the ball, so that any dynamic of progression in the unfolding of the plot appears overlaid on to a basic stasis, which is that incarnated by Lol herself, in the manner of Anne-Marie Stretter, Alissa, or 'the woman' of *L'Amour*. These latter three women are portrayed as progressively more changeless, existing apparently outside the movement of history, and whose desires, if they exist at all, do not provide a motiva-

---

62 *Le Ravissement de Lol V. Stein*, p 48.

ting force behind the narrative of events. Instead of subjects of desire, each of these figures stands for a point of 'love' as Duras means it, where the subject breaks down and meaning dissolves.

It is not really until she introduces herself as narrator into her narratives, in *L'Homme Atlantique* and more importantly, in *L'Amant* and *La Douleur*, that Duras begins once more to present women figures as subjects of desire and intitiators, rather than catalysts, of action. The eponymous heroine of *Agatha* is an exception to the rule. But then, as I shall elaborate below, women subjects of incestuous desire are a special case in Duras's work. Otherwise, the role of the purely fictional woman figure seems finally to have become firmly established as the silent site of love and oblivion.

THE POWER OF THE WOMAN

So it is in relation to the woman figures of her texts that the 'blanks' in Duras's work are most often produced. I have already discussed the fetishistic attitude these texts require from the reader, the simultaneous possibility and impossibility of knowledge, and I think that the position of the text as fetish becomes increasingly dependent upon the position of the central woman figure as fetishized: she is all-powerful, and yet a point of non-sense, present and absent in the 'blanks'.

This is not really surprising, since it is precisely the problem of the woman's having or not having the phallus which is, according to psychoanalytic theory, at the root of the development of fetishism. The discovery that the mother is castrated – does not have the phallus – raises for the child the whole problem of her desire which the child cannot meet because s/he is not and cannot be the phallus. Seen in this light, the fetish is a block against recognition of the existence of the mother's desire arising from a (fantasised) lack in her, and it is possible to extend the idea of fetish from an object which specifically stands as a substitute for the maternal phallus to any representation which avoids or compensates for castration. Thus a part of the woman's body may be fetishized, particularly the breast, archaic object of desire; or she may be represented visually holding a phallic object, the classic example being a whip; or she may be represented as self-sufficient, desireless and complete, phallic as in the child's pre-oedipal fantasy of her she was. Such fetishistic representations of women can, I think, be seen in Duras's work.

The structural importance of the desire of the women figures moves from its place in the earlier, pre-*Moderato cantabile* novels, where it is more or less explicitly stated and is the point from which problems are explored, through a middle period between *Moderato cantabile* and *L'Amante anglaise*, where, with the exception of *Dix heures et demie du soir en été*, the texts portray a woman figure who is seen in terms of some other figure's desire and whose own desire is somehow beyond the grasp of that figure, a 'blank'. This leads on a further shift, so that with the last three novels, the woman figures have become largely desireless incarnations of 'love itself' (which was only a twinkle in Lol V. Stein's eye).[63] This represents a process of increasing fetishization, which ends, in *L'Amour* and subsequent short pieces, with the woman figure occupying the position of the phallus, all-powerful with respect to the men, unknowable and desireless.

It is in relation to visual images of women's bodies that the idea of fetishism has most often been discussed, and in everyday life much emphasis is placed on the appearance of women as objects of desire for men. Thus, the desirable woman is often described in terms of some adjective relating to her appearance, 'beautiful', 'pretty', 'blonde' (in the tabloid press, for example). Perhaps this is because Lacan is right and the scopic drive 'is the one that most completely avoids the limit of castration' and can apprehend its object as an integrated whole. In relation to this, Stephen Heath says, 'for beauty is exactly *the woman as all*,' – as opposed to Lacan's 'not-all-there' – 'undivided in herself, the perfect image'[64], the (male) subject of desire can look at the woman as a whole and integrated object, which allows him the fantasy of himself as whole and integrated subject, the ideal-ego.

I think that such an account makes sense in relation to one aspect of possible pleasure to be had by anyone in looking at the fetishised image of a woman (and, why not? a man, come to that), though by no means all. For in addition to the fetishised woman appearing self-contained and complete, such images portray women in terms of culturally defined ideas of beauty. Variables such as age, colour of skin (both in relation to race and, amongst images of white women, suntan), quantity of body hair, all come into play. Images produced for different groups of spectators will combine these and a myriad other factors in different ways in order to be effective. It is not any and every image of a self-contained woman that will make a fetishised object of desire. Or perhaps it is that only certain attributes carry the connotation of 'completeness'.

Given the emphasis placed upon the appearance of the woman's body by fetishistic images of women and the different forms such images take, I want to look at the evolution of the physical des-

63   ibid, p 105.
64   Heath, 'Difference', p 90.

criptions given of the women figures in Duras's work. In *La Vie
tranquille*, Françou contemplates her body whilst she is staying at
T...:

> In the sun. My hands on my thighs. I caress them. The warm
> palm of these hands meets the coolness of these thighs which are
> happy. From my half-open arm-pits rises that smell of fresh earth
> which is mine...This twenty-five year-old body of mine is beauti-
> ful. These feet are hardened, finished, feet that have walked. It's
> here in this little space of flesh that everything has happened and
> that everything will happen. Where one day death will bite, hang-
> ing on by its jaws until the pair of us turn to stone.[65]

This description is, I think, not at all fetishistic. The reader is not
presented with a picture of a whole body, nor even any isolated part
of a body, as the object of a look. Françou perceives her body through
all her senses and each part she thinks about is perceived differently.
Moreover, she situates her body in its own history, with her death at
the end, its beauty lying in its transience, its capacity for change.
This is a far cry from the fixity of the fetish. At another point, Françou
says of herself: 'I look like other women. I am quite an ordinary-
looking woman, I know.'[66] Although she somewhat narcissistically
looks at and describes her body, it is not as a finite object, but more
as a moment in a process, that of her own life from birth to death.
The reader is invited to imagine a woman who is one of many, an
idea built up from many different impressions. Above all, Françou is
constructed as a subject of desires and her contemplation of her body
is not their only manifestation. In fact they provide the driving force
behind the novel.

Neither Suzanne, in *Un barrage contre le Pacifique*, nor Anna in *Le
Marin de Gibraltar*, nor Sara in *Les Petits Chevaux de Tarquinia* are
given much physical description, although all three are seen as desirable by at least one man figure within the text. Whilst the desire of
the men is important, the reader is not invited to dwell on the
physical appearance of these women. In *Le Boa*, the narrator describes the effect on Mlle Barbet of never having had her body looked
at by a man, in a story which may provide insight into the reasons
why Duras always portrays her central women figures as objects of
men's desire. 'Lack was eating her up, the lack of the man who had
never come.'[67] But, unlike later stories, in *Le Boa* the narrator has
no male admirer and the story is about the structuring of a woman's

65 *La Vie tranquille*, pp 139–40.
66 ibid, p 125.
67 *Des journées entières dans les arbres*, p 105.

sexual desire from a woman's point of view. It describes the development of the narcissism of a young girl, analysing rather than presenting the girl as a narcissistic object. *Les Chantiers*, in the same collection, does portray a woman figure who is the object of a man's desire, offering the reader a position close to his from which to observe her. A physical description of her is given:

> There was nothing obviously remarkable about her. She was not exactly beautiful. And she did not behave like a woman who knows she is beautiful, or who wants to appear so. There were many women who were more beautiful than her at the hotel and towards whom men gravitated. And she watched those women, and like everyone she no doubt thought them beautiful, in her ignorance of the fact that she was already more beautiful to him than the most beautiful of all those she thought beautiful. So what did she look like? Tall. She had black hair. Her eyes were pale, she walked a little heavily, she had a solid body, perhaps even a little weighty. She always wore light-coloured dresses, like the other women, who had, like her, come to spend their holidays by the lake.[68]

This description does not fetishize the woman in her position as object of desire, although it presents her as seen from the outside, from a distance, object of a man's desire. She is presented, as was Françou, as one woman among many, not the most beautiful, nor the one that the other men staying in the hotel are interested in. She herself also watches the other, more beautiful, women, which rather detracts from any self-sufficiency she might have. She has nothing distinctive about her in terms of her appearance, unless it be that she is less beautiful than the other women, that her body is 'solid, perhaps even a little weighty'. What makes her desirable to the man who watches her is the result of his having come upon her 'in one of the most secret moments of her life'.[69] Later this, perhaps more voyeuristic, desire, stimulated by the sight of something secret, is echoed in another physical description:

> At one moment she leant forward, her hair lifted. He could see that the collar of her blouse had been dirtied slightly on the inside by rubbing against her neck.
> This suddenly filled him with great emotion. The sight of that collar, dirtied and rubbed by that neck, the nape of that neck, half hidden by hair, that linen and that hair and that neck, which could make something dirty, these things which only he could see,

68 ibid, p 205.
69 ibid, p 190.

which she did not know he could see and which he could see better
than she could, made him relive the situation he had been in on
the evening of their meeting, in front of the building site. It was as
if they both been living in that body of hers and still she did not
realize it.[70]

Here the man's desire is described as stimulated by a sight, but it
seems more voyeuristic than fetishistic, the sight of a process rather
than an object. Moreover, because the narrative goes on to analyse
the causes of the man's desire, any fetishistic effect on the reader is
here disturbed. The woman is described as the object of a specific
man's desire, but not of that of other men. Her status as an object
of desire is thus rendered circumstantial. The analysis of the man's
desire forces the reader/narratee, who has been offered his place
from which to watch the woman, to step out of this position and to
contemplate the man's desire, analyse it, and therefore to distance
her/himself from it. For the reader/narratee, the woman is thus produced as an object of desire in a specific relation, and not simply as an
object of desire. S/he may be offered the man's position from which to
view the woman, but s/he is also offered the narrator's position from
which to view the man.

Because all these early works offer a certain amount of analysis of
the workings of (sexual) desire, they do not produce fetishized images
of women. The problem being explored in each of the texts I have
mentioned is posed as a process, whilst fetishism concentrates on a
representation of the object. In this respect *Moderato cantabile* once
more provides a break. As I have tried to show, Anne Desbaresdes is
produced in this text as an object of contemplation for the 'look' of
both Chauvin and the narrator and, because the text is written as a
description of the visible, the narration does not analyse, as it did in
earlier novels. Instead it purports merely to present things, people
and a dialogue, and their significance beyond their physical presence is not ostensibly given. In the case of Anne Desbaresdes then,
her physical presence falls within the scope of the narration, although
no physical description of her is given, but the existence and nature
of her desire must be inferred. However, it is crucial for a reading
of this text that is to make anything out of it at all that the reader
should infer the presence of Anne's desire. This disturbs the fetishization of her as an object of desire although it makes a kind of fetish of
the text itself. Chauvin's description of Anne is somewhat fetishistic,
particularly given that it focusses on her breasts, or rather, on the

70   ibid, p 213.

magnolia flower which comes to stand in for them in a very fetishistic manner: 'You were resting your elbow on the grand piano. Between your breasts, naked under your dress, is that magnolia flower.'[71] However, most descriptions of Anne given by the narration are of expressions and attitudes which signify emotions and desires.

I think there is a tension in the portrayal of Anne Desbaresdes in *Moderato cantabile*. On the one hand she has the role of what I would call an instance of Woman, where Woman is culturally defined as the universal object of masculine fantasy and desire (irrespective of the permutations on actual relations between individual women and men). Woman is always simply Other, since the differences between individual woman as subjects (even, on a basic level, as objects) are outside the scope of that particular construction. So to the extent that Anne Desbaresdes has that role, she is also Other. On the other hand there is Anne Desbaresdes, the subject of (unnamable) desire. Insofar as Chauvin's desire for her is conveyed through the magnolia flower, which refers back to her breasts and a fetishisation of her body, she is constructed as an instance of Woman. Also, as the idle wife of a rich man she is an object of status for her husband in relation to other men, whilst in herself she has no other social role, except as a mother. However, insofar as her desire is the problem explored by the text, she is a woman subject, more than just an object of desire and exchange, and the reader must partially identify with her in order to continue reading.

In contrast, Valérie, in *L'Après-midi de Monsieur Andesmas*, is undoubtedly fetishised, particularly as it is her blonde hair which stands as the signifier of her desirability as an object. Indeed, Valérie's physical attribute, blonde hair, is refined to an abstraction: *blondeur* ('blondness'). The fetishization of Valérie's blondness is made crystal clear in Mme Arc's account of her first sight of Valérie, when the former exchanges glances with two men who are – not coincidentally, considering Duras's portrayal of women through the look of men – also present: 'We were still wondering what man possessed this blondness, and the blondness alone, since we had not yet seen the face. So much useless blondness was unthinkable.'[72] The problem which Valérie's hair presents is not about Valérie's desire, but around her position as object. Who has claimed this object? For an object without a desiring subject is 'useless', as, presumably, is the undeclared desire of Mme Arc and the two men, none of whom 'possess' this blondness. A fetish is a fixed object, but it can only exist in a relation of subject

71 *Moderato cantabile* p 79.
72 *L'Après-midi de Monsieur Andesmas*, p 90.

and object. Valérie's blondness constitutes the potential object, so where is the subject? The answer, of course, is not long in coming: it is Michel Arc.

This fetishization of the figure of Valérie follows very conventional lines for the young blonde is a traditional object of desire for men. Valérie is fixed in the memory of Mme Arc. The unwitting object of admiring looks, she is tall and blonde, positively glowing with self-sufficiency, bathed in light. 'She was walking across, the square is big, across...A year ago when she was still unaware of the splendour of her walk, in the light of the village square.'[73] The text presents this fetishized image as one of devastating power and concerns itself with M. Andesmas and Mme Avc, the victims of Valérie's splendour, not with Valérie herself. The tension between Woman/fetish and desiring subject is absent.

In *Le Ravissement de Lol V. Stein* that tension returns to some extent, although not in terms of physical description. Lol herself is described little, except as regards her 'blondness'.[74] Indeed, Jacques Hold says of her, 'Lol's blondness will never be talked about, nor her eyes, ever', although he mentions them enough for the descriptions to stick, in my memory at least.[75] Perhaps it should be mentioned, however, in the context of this novel, that Tatiana Karl's hair, which is long and black, is concentrated on in a way which is not without a fetishistic quality. Lol remembers: 'Ah! your hair, when you let it down, in the evenings, the whole dormitory would come and look, we helped you.'[76] However, Tatiana herself is described as positively oozing desire and a feeling of lack:

> When she changes position, gets up, rearranges her hair, sits down, her movements are carnal. Her girl's body, her wound, her blessed calamity, cries out, calls out for the lost paradise of its unity, it will call out ceaselessly, from now on, for consolation, it is only whole in a hotel bed.[77]

It is Anne-Marie Stretter who fills the position of fetishized woman figure in *Le Ravissement de Lol V. Stein:*

> She was thin. She must always have been so. She had dressed this thinness, Tatiana clearly remembered, in a black dress cut very low, with a double sheath of tulle, also black. She wanted herself formed and dressed in this way, and she was as she had wished to

73 ibid, p 87.
74 *Le Ravissement de Lol V. Stein,* p 33.
75 ibid, p 79.
76 ibid.
77 ibid.

be, irrevocably. One could make out the admirable bone structure of her body and of her face. Such she appeared and such, henceforth, she would die, with her desired body.[78]

This description of Anne-Marie Stretter fixes her as the unchanging object of desire, both that of others and of her own narcissism. She is completely in control of her appearance and requires nothing from anyone, forever beyond reach in Tatiana's memory. Her appearance has a certain conventionality: she is thin, as was perhaps even more fashionable in 1966 than now, she is dressed in black, a colour often associated with fetishistic images of powerful women, women who are in control, women with whips, for example, or in fetishized clothing such as black leather, black underwear, etc., and her dress is low-cut and lets the onlooker make out the shape of her body. Slightly out of the ordinary is the fact that she is the mother of a grown-up daughter, whom she has brought with her, but the daughter soon disappears from the attention of the narration and the power of the physical description of the mother ensures that neither age nor motherhood detract from the effect of her 'desired body'. In *Le Vice-consul*, Anne-Marie Stretter continues her career, although the description given of her here is not quite so homogeneous:

This evening in Calcutta, the ambassador's wife Anne-Marie Stretter is by the buffet, she is smiling, she is dressed in black, her dress has a double sheath of black tulle, she is holding out a glass of champagne. She has held it out, she is looking around her. With her advancing age, a thinness has come upon her, which clearly reveals the length and delicacy of her bone structure. Her eyes are too pale, like the cut out eyes of statues, her eyelids have grown thin.[79]

This description fixes Anne-Marie Stretter as if in two photographs taken one after the other; the first as she holds out the glass of champagne, the second, a close-up perhaps, after the glass has been taken. It describes a woman's body with a history ('with her advancing age'), but the use of tenses, 'she is holding...' 'she has held...' has the effect of catching two moments and freezing them in the text for all time. As in *Le Ravissement de Lol V. Stein*, Anne-Marie Stretter is described in terms of abstracts such as her 'thinness' and also 'the length and delicacy of her bone structure' which, as in the case of the 'blondness' of Valérie's hair, takes the description away from the specific woman being described and into the realm of arche-

78 ibid, pp 15–16.
79 *Le Vice-consul*, p 92.

types and the 'absolute object of desire'. A 'good bone structure' is a traditionally admired feature in women. Such a depersonalised description of a woman is not an uncommon phenomenon but it does have something of a description of a racehorse about it. Certainly, beyond the allusion to her age, there is not much here, or elsewhere in *Le Vice-consul*, that individualises Anne-Marie Stretter as a particular woman amongst others. She stands as a powerful incarnation of Woman, the object of desire.

The description of Anne-Marie Stretter cited above, long and thin, with her fine bone structure, her black dress, the only woman in the novel who is described in this fashion, or given any description at all, apart from the beggar-woman (an object of fear for Charles Rossett in the only physical description given of her), is a long way away from the description of Françou's body in terms of smells and touch, and from that of the woman figure in *Les Chantiers*, with her solid body and the dirt on her collar. These are both specific women with their own individuality. It seems that, as Duras's texts, and the role of women within them, become more fetishistic, so her physical descriptions of women become more conventional: Valérie, the young blonde, Anne-Marie Stretter, the more mature and subtle society beauty. When Duras shifts from portraying figures in specific relations, as in *Les Chantiers*, she gives her women figures more conventional physical attributes of objects of desire. She forsakes evocations of individual presence, the particular smell, the private dirtiness of a grubby collar, for the abstracted 'blondness' or 'thinness' of desirable Woman. The woman's body becomes a signifier of (sexual) desire itself and its materiality is largely dissolved.

In novels following *Le Vice-consul*, there is no physical description of the bodies of the woman figures in the manner of Anne-Marie Stretter, or even Lol V. Stein, although the women figures are constantly portrayed as the object of a man's look. Possibly this is because any description would give these figures a specificity which might undermine their positions as 'ravaged beings', incarnations of love. The roles of Alissa and the woman in L'Amour in particular as fetishized, self-contained objects of desire are built up in ways which do not require that their bodies be specifically described. It is not until *L'Amant* that Duras returns to the kind of 'photographic' description that she gives to Anne-Marie Stretter in *Le Vice-consul*, in this case it is a description of herself at fifteen when she meets the man from Cholon on the ferry. 'Look at me' she commands the reader.[80] Here she makes explicit the link between photography and her own project of description:

---

80   *L'Amant*, p 24.

It is during this voyage that the image would have become separated, that it would have been taken out from all the rest. It could have existed, a photograph could have been taken, like any other, elsewhere, in different circumstances. But it was not taken. The subject was too insubstantial to provoke its taking. Who would have thought of it? It would only have been taken if it had been possible to foretell the importance of this event in my life, this river crossing. Well, while it was happening, even its existence was unknown. Only God knew of it. That's why, and it could not have been otherwise, this image doesn't exist. It was left out. It was forgotten. It did not stand out, was not taken out from all the rest. It is to this failure to have been taken that it owes its power, that of representing, in fact of being the author, of an absolute.[81]

Here Duras gives us an interesting insight into the function of the verbal 'photograph' for, spared the specificity of its existence as an image, it can more easily generate an absolute in the image fantasised by the reader, any reader, to fit the occasion. Duras describes her appearance, the dress, the shoes, her hair, her makeup and, most important of all, the hat, in detail. It is not a conventional image, 'this appearance that could have made people laugh and which no one laughs at'.[82] But it does have a self-sufficiency and unity about it and the unifying principle behind this image is the adolescent's desire to appear as she does. At fifteen she is as much in control of her image as Anne-Marie Stretter. 'That's how I want it' she says.[83]

Duras's portrayal of herself in *L'Amant* has a certain ambiguity: she is both subject and object, not just because she is writing about herself many years ago, but also in the way that she portrays herself always as an object of someone's desire. The book begins with an anecdote, a man comes up to her to tell her he thinks her ravaged face more beautiful than it was when she was young. Duras says she recognises herself in the image of this event: 'I often think on this image, which only I can still see and of which I have never spoken. It is always there in the same silence, wondrous. Of all the images of myself it is the one I like, the one in which I recognise myself, in which I delight.'[84] This sets the tone for all that follows. She then goes on to describe the way her face has changed over the years, inviting the reader to imagine this face, prematurely aged and later ravaged by alcohol. It is through her face that she offers her contemporary

---

81 ibid, pp 16–17.
82 ibid, p 29.
83 ibid, p 19.
84 ibid, p 9.

self to the reader's imagination, describing herself from the outside rather than the inside. And in her account of herself at fifteen, she builds up the image of herself on the river crossing, as she would have appeared to an external observer, inviting the reader to contemplate this other, different self with her. When she describes the Chinese man's feelings for her, she sometimes uses the first person, sometimes the third, turning herself into a character, one step more distanced from the reader. In relation to the lover she portrays herself as an 'absolute object of desire' and even his desire for his wife has to pass through the fifteen year-old's body:

> He must have been unable to be with [his wife] for a long time, unable to give her an heir to the family fortune. The memory of the little white girl must have been there, the body, lying there, across the bed. For a long time she must have remained the mistress of his desire, his personal reference for emotion, for the immensity of tenderness, for the dark and terrible depths of the flesh. And then the day came when it must have been possible. The day, in fact, when the desire for the little white girl must have been such, unbearable to such a degree that he was able to grasp her entire image, as in a great, strong fever, and to penetrate the other woman with this desire for her, the white child.[85]

In *L'Amant* Duras also writes 'from the inside'. She describes her thoughts and feelings in relation to her mother and brothers, to her writing, to Hélène Lagonelle, and to herself, but the story of the Chinese lover maintains her as an object of desire all the way through, until the very end of the text. It is this ability to be the object of a man's desire which she describes as allowing her to separate from the emotional disaster of her family and it is that which gives her the independent existence which allows her to write. So it is perhaps hardly surprising that in an autobiographical work, she should maintain herself in the status of object of desire, inviting the reader to see her image through the desire of men.

The images she presents of herself, either now, ravaged and lined, or at fifteen, 'dressed like a child prostitute'[86] are more individualised than the fetishistic descriptions of Valérie's 'blondness' or Anne-Marie Stretter's black-clad bone structure, but they have something of a similiar function. For the reader is invited to dwell on the unified image Duras presents of herself, and the familiarity with desire (and death) that these images represent. And whatever else she says

85　ibid, p 140.
86　ibid, p 33.

about herself and her life, the power of the images remain. Duras must be seen – in the mind's eye at least – to be believed.

I think the fetishized woman figure is the most important element of the fantasy which Duras invites the reader to build around her texts, certainly in her fiction. The part it plays in *L'Amant* is slightly different, since Duras is apparently portraying herself as a specific individual (as well as an absolute). These women are clearly the most powerful figures in Duras's work in terms of their structural position within the texts, and they are the ones who remain in the reader's imagination. Writers such as Stephen Heath and Laura Mulvey have analysed the power of fetishised images of women in terms of visual imagery, relating its effects specifically to men. I would not wish to imply that I think such analyses can be simply transferred to literature, but I do think that the fetishism of visual representations of women both draws on and generates a structure which is already built into the psychic organisation of the person who responds to the image.

Similarly, I think that the fetishism of the reader is brought into play in the reading of a novel by Duras which invites her/him to imagine, for example, Valérie, in the light of all the other images of young, blonde women which s/he has come across and the meanings attributed to youth and blondness (as opposed to the specific characteristics of individual young women with fair hair). This is not to mention the reinforcement those meanings are given in relation to Valérie in *L'Apres-midi de Monsieur Andesmas*. I do not think the reader would need to make, project and watch a film of *Le Vice-consul* before Anne-Marie Stretter can assume her role as fetishized object (and I am not speculating here as to why Duras made *India Song*) as the cinema of the unconscious will suffice. Undoubtedly, some representations of men could also be described as fetishistic, and would draw on the fetishism of their audience in the same way, although I think this operates far less frequently than in representations of women. However, given that in Duras's work I see an increasing polarity in the way in which men and women figures are represented, with the women portrayed more and more as the fetishized objects of the men's desire, the problem which my discussion has raised, and which I now want to address is: what is the power of a fetishized representation of a woman for another woman (reader)?

In her article 'You don't know what's happening, do you Mr. Jones?', Mulvey describes fetishistic images of women as products of male castration anxiety. According to her, the fetishistic attitude demands that the castrated woman must either show herself to be phallic, or be punished. In her analysis of fetishistic visual representations of women, she identifies three possible ways in which the image offsets the threat posed by the woman's castration: 'First: woman plus phallic substitute. Second: woman minus phallus punished and humiliated, often by woman plus phallus. Third: woman *as* phallus.'[87] In the first and third instances, the image provides a filler for the gap left by the woman's missing phallus, either by substituting something for it, or by making the image of the woman stand for the phallus. However, in the second instance, there is no phallus or phallic substitute present and the castrated woman is punished for its absence. According to Mulvey, such images thus reproduce a titillating ambiguity around the castratedness of women for the anxious male, and ultimately reassure men that they themselves are not castrated. Mulvey discusses these images entirely in relation to the psychic organisation of men and sees them as an effect of masculine narcissism:

> The message of fetishism concerns not woman, but the narcissistic wound she represents for man. Women are constantly confronted with their own image in one form or another, but what they see bears little relation or relevance to their own unconscious fantasies, their own hidden fears and desires. They are being turned all the time into objects of display, to be looked at and gazed at and stared at by men. Yet in a real sense women are not there at all. The parade has nothing to do with woman, everything to do with man. The true exhibit is always the phallus. Women are simply the scenery onto which men project their narcissistic fantasies.[88]

Whilst I find Mulvey's analysis of fetishistic images of women interesting and quite convincing, I think she has fallen here into the trap of the 'excluded woman' theory which I discussed earlier in relation to language, the one that holds that women are somehow excluded from culture, which has been constructed entirely by men and which has nothing to do with us – a line implicit or explicit in the work of Irigaray and Spender, for example, and much espoused by feminists in the late seventies and early eighties. However, such a line does not deal with the fact that women and men are born into the same cultures and that, although their respective positions may be different, the archetypes in relation to which they establish those positions, such as the Mother, the Father, the fetishized or castrated Woman, to take those under scrutiny here, are the same. The advertising hoardings and films that men see in this country and elsewhere I and other women also see. Woman have to find a place within patriarchal culture as well as men do, and our unconscious fan-

87 Laura Mulvey, 'You don't know what's happening, do you Mr Jones?', in *Spare Rib*, no 8, London, February 1973, p 14
88 ibid, p 30.

tasies will be shaped in relation to the culture that we grow into as men's are.

Furthermore, it is quite clear that images of women that men may find powerful or compelling often affect women too, perhaps even more so, in some cases. Women have been fascinated by film stars such as Marilyn Monroe or Marlene Dietrich, for example, women watch other women, and look at fashion magazines where the faces and bodies of the models and the clothes they are wearing form a homogenised 'image', women look at themselves in mirrors to assess the overall effect they create and comment on each other's clothes and bodies. Not as men do, maybe, but we are very aware of each other's presence and the meanings of the way we present ourselves.

And women find Duras compelling reading as well as men, quite possibly more so. It is women who have described her writing as 'feminine'. And Duras herself is a woman, writing not an elaborately constructed pastiche of what a man might write, but from her own fantasies:

> I was at Vinhlong and one day there was a new Governor. He arrived with his wife. They might have been called Stretter. I can't remember. They had two daughters. The wife was a redhead, completely lacking in colour, who did not wear makeup, who didn't dress to be noticed (*qui ne* paraissait *pas.*) You could say that was where I saw the difference between being and appearance, I felt it then. Very shortly after their arrival at Vinhlong I learnt that a young man had just killed himself for love of her. This invisible woman, you see, who did not attract notice and who attracted me because of this sort of lack of colour in her face, her eyes, well! I learnt that she had power, a kind of power of death, very hidden, very secret, and I remember the extraordinary shock it was, the death of that young man...[89]
>
> ...To give me such a shock, you know, I think that it must have concerned me, for it to reappear forty, fifty years later, it must have concerned me very, very closely.[90]

As I have indicated above, Duras's portrayal of herself in *L'Amant* is not without elements of fetishism, particularly in relation to the 'man's fedora', a male (phallic) attribute, which is made the condition of the fifteen year old's seeing herself as an object of other's desire. She puts it on for the first time and, 'Suddenly I see myself as another, as another would be seen, outside, made available to all, open to all looks, brought into the traffic of towns, roads, desire.'[91]

89 'Dépossedée', in *Marguerite Duras*, p 83.
90 ibid, p 85.
91 *L'Amant*, p 20.

I think one can see parallels between the kind of fascination such images can have for women, and the kind of fascinated exchange of looks identified by Montrelay and Lemoine-Luccioni, or the 'neither one nor two' of femininity described by Irigaray. Perhaps part of the fascination lies in the relation of women to the mOther, all-powerful and all-satisfying object of desire. However, the women figures in Duras's texts, as in other fetishized representations, are not simply incarnations of the mOther. They are always constructed primarily as an object of desire for men. Such images of women are produced as other in relation to the position of the narratee, from which the reader of either sex is invited to read. They are shown in terms of men's desire and ostensibly allow no place for other women to occupy in relation to them, since the narratee is implicitly constructed in the masculine position. So what is their power for women?

I think Duras herself goes some way towards providing an answer in the conversation cited above, when she mentions the 'power, a kind of power of death' that she attributed to the Governor's wife. For the power of the fetishized image is the power to call up desire – indeed, to signify desire, as the fifteen year-old of *L'Amant* knows: 'It wasn't a question of attracting desire. It was there in she who aroused it, or it did not exist.'[92] Duras's women figures are in control of (men's) desire, they could perhaps drive men to their deaths, although in fact they do not do so.

This power is the only one specifically allotted to women as women by patriarchal culture. In saying this, I do not want to gloss over the success of a woman like Margaret Thatcher, whose very powerful image has everything to do with her being a woman. Clearly, it is another version of the phallic woman, the archaïc mother. She is constructed as a woman with masculine power, the Iron Lady, who wields absolute power, as the mother did in the fantasy of the child, and who is cruel to be kind. This position is reinforced by her dissociation from other women with whom she might be identified, for example, we are told she does not get on with the Queen. She is usually portrayed as one woman surrounded by men – her Cabinet – in inferior power positions. Any other women with whom she might be associated are seldom seen with her and thus comparisons are never made. There is only room for one woman at the top.

Such a construction of a woman as an all-powerful figure is, however, relatively rare in our culture. Undoubtedly the image of the archaïc mother has its place in the unconscious, but it is seldom directly represented. It is usual for women portrayed as powerful to be seen as wielding their power entirely through sexuality – the

92   ibid, p 28.

'power behind the throne' of the wife, or mistress – or in ways which are specifically sexual. Sexuality is absent in the construction and self-presentation of Margaret Thatcher, the phallic subject is not also an object of desire. Perhaps the image of the phallic Mother, in whom both these positions are fused, is too threatening in the context of patriarchal culture for a woman to hold both positions or perhaps they somehow cancel each other out. But whatever the reasons, the power which usually accrues to images of women, though it must be related to the total power of the (phallic) mother, is specifically channelled through sexuality. The woman acts by proxy: the man realises her desires precisely because she is object of his desire.

This construction makes women-objects of desire appear as the condition for the existence of the desire of men – as Lemoine Luccioni suggested. In the patriarchal context, this is a considerable power, a power which comes from the position of being the phallus rather than having it. However, there are pitfalls for women here, for no woman can fully occupy the position of the phallus, anymore than any man can simply have it. Either her position as object of (men's) desire is precarious, or else, if her position in relation to a man or men is at all established, it is undermined by the inability of men to confer what they do not have. Perhaps this last effect is why it is not until she is leaving Indo-China that the adolescent of *L'Amant* begins to think that she might in fact have loved the man from Cholon with a love that she did not feel at the time, perhaps he is only able to confer the phallus in retrospect. Furthermore, in order to be in the position of the phallus, the woman must construct herself as an object of desire for others, her narcissism has to pass through (a fantasy of) the other's desire. This must require a split between the subject and object of narcissism, as demonstrated by *L'Amant*, with its constant restaging of the split between Duras the author/subject and Duras the object of desire, both aged fifteen and more recently (by implication, now). Women's fascination with the fetishized image of a woman may arise partly from desire for the Mother, but their desires are most often channelled through those of men to reach the unattainable object.

In Lacanian terms, any subject is always an object for the Other ('the look which I imagine in the field of the Other'), but Lacan's Other is not personified, and the Other's desire, which is what the subject desires, can manifest itself in an infinite number of different ways, depending on which of any possible 'o' objects are standing in the place of the Other at any given time. In the context of heterosexuality, which is the relevant one to a discussion of Duras's work, it is men (or certain men, or even perhaps one man) who stand in the place of the Other for the paradigmatic woman who identifies herself in the place of the phallus. (Obviously no subject identifies her/himself in one position alone in relation to only one form of narcissism, but I am elaborating a model here, rather than trying to describe a total reality.) The woman's narcissism also passes through the desire of other women, though this is more supressed in the strictly heterosexual context expressing itself, perhaps, in the competitiveness 'of commodities between themselves' that Irigaray noticed, perhaps also in admiration and imitation. But the woman's narcissism passes openly through the desire of men, or at least, that of the men for whom she wants to be the phallus.

In this model, for the paradigmatic woman the Other is a man and, in order to construct herself as object of desire, she must look at herself through her fantasy of a man's eyes, so that, in her narcissistic relation to herself, the she who looks is gendered masculine, whilst the she who is looked at (or talked to, danced with, etc.) is gendered feminine. What is 'desirable' in masculine eyes is already defined, though constantly being modified, before any woman begins to try to identify herself in relation to the phallus. Thus, she has to try and make herself into an object of desire in terms of those pre-existing images, playing with the signifiers of desirability. Hence, no doubt, many women's alienated relations to their own bodies, which they starve, have re-modelled, or just simply hate because they do not conform to these women's fantasised images of the object of desire.

But whatever women do, it is impossible to be the phallus. No woman can simply be the fetishized image of herself that she may, to a greater or lesser extent, create. For she is always still a subject. What the fetishized image of a woman that she sees on an advertising hoarding, or in a film, gives her is the image of an instance of Woman, an image which is, in terms of that particular advertisement or film, in the position of the phallus, the self-sufficient object of desire. It is an image to which she can compare herself and find herself wanting, as many feminists have pointed out. However, it is also an image with which she can identify and it offers her power too. So such images of women can have an ambiguous effect for women who look at them: they bear witness to the power of Woman, signifier of desire, and at the same time to the failure of individual women to attain that power (or any other).

I think it is in this dual effect that part of the fascination of Duras's work for some women lies. For what Duras does, to a greater or lesser extent in different works, is to present women figures who are primarily objects of desire, but with whom the reader is also invited to identify. This is most apparent in *Moderato cantabile*, *Le Ravissement de Lol V. Stein*, *Le Vice-consul* and, above all, *L'Amant*, where identification is the easiest. It is surely not purely coincidental that the first three are the novels most frequently discussed in relation to questions of femininity, or that *L'Amant* has thus far proved the most successful of all. As we have seen in each of the novels 'blanks' are produced around women's desires, desires which must be assumed, but remain inaccessible. The text demands a precarious identification with the central woman figure. In *L'Amant* it is not so much that there are 'blanks', but in terms of the sexual relationship, the fifteen-year-old Duras is portrayed principally as object of the Chinese man's desire. His is the passion. She, meanwhile, goes about the business of taking charge of her life. In all these books the woman reader is offered an image of a woman who could be, and insofar as she infers her desires becomes, herself. And this image is a powerful one of the woman-object of men's desire, who is also, by inference and implication, a subject of other desires. Woman-as-phallus and (just) subject too: Lacan's impossibility.

Duras's earlier novels, before *Moderato cantabile* lack the powerful concentration of her later work. The reader is distracted from the production of the fixed image by psychology, analysis and the details of everyday life. The texts are structured around problems of plot, which are resolved, rather than an effect of fascination. In some of her later work the balance of tension between the possibility of identification and the status of the woman figure as object of desire is less finely tuned, and the power of fascination correspondingly less, to judge from what has been written about them. In novels following *Le Vice-consul* I personally find any identification with the figures difficult, due to a withering away of character and setting so extensive that I find it unbelievable that these are 'beings like us', and this particularly in relation to the women figures, although I cannot identify in the position of their male desirers either without effort. For me these texts fail in their effects of fascination, although I can see that they exhibit structures which might draw in other people's imaginations. Blanchot's, for example, was apparently drawn by *Détruire, dit-elle*.

To sum up then, insofar as Duras's novels do fascinate their women readers, as sometimes they clearly do, it must be in part because they offer the pleasure of perceiving a woman who is both subject and object of desire at the same time. And doubtless this offers a pleasurable form of identification to some men too, why not? Gender is not the preserve of anatomical sex. However, I do think that on a fundamental level, in relation to sexual difference, women's narcissism is beset by the problem of identification with an image which is always an object of desire, where the only position available as subject is implicitly masculine, or else that of the child in relation

to the archaïc Mother. Duras portrays women who are already constituted as objects of (masculine) desire and they are to this extent
gendered 'feminine'. They are in the position of the phallus, but at the
same time the reader infers the presence of their desires. This is no
doubt why Marini hears femininity resounding through Duras's writing. She hears it in the echoes of the unspeakable desire of the woman-
as-phallus. Certainly Duras's texts suggest the presence of desire that
emanates from the 'feminine' position, and it this aspect of her writing
that has led to its being claimed as feminist. But, in order to be inferred, this desire must be constructed in relation to something, some
object, and the form the woman's desire takes is also of relevance to
the meanings of the texts in relation to feminism. So what is it for?
What does (Duras's) woman want?

CHAPTER 7
Was das Weib will

According to Marini, 'the feminine' not only resounds, but also speaks through Duras's work, and indeed, it would be almost impossible to infer the presence of desire in a text without also having some idea of the direction it was taking. In Marini's terms, 'the feminine', while remaining a somewhat ill-defined concept, appears to refer to a form of psychic organisation she sees as specific to women and which in other texts does not get a hearing. But if it did speak, what would it say? In this section I intend to look at the presentation of women as subjects of desire in Duras's work, at the way in which the presence of their desires is conveyed and the directions they take.

The presentation of the desires of the women figures in Duras's writing – to the extent that is articulated – undergoes, as might be expected, a transformation over the course of time. There are two main areas in which these desires are discernible: in sexual desire and in relations between mothers and their children. These areas are treated quite differently and appear to a large extent to be mutually exclusive. Such a separation makes it possible to look at each in turn.

SEXUAL DESIRE

In early novels, particularly *La Vie tranquille*, but also *Le Marin de Gibraltar*, the central women figures express quite clearly their sexual desire for a man or men. Françou's desire for Tiène is articulated plainly: 'As I talked, I could see Tiène half sitting up in bed, the shape of his body. Why is he so beautiful that one can't help looking at him even in anger? Why is he so desirable, so disconcerting, so filled with silence that any word spoken in his presence becomes a lie?'[1] Elsewhere Françou says:

> I love Tiène. Even at a distance, I feel quite clearly that I no longer want anyone but him. The thing that I thought was most important to me until now has faded away. But I am still left with this desire for Tiène. It's there, contained between my hips, a sort of wisdom that is wiser than I am and which knows better than I do what I want.[2]

Tiène is clearly the object of Françou's (and Luce Barragues's) desire, and the resolution of the problem which this desire poses for Françou comes when she announces that she and Tiène are to marry and that her mother will have grandchildren.[3] Given that the usual structure of relations between the sexes underlying not only works of fiction, but also, if we are to believe Claude Lévi-Strauss, the organisation of human societies, is based upon the exchange of women between men, the way in which the determined and active Françou and Luce do battle for Tiène the object of desire, almost constitutes a role reversal, with Françou's final announcement settling the business and making Tiène 'hers'.[4] Certainly there is a passivity in both women's approach to Tiène which in fact ensures the maintenance of more traditional relations between the sexes. However, the desire of both women is explicitly stated; its object being a man, either Nicolas or Tiène.

Le Marin de Gibraltar is the only other novel by Duras in which a man is the object of a woman's explicitly stated sexual desire but here the man – the sailor from Gibraltar – is an elusive creature, whose charm lies as much in his absence as in his presence. Whilst on her travels, Anna picks up various men, whom she takes with her on her yacht, but although she tells the narrator that she took them on board because of an 'essential need' left in her by the sailor, she speaks of them as objects of ridicule rather than desire. They are her 'mistakes'.[4] The nature of her feelings in relation to the narrator are left to the reader's inference, although near the end of the novel, the narrator says of himself and Anna 'we love each other'.[5] Anna articulates nothing directly, but the reader must assume that some of her sexual desire is directed towards the narrator in order to make sense of the narrative. However, the articulation of that desire is not constructed as a 'blank',

1 *La Vie tranquille*, p 48.
2 ibid, p 130.
3 ibid, p 216.
4 *Le Marin de Gibraltar*, p 209.
5 IBID, P 427.

since it is not really posed as a problem. The novel is far more concerned with exploring the narrator's desires.

But, if Anna's desire for the narrator is left largely to the assumption of the reader, in the case of Sara in *Les Petits Chevaux de Tarquinia*, any form of sexual desire seems simply absent, although the novel is largely structured around whether or not she will embark on an adulterous relationship. Sara appears completely passive and desireless in her sexual adventure with Jean, 'the man'. She is bored with her husband Jacques and 'the man' seems very interested in her but the narration conveys no sense that he excites any desire on her part, nor is her lack of desire constructed as in any sense a problem in her relations with him. She simply finds herself 'the object of his desire'[6] and allows him to decide for her what will happen:

> He kissed her. Then he took a step back. She did not move. They looked at each other. Sara saw the river glistening in his eyes.
> 'I don't want to go', he said.
> Sara did not move. His kissed her again.
> I'm not going', he repeated.
> He kissed her once again. They went into the villa.[7]

The only decision Sara makes in the course of the novel is to discontinue her affair with 'the man'. Otherwise, she is passive in relation to him as to everyone else. And whilst the reader gains some idea of what she does not want, she evinces very little in the way of active desires.

Like Sara, Suzanne in *Un barrage contre le Pacifique* adopts a very passive position in relation to 'young Agosti' and drops him without compunction when the chance comes to leave the plain with Joseph. It is Joseph who appears to be the object of Suzanne's somewhat undefined desire and the explicitly stated incestuous love of the later film/narrative *Agatha* is perhaps hinted at here, although, being tangential to the main direction of the plot, need not command much of the reader's attention. However, it is there to be noted: at one point the narrative gives Suzanne's thoughts about Joseph through free indirect speech: 'When, like this evening, he was thinking with difficulty and disgust, one couldn't help finding him very beautiful and loving him very much'[8] and it is on the strength of his resemblance to Joseph that she encourages 'young Agosti'. But Suzanne's overwhelming desire is to leave the plain. Sexual desire is primarily the means to achieving that end, by finding a man who will want her enough to take her away with him.

6 *Les Petits Chevaux de Tarquinia*, p 112.
7 ibid, p 108.
8 *Un barrage contre le Pacifique*, p 144.

In these early novels, excepting as ever *La Vie tranquille*, the women figures' sexual desire is not articulated, even though the narrative might be concerned with their sexual relations. As this lack of articulation is in no way presented as a problem, the active sexual desire of the women figures is constructed as largely irrelevant to the progression of events, to be assumed present by the reader if necessary. However, with *Moderato cantabile*, again as might be expected, comes a change. In this latter novel, Anne Desbaresdes's desire is constructed as very important, a motor force behind the movement of the narrative, but unarticulated and inarticulable, its presence can only be inferred by the reader in the 'blanks'.

In order that it might be inferred, Anne Desbaresdes's desire must be constructed as being in relation to something, and the reader is encouraged to infer a particular form of desire on her part, namely, a desire for her own anihilation. For example, in the following passage, where Chauvin describes Anne listening to two men passing outside her bedroom window:

> 'Sleeping or awake, decently dressed or not, your existence was being disregarded.'
> Anne Desbaresdes struggled, guilty, and yet accepting it.
> 'You shouldn't', she said, 'I remember, anything could happen...'[9]

It seems fair to assume that the reader/narratee will infer that Anne Desbaresdes is in some way moved by the thought that people – men – are disregarding her existence. This is of course paralleled in *Le Ravissement de Lol V. Stein*, where Lol's desire is locked into the scene in which she is a witness to her own obliteration from the thoughts and feelings of Michael Richardson, a scene which she was unable to watch to its conclusion because at the end of the ball she was separated from her fiancé and Anne-Marie Stretter:

> A breath away from replacement by this woman. Lol holds that breath: as the woman's body appears to this man, her own fades, voluptuousness, from the world.
> 'You. You alone.'
> This very slow tearing off of Anne-Marie Stretter's dress, this velvet annihilation of her own person, is something Lol has never managed to bring to its conclusion.[10]

More than annihilation in the form of others' ignorance of her existence, it is the annihilation of death which seems to fascinate

---

9 *Moderato cantabile*, p 57.
10 *Le Ravissement de Lol V. Stein*, p 50.

Anne Desbaresdes. Her desire seems to have been awakened by the murder of the woman in the café and it is the story of events leading up to that murder which she apparently wants to elicit from Chauvin. I say apparently; Anne's desire in relation to the murder is suggested in the first conversation between herself and Chauvin, as for example in the passage cited above, and continues to be suggested by her constant questioning in subsequent conversations. The story of the lovers as told by Chauvin is one in which the woman becomes increasingly abject, and it is this which seems to excite Anne:

> 'So this house was very isolated', Anne Desbaresdes began again, slowly. 'It was hot, you were saying. When he would tell her to go away, she would always obey. She would sleep under trees, in fields, like...'
>
> 'Yes', said Chauvin.
>
> 'When he called her, she would come back. And in the same way that she would go when he shooed her off. Obeying him to this extent was her way of hoping. And even, when she arrived on the doorstep, she would wait for him to tell her to come in.'
>
> 'Yes.'
>
> Anne Desbaresdes leaned her stupified face towards Chauvin, she did not reach him. Chauvin drew back.
>
> 'It was there, in that house, that she learned what you said she was, perhaps, for example...'
>
> 'Yes, a dog',[11] Chauvin stopped her again.
>
> She drew back in her turn. He filled her glass, held it out to her.
>
> 'I was lying', he said.
>
> She tidied her profoundly disordered hair, came back to the present with weariness and contained compassion.[12]

Anne seems to identify with the woman in Chauvin's story, as Chauvin does with the man. The reader is strongly encouraged to assume that the dog-like behaviour and final death of the woman correspond in some sense to Anne's desires, even if she and Chauvin stop at a kind of symbolic resolution, rather than an actual killing. The masochism of her position is evident, both in the content of the dialogue, building up to Chauvin's 'I wish you were dead', and the interspersed moments of brutality on his part: 'Chauvin uttered a word in a low voice. Anne's gaze slowly dimmed under the insult, filled with drowsiness',[13] or, at the end of their fourth conversation:

---

11 The word Chauvin actually uses is *chienne*, literally 'bitch', but 'bitch' has connotations of hardness and spitefulness which are not intended here, I think, the principal being abjection and obedience on the part of the woman. So I have translated as 'dog', which carries these latter connotations slightly better.

12 *Moderato cantabile*, p 87.

13 ibid, p 81.

'she closely observed the inhuman tensing of Chauvin's face, could not get enough of it.'[14] It is also apparent in the form, which has Anne as the questioner and Chauvin in the position of authority, even if he says constantly, 'I know nothing'.

The masochism apparent in *Moderato cantabile* is given further weight by Duras's own description of how she came to write it:

> ...I once had a love affair and I think that's where it started [...] A very, very violent erotic experience and – how can I explain it? – I went through a crisis that was...suicidal, I mean... that the story I tell in *Moderato cantabile*, the woman that wants to be killed, I experienced that...and after that the books changed ...I've been thinking about that for two years, two, three years, I think that the turning point, the turn towards...towards sincerity took place then. And, like in *Moderato cantabile*, the personality of the man I was involved with didn't matter. It wasn't a...let's say a love story, but it was a – how shall I say? – a sexual story. I thought I wasn't going to get out alive. It was very odd, because I told it from the outside in *Moderato cantabile*, but I have never talked about it otherwise.[15]

However, whether or not Duras has consciously written about her experience other than in *Moderato cantabile*, the same kind of masochistic relation of woman to man can be found in other work by her. In *Le Ravissement de Lol V. Stein*, it is seen from the position of the slightly sadistic Jacques Hold in relation to Lol: 'Through her face and her face only, as I touch it with my open hand in a more and more urgent and brutal way, she feels sexual pleasure',[16] but more obviously in relations between the narrator and Tatiana Karl: 'Jacques Hold possessed Tatiana Karl mercilessly. She put up no resistance, said nothing, refused nothing, marvelled at such possession.'[17]

He hides Tatiana Karl's face under the sheets and thus he has her decapitated body in his hands, entirely at his disposition. He turns it over, turns it back, arranges it as he wishes, parts the limbs or draws them back together, looks intensely at its irreversible beauty, enters it, becomes immobile within it, waits to become sucked into oblivion, oblivion comes.[18]

There is violence in these descriptions, particularly in the use of language such as 'mercilessly', or 'decapitated body', as well as in

14 ibid, pp 87–8.
15 *Les Parleuses*, p 59.
16 *Le Ravissement de Lol V. Stein*, p 173.
17 ibid, p 123.
18 ibid, pp 134–5.

the portrayal of Tatiana Karl's total passivity and Jacques Hold's unimpeded control of her depersonalised body. In *Le Vice-consul*, the violence suggested at here is made more explicit in Charles Rossett's fantasy about Anne-Marie Stretter:

How he would have liked, oh, to raise his hand... His hand is raised, falls back, begins to caress the face, the lips, gently at first, then more and more curtly, then harder and harder, the teeth are offered up in an unsightly, painful smile, the face comes as much as possible within reach of the hand, it is placed at its entire disposition, she lets it happen to her, he shouts as he hits her: she must never cry again, never, never, never again; you would think she was beginning to lose her memory, no one is crying now, she says, there is nothing more to understand, the hand strikes, each time more precisely, it is reaching the speed and precision of a machine, perfection soon. Anne-Marie Stretter suddenly has a dark beauty, smooth, she accepts the rending of her sky, the mobility of her head is wonderful, it moves on the neck at will, oiled, an incomparable mechanism, it becomes, for Charles Rossett's hand, organic, instrumental.[19]

What form Anne-Marie Stretter's own desires might take is left mainly to the reader's inference. She certainly shows no obviously masochistic traits. But, more than the somewhat frantic Tatiana Karl, she is shown as completely passive, 'a woman who has no... preferences',[20] as the vice-consul describes her. Although she is seen largely in terms of the sexual desire men have for her, she seems to have none of her own, beyond the narcissism apparent in her appearance in *Le Ravissement de Lol V. Stein*.

The most overt and explicit example of sadomasochism in Duras's work is the narrative *L'Homme assis dans le couloir*, which recounts what appears to be simply a sadomasochistic sexual fantasy, in which the woman takes a highly masochistic role. Towards the end of the narrative, 'she says that she wants to be hit, she says on her face, she asks him to do it, come on'.[21] He complies, until at the end of the narrative, it is unclear to the narrator, who is constructed primarily as an observer of the scene, whether the woman is alive or dead: 'I can see that the man is crying, lying on top of the woman. I can see nothing of her but immobility. I don't know, I know nothing, I don't know if she's asleep.'[22] This final scene, and the expressed wish of the woman, 'she says that she would like to die',[23] echo the description of

19 *Le Vice-consul*, p 203.
20. ibid, p 171.
21 *L'Homme assis dans le couloir*, Paris, Minuit, 1980, p 32.
22 ibid, p 36.
23 ibid, p 33.

the murder in the café and the desire of the woman/Anne Desbaresdes
in *Moderato cantabile*. There are many similar echoes and resonances
throughout Duras's work; for example, this description of the man
beating the woman is very close to Charles Rossett's fantasy cited
above, and the sentence: 'She has become ugly, she has become what
she would have been, had she been ugly'[24] is an almost exact repetition of a sentence from *Le Vice-consul:* 'She has suddenly become the
woman that, had she been ugly, she would have been.'[25]

L'Homme assis dans le couloir, because of its close links with other
texts by Duras, which in turn reflect and echo each other, crystallises
certain aspects of heterosexual relations as portrayed in her work.
It brings together many different threads in her depiction of sexual
desire: on the part of men, a certain brutality and a degree of voyeurism; on the part of women, the desire to be looked at, the abjection
of their sexual desire insofar as it manifests itself, and the desire to
be beaten, perhaps to death, by their lovers. Traces of these different
aspects can be found in most of Duras's work, though not all, but
they are most clearly apparent in those novels where the central problem of the text is constructed as being that of the central woman
figure's (sexual) desire, and where the man for whom she is an object
of desire is the investigator of the problem. In other words, it is those
women who are portrayed as being in the feminine position, the
position of object of desire, and whose own desire is perceived by
the reader in the 'blanks' of the text (*Moderato cantabile*), or is
articulated as an inference on the part of the male investigator (*Le
Ravissement de Lol V. Stein, Le Vice-consul*), who are portrayed as
masochistic in their (never articulated) sexual desire.

If we consider the masochism of these figures in the light of the
fetishism perceptible in their portrayal, it seems quite in keeping, for,
as Freud discusses in his essay on fetishism, there is an ambivalence
in the way in which the fetish is cathected:

> In very subtle instances both the disavowal and the affirmation of
> the castration have found their way into the construction of the
> fetish itself...In other instances the divided attitude shows itself
> in what the fetishist does with his fetish, whether in reality or in
> his imagination...Another variant, which is also a parallel to
> fetishism in social psychology, might be seen in the Chinese custom
> of mutilating the female foot and then revering it like a fetish after
> it has been mutilated. It seems as though the Chinese male wants
> to thank women for having been castrated.[26]

24 ibid, p 12.
25 *Le Vice-consul*, p 197.
26 Freud, 'Fetishism', p 157.

Mulvey would no doubt see the practice of foot-binding in terms of punishment for castration, following her view that the fetishistic attitude requires that the woman who does not appear as phallic be punished for being castrated. However, I think this idea raises the question: why should the castrated woman be punished? Does not castration already constitute a form of punishment in itself? It seems to me that what the woman is being punished for is not simply her castration but that she is also at the same time a subject of desire. In the first and third instances, she is woman-plus-phallus, the phallic mother, the all-powerful object of infantile desire, and at the same time satisfier of desire on the level of fantasy. Both types of image offer a possibility of plenitude – *jouissance* – to the onlooker in the masculine position, plenitude which would be attained by possession of the woman represented. It is insofar as she is represented as neither having a penis nor being the phallus, but rather as a woman subject of desire that I think the image of the woman Mulvey describes threatens the (masculine) subject who looks. For like any image, it invites identification and also makes the looker the object of a look. But if the woman's lack of penis is conflated with a lack of (Symbolic) phallus, then the phallus necessary to desire and subjecthood is missing from the exchange of looks between subject and image. If penis and phallus are not conflated, then such an image affirms that it is possible to be 'castrated' (in the sense of penisless) and yet also a subject of desire. For the anxious masculine subject, either of these two possibilities could mean an undermining of his position as phallus-bearer for he is being asked to accept that the hierarchy of subject the object does not necessarily correspond to possession of a penis.

This is a rather schematic account, which disregards any feminine identifications on behalf of the masculine subject. However, most women will have felt the effects of the threat posed to the would-be phallus-bearer by the woman subject. Being told to 'cheer up, love' by a strange man in the street is not just to receive a solicitous exhortation to escape from one's miseries. It is an exhortation to remember one's primary role and make an effort to appear decorative and desirable, rather than locked away in one's own (grim?) thoughts, an exhortation many men seem to feel free to make to any woman, although never to other men. An extreme example of this kind of thing is the hate shown in the tabloid press for women who refuse to wear the badges of desirability to those who 'burn their bras', do not shave their legs or wear makeup, and who then make their non-sexual desires manifest in political action. The Greenham Common women have long suffered such vilification, and their worst crime often seems to have been 'ugliness'. I think that women who behave in this way threaten because they are asking to be seen in the first instance as subjects of desires which are not confined to narcissistic sexuality and only in the second instance (or sometimes not at all) as objects of the desires of others. They are accused of 'wanting to be men', but in fact what they are saying is that the Other sort of human being, the 'castrated' sort, the sort that doesn't have a penis (and does have different attributes), can enter the world of the masculine subject.

This account of the threatening nature of the woman subject also fits with feminist analyses of *film noir* (in particular). According to such analyses, *film noir* portrays women as subjects of (sexual and other) desires, represented as uncontained within a particular relationship and as a highly destructive force, particularly for the male figures whom they 'ensnare'. They are eventually punished for this excess of destructive desire, frequently by death. The central woman figure of such films is portrayed as either being outside the family structure – unmarried and independent – or as breaking it up as an adulteress. Her position constitutes a transgression of the Law and she invites a man to transgress with her. This he does, apparently assuming that her desire is directed entirely towards him and that all will be resolved with himself taking the position of the Father. However, the woman proves treacherous – her desires are moving in unforseen directions – and the problem posed by the transgression is resolved by the punishment meted out to both in the ensuing disaster. The moral is that the woman subject is dangerous but that ultimately she will be punished.

Duras's fetishistic texts obviate such need for punishment of the woman subject. For although in *Moderato cantabile*, and also, more oblilquely, in *Le Ravissement de Lol V. Stein* and *Le Vice-consul*, she portrays women whose desire invites and in itself constitutes transgression of the Law, these are not the duplicitous and determinedly amoral figures of *film noir*, whose overweening desires must be punished by external forces. On the contrary, their desires are self-regulating in terms of the Law, always manifesting themselves as desire for death, or sleep, or 'oblivion', or in other words, for their own end. Given the position in which the woman figure is constructed, the 'feminine' one, this is not surprising. What else indeed could this feminine say when it speaks? For if it uttered its desire as being for anything other than its own destruction, it would be breaking that Law which defines its place as feminine and gives it its position in the scheme of things. Feminine masochism ensures the maintenance of the Law and, in return, the Law legitimises the feminine position.

This is not to say that women's desire has to be masochistic, for the feminine is a position, not a sex-specific essence. And indeed, not all of Duras's women figures are constructed as masochistic in their sexual desires. In the portrayals of Anna in *Le Marin de Gibraltar* and Claire Lannes in *L'Amante anglaise*, both figures are made to tell their stories to a questioning male narrator and both tell stories of sexual desire for men from which all traces of wishes for annihilation are absent. However, in neither case is the Law seriously threatened, for both these women's desires are locked into inaccessible objects: Anna's sailor may or may not exist, but in any case she has not seen him for three years; Claire Lannes relationship with the 'policeman from Cahors' is a thing of the distant past and could not be returned to. Furthermore, the appellation of both of these men in terms of their jobs and a place helps them to occupy the position of fantasy objects without really appearing as individual people at all. The male investigator is not confronted with an actual rival. In each case, the threat that the woman's uncontained (by him) desire might pose to the investigator/narrator is neutralised: in *Le Marin de Gibraltar* by the narrator's reaching a point where he understands Anna and establishes that she loves him, even though they go on looking for the sailor to stop their relationship from becoming boring; in *L'Amante anglaise*, by the narrator losing interest precisely at the point where Claire Lannes makes a demand on him, 'listen to me'. In each case, the text ends at the point where the narrator has established that the woman's desire, insofar as it eludes his grasp, is caught up in a fantasy that can have little effect on the world outside that woman's head, and in particular, on the narrator himself.

These two texts in which the woman's sexual desire is for an inaccessible or lost male object can be seen as points where an underlying theme, which runs throughout Duras's work, and which is related to the question of why the Law is never broken, surfaces and is given expression. I see this theme as dividing into two strands, which intersect at various points. The first is that of the dead brother.

The dead brother, who can be linked to the favourite 'little brother' portrayed in *L'Amant*, appears first in *La Vie tranquille*. Here, although Françou expresses love for Nicolas, her sexual desires are directed towards Tiène. The brother then reappears in *Les Petits Chevaux de Tarquinia*, in a passage which is striking, partly in its resemblance to descriptions in *Un barrage contre le Pacifique*, and partly because it is totally unconnected to the rest of the narrative in any immediately obvious way:

A memory comes back to Sara of other fishermen who, in grey rivers with swampy mouths, resonant with monkeys, cast their nets in the same serene, perfect way. With a little concentration, she could still hear the screeching of the monkeys in the mangroves, mingled with the rumbling of the sea and the creaking of palm trees stripped by the wind. They were both, the brother and she, Sara, in the bottom of the boat trying to catch teal. The brother was dead.[27]

There is no further mention of the brother in this novel, although anyone who had read *Un barrage contre le Pacifique* or *L'Amant* would no doubt connect him with Joseph or the 'little brother'. I would include in this thematic strand the portrayal of the dead lover of *Hiroshima mon amour*. The actress' love for the German soldier is just as taboo in occupied France as a sister's incestuous love for her brother would be, and she is punished for it.

Although the brother/sister relationships I have mentioned above are not specifically portrayed as incestuous, I think such an interpretation is sanctioned by the narrative *Agatha*, which portrays sexual desire between brother and sister, a desire which condemns them to be separated from one another, since it is forbidden. Furthermore, as I have suggested above, it is possible, although not necessary to the novel, nor particularly encouraged, to construct Suzanne's love for Joseph in *Un barrage contre le Pacifique* as partly sexual. One could also speculate about the link between the relations Duras describes between herself and her older brother and other portrayals of death and desire in her work, although I do not think this is really relevant to a discussion of the possible effects of her work on the reader.

The second thematic strand I would identify in relation to the lost object is that of the man's desire for another woman. Elements of this theme appear in many of the novels. In *La Vie tranquille*, Luce Barragues is the rival to whom the brother succumbs and whom the lover rejects, and in *Un barrage contre le Pacifique*, a sister is again witness to her beloved brother's overwhelming desire for another woman, notably in the section in which Joseph relates his meeting with Lina. I would link these two instances to those portrayals in other texts of women figures who find themselves losing the love of a man to another woman: *Dix heures et demie du soir en été*, *L'Après-midi de Monsieur Andesmas*, *Le Ravissement de Lol V. Stein* and *L'Amante anglaise*.

Obviously, these scenarios involving separation from the lost object lend themselves to all sorts of psychoanalytic explanations, but I do not intend to explore those here. What I do want to stress is that in Duras's work after *La Vie tranquille*, the sexual desire of the central woman figures is always presented as either directed towards

27 *Les Petits Chevaux de Tarquinia*, p 54.

a lost or forbidden male object, or as a masochistic desire for annihilation, or, as in the case of Lol V. Stein, both. Otherwise, the central woman figure is portrayed as passive and largely desireless as far as objects external to her own person are concerned. She is either shown in the narcissistic manner of Sara or Suzanne, or in the fashion of the 'ravaged' Alissa, or 'the woman' of *L'Amour*.

Given the way Duras portrays women's sexual desires, I think it is possible to read the relatively desireless attitude of Suzanne and Sara as regards their sexual adventures as an effect of the incest taboo, which prohibits the expression, or even the admission, of an incestuous desire present as an undercurrent in *Un barrage contre le Pacifique*, and which I suggest could be read into the reference to the dead brother in *Les Petits Chevaux de Tarquinia*. Perhaps the sexual desire of these women cannot be directly articulated in the text because it is prohibited; perhaps this is why they seem somewhat listless and sexually passive.

This interpretation could also be applied to Duras's portrayal of the adolescent in *L'Amant*, for whom sexual desire appears initially as a lack of dislike: 'She has no clearly defined feelings, no hate, no repugnance either, so doubtless there is already desire there'[28] In this text, relations between the girl and her brothers are portrayed as intense, but not incestuous. They are split between love for the 'good' but powerless 'little brother', reminiscent of Nicolas of *La Vie tranquille*, and on whom, says Duras, is based Joseph of *Un barrage contre le Pacifique*, and the 'bad', all-powerful older brother, who bears a resemblance to Jacques of *Des journées entières dans les arbres*. However, whereas Duras clearly states her feelings for the little brother, the older brother is portrayed with more mystery and a definite 'blank'. She describes him as 'the night murderer of children',[29] and later in the context of the memory of her older brother, she says, 'Around the memory, the livid clarity of the night of the hunter. It makes a strident sound of alarm, a child's cry.'[30] But whether or not the brother actually murdered a child at night, we are not told. And then there is a certain ambiguity in the portrayal of the murderous brother; he holds a fascination:

> I never dance with my older brother, I have never danced with him. Always prevented by the disturbing apprehension of a danger, that of the evil attraction that he exerts over all of us, that of the closeness of our bodies.
>
> We look strikingly alike, particularly our faces.

28 *L'Amant*, p 47.
29 ibid, p 12.
30 ibid, p 67.

...I tell (the Chinese man) about the violence of my older brother, cold, insulting, it accompanies everything that happens to us, everything that comes to us. His first movement is to kill, to obliterate life, to dispose of life, to despise, to hunt, to cause suffering. I tell him not to be afraid. That he himself risks nothing. Because the only person the older brother is afraid of, before whom, curiously, he becomes nervous, is me.[31]

Later, when describing her relation with the Chinese man, she says: 'The shadow of another man must also have passed through the room, that of a young murderer, but I didn't yet realise that, nothing of that had yet been shown to me.' The little brother is clearly there though: she goes on:

The shadow of a young hunter must also have passed through the room, but with that one, yes, I knew, sometimes he was present in orgasm and I told him, the lover from Cholon, I told him of his body and of his penis to, of his ineffable softness, of his courage in the forest and on the rivers with black panthers at their mouths.[32]

I do not think it is too far-fetched to see the other form of passivity of Duras's women figures, that is the 'pure love' of Alissa or the woman in *L'Amour*, as an expression of the madness that results from 'capital destruction', from transgression of the Law, one means to which is the breaking of the incest taboo. Alissa has not actually broken this taboo, as far as we know and the origins of her madness are not known. But Max Thor does say of her to Stein, 'My wife is very young. She could be my daughter.[33] If the Law is transgressed, then everything is permitted but the order of things collapses. In Duras's work, 'destruction' seems to lead to the madness of the woman figure, who becomes, now that her role as object of controlled exchange has become obsolete, available 'to whoever wants her'.

The possible positions in relation to sexual desire open to most of Duras's women figures would appear to be fourfold: repression of all active desires, resulting in narcissistic passivity; nostalgia for and/or attempts to restage a lost relation which is irretrievable; masochism; madness. In the second instance, the woman figure may articulate her desire, but always in the past tense, or it is produced as a 'blank', to be inferred by the reader or another (male) figure in the text. Otherwise the text makes no place for it at all, and it is thus

---

31 ibid, p 68.
32 ibid, p 122.
33 *Détruire, dit-elle*, p 19.

constructed as irrelevant, even though the events described concern sexual relationships of varying sorts in which the woman figure is always the object of men's desire.

The first three of these options show similarities with Freud's account of the three possibilities for the psychic development of the little girl after she has realised 'the fact of her castration': suppression of sexuality, the 'masculinity complex', where the little girl refuses to abandon her narcissistic desire to be herself the possessor of a penis, and 'normal femininity'.[34] They do not correspond entirely. Both narcissism and masochism have their place in Freud's account of 'normal femininity, but they certainly do not conflict.

So in this respect, Duras's portrayal of women is consonant with the established accounts of women's sexuality offered by (phallocentric) psychoanalytic theory. Certainly, it does not subvert either this theory, or the Law which it describes.

MOTHERHOOD

The theme of relations between mothers and their children runs through much of Duras's work. It is treated quite differently from that of sexual desire, and treatment also differs depending on the sex of the child.

However, whatever the sex of the child, the importance of the relationship of the mother to her children seems to be an index of the mother's sanity. Children provide a focus around which the mother can identify herself as a subject of desire and a centre of meaning. It is when Anne Desbaresdes finally goes to the café without her son that she can succumb to her desire for death, even if Chauvin does not actually kill her, whilst Lol V. Stein, who is in a way mad, does not seem at all interested in her hardly-mentioned children. The beggar-woman finally goes mad after giving away her daughter and thus having nobody to talk to, nobody in relation to whom her desire can form, so that it no longer exists other than in the word 'Battambang'. After the birth of her daughter, the beggar-woman has many other children before she becomes sterile, but she always abandons them almost without realising, as does the mad woman of *L'Amour*, whose madness also seems to manifest itself in, amongst other things, a great quantity of unnoticed babies: '"Her children are in there, that thing, she had them, she gives them away", he adds, "the town is full of them, the earth."'[35]

34 Freud, 'The Psychology of Women', p 162.
35 *L'Amour*, p 52.

When the mothers are not mad, the relations of love and desire between them and their children do not undergo the same textual repression or suppression as that of women's sexual desire. In *Les Petits Chevaux de Tarquinia* and *Moderato cantabile*, the two different relations of desire, the sexual desire between the central woman figure and a man and the desire of the woman figure in relation to her child, are contrasted with each other in a striking manner. In the former novel, Sara's clearly-stated and all-pervasive love for her child is constantly stressed, both in her actions, as for example when the first thing she does on returning to the house with 'the man' is to check on the sleeping child, and in words, as, describing her love for her child and the effect of this love on her, she says, 'since he was born I've been living in madness'.[36] In contrast, her desire in relation to 'the man' is, as I have already discussed, scarcely perceptible in the text. Indeed, Sara's would-be lover is apparently somewhat disconcerted by her love for her child. He says, 'It's even sometimes a bit. . . a bit difficult to bear',[37] implying perhaps that Sara's feelings for her child exclude him (and everyone else), and make her less available to, or aware of, him.

In *Moderato cantabile*, the contrast between the two aspects of Anne Desbaresdes's desire is even more obvious, both in the way each manifests itself in the text, and in their apparent mutual exclusivity. Anne's sexual desire is only present in the 'blanks' of the text, but she articulates her love for her child without hesitation: 'If only you knew how much happiness one wants for them, as if it were possible. Perhaps sometimes it would be better if they were taken away from us. I can't seem to be reasonable about this child.' The reader is not asked to infer either the presence or the nature of Anne's feelings in relation to the child. Furthermore, the passages portraying the piano lessons with Mlle Giraud, where Anne is seen solely in relation to her child, are written without 'blanks' and in a style of psychological realism, providing interpretations of the thoughts of both the child and the woman, and expressing Anne's love as much as Mlle Giraud's exasperation:

> The scale came to an end. The child, perfectly disinterested in the present moment, raised himself slightly from his stool and attempted the impossible, to glimpse what was happening down below, on the quayside.
> 'I'll explain to him that he must,' said the mother, falsely repentant.
> Mademoiselle Giraud took on a bombastic, saddened air.

36 *Les Petits Chevaux de Tarquinia*, p 28.
37 ibid.

'You don't have to explain anything to him. He doesn't have the choice whether or not to learn the piano, Madame Desbaresdes, it's what is called education.'[38]

As in *Les Petits Chevaux de Tarquinia*, an effect of mutual exclusivity is set up between the two areas in which Anne Desbaresdes' desires are shown; firstly in the way that she appears to talk about her child to Chauvin so as to avoid hearing what the latter wishes to say to her, as in the passage of dialogue that I have analysed above, and secondly in the way that, as her interest in what Chauvin tells her grows, she becomes increasingly distracted in relation to her child and it is not until she goes to the café without the little boy that the 'consummation' of her relationship with Chauvin occurs.

Like 'the man' in *Les Petits Chevaux de Tarquinia*, Chauvin seems disturbed by the relationship of mother and child. For example, towards the end of the penultimate meeting in the café: 'The child came in, snuggled against his mother for a moment. He was still humming the Diabelli sonatina. She stroked his hair very close to her face, blinded. The man avoided seeing them. Then the child went off.[39] In the portrayals of Sara and Anne Desbaresdes both women's lives and active desires appear to be organised entirely in relation to their children, anything else being buried in the inaccessible depths of their psyches. In both cases their love for their children is seen as excessive and disturbing to the smooth running of things: in Sara's case, it is a contributing factor to her staying in every night whilst the maid goes out with her boyfriend, a state of affairs the other figures in the novel disapprove of; in the case of Anne Desbaresdes it is the motivation both for her wish that the child should learn the piano, and for her complicity with him in his refusal to cooperate with his teacher. At the same time, in both these novels, the love of their children seems to be the foundation for stability in the women's lives, as opposed to the disturbing and exciting, but potentially destructive effects of sexual desire. For both of them, the only positive and constructive area in which their desires are in evidence seems to be the care and happiness of the child. In relation to their children, Sara and Anne Desbaresdes seem to come alive as subjects of desire, whilst otherwise, as objects of men's desire, they are either indifferent and passive, or reduced to silent disarray.

Sara and Anne Desbaresdes are both mothers of sons. In both cases, the son plays a crucial role as focus of the mother's desire, and his presence appears as a major factor in the conflict she faces when confronted by the sexual desire for her of a man who is not the

38 *Moderato cantabile*, p 72.
39 ibid, p 86.

father of the child. In this sense, the son comes to represent the incarnation of the Law of the Father, in a way which the father himself does not do; neither woman seems particularly interested in her husband, certainly not in comparison with her son.

Neither Sara nor Anne Desbaresdes in fact transgresses this Law in any permanent way; Sara renounces her affair with 'the man' and Anne Desbaresdes's adventure ends when 'It's done'.[40] Everything apparently returns to the order of the family unit. But in the portrayal of Maria in *Dix heures et demie du soir en été*, and Anne-Marie Stretter's two incarnations, things turn out otherwise for these mothers of daughters. Maria has one daughter, Judith, whilst Anne-Marie Stretter has one in *Le Ravissement de Lol V. Stein* and two in *Le Vice-consul*. None of these daughters are the objects of their mother's desires in the way that the sons of Sara and Anne Desbaresdes are. Maria seems more interested in Claire, her rival, than in Judith, as is indicated by the following passage, in free indirect speech from Maria's point of view:

> She, in her turn, Claire, smiles at Judith. At Judith's tiny little form, lop-sided, enveloped in her brown blanket. Her hair is still wet from the rain on the balcony. In the yellow light of the paraffin lamp I see your eyes, he was saying to her, your eyes. The youth of her breasts shows precisely under her white jumper. The blue gaze is hagard, paralysed by insatisfaction, by the very fulfillment of insatisfaction. The gaze has turned away from Judith and back towards Pierre.[41]

The entire passage, after the second sentence, clearly refers to Claire. The narration does not bother to make clear the fact that 'her hair' is Claire's and not that of the last person mentioned, Judith. The reader/narratee is invited to infer that Judith's appearance in the text has not been enough to deflect Maria's attention from her main subject of interest, Claire. The impression s/he has already gained of the relative importance of Claire and Judith for Maria is strengthened. Judith, small and huddled in her blanket, does not hold her mother's interest for more than an instant. The novel shows Maria as caring for her child, she makes affectionate gestures towards her and looks after her, but the almost excessive love of Anne Desbaresdes or Sara is absent. Later, Maria reveals a mixture of feelings in relation to Judith:

> 'Judith', says Maria.
> She holds her at arm's length and looks at her. She's a little girl

40   ibid, p 114.
41   *Dix heures et demie du soir en été*, p 53.

who slept well last night. Her eyes are blue. The shadow of fear has disappeared from under her eyes. Maria pushes her right away, distances her. He must be in the wheatfield. He is asleep. The shadow cast by the stalks is slight and he has begun to get hot. Whom would one be saving, definitively speaking, if one saved Rodrigo Paestra?

'She ate masses at breakfast this morning', says Claire. 'One cool night and she eats masses.'

Judith has come back towards Maria. Maria holds her again, looks at her again, then lets her go again, almost shoving her. Judith is used to it. She lets herself be looked at, then shoved, by her mother as much as the latter wants, then she goes off round the dining room and sings.[42]

The similarly long-suffering son of Anne Desbaresdes does not have to put up with such ambivalence:

'Lift your head up', said Anne Desbaresdes. 'Look at me.'

The child obeyed, used to her ways.

'Sometimes I really think I've invented you, that it's not real, you see.'

The child lifted his head and, facing her, yawned. The inside of his mouth filled with the last gleams of the sunset. Anne Desbaresdes' astonishment, when she looked at the child, had remained the same since the first day. But that evening no doubt she felt as if her astonishment was redoubled.[43]

None of this constant astonishment is discernible in Maria's attitude towards Judith, nor does the narration describe the latter in ways comparable to that of filling her mouth with sunset. Judith is given none of the importance accorded to the child in *Moderato cantabile*.

Anne-Marie Stretter's daughters are given an even lesser role to play. In neither *Le Ravissement de Lol V. Stein*, nor *Le Vice-consul*, are they given more than cursory mentions, and they appear to have absolutely no effect on their mother's feelings or actions. Benign indifference is about the most a reader could glean of Anne-Marie Stretter's feelings in relation to her daughter(s), should s/he wish to consider them, but this is not encouraged by the texts in which she appears.

Both Maria and Anne-Marie Stretter are portrayed in irregular situations concerning their position within the family and in relation to the Law: Maria decides to end her relationship with Pierre, which

42 ibid, pp 121–2.
43 *Moderato cantabile*, p 35.

leaves her a free subject, unattached to any man; Anne-Marie Stretter, although remaining married to the ambassador (who never appears in any of the texts), has an apparently limitless capacity for taking lovers. In neither case does the daughter appear to be of any consequence as a factor in deciding the mother's course of action or position. The daughters are presented as the mother's appendages, whose presence do not affect events.

Elizabeth Alione, *Détruire, dit-elle*, is also the mother of a daughter, Anita, but unlike the other two, she does return to the fold. Nevertheless, it is her husband, rather than her daughter, who seems to influence her decision. Like Maria, Elizabeth Alione seems rather ambivalent in her attitude towards her daughter, who, in any case, has a relatively small and insignificant part to play in *Détruire, dit-elle*. Her mother says that 'she is bad-tempered...she's going through an awful phase, but it's just her age, she'll grow out of it'[44], although being bad-tempered, insofar as it means not conforming to accepted patterns of behaviour, is not necessarily a bad thing in *Détruire, dit-elle*, where conventional values attached to human behaviour do not necessarily apply. Later Elizabeth says of Anita: 'She is a very affectionate little girl, underneath, who I expect will suffer. But it's hard to judge when it's your own child.'[45] No sign of the 'madness' of Sara or of Anne Desbaresdes here. Elizabeth, like Maria, describes her child with more distance than Duras's mothers of sons: the French uses the construction *C'est une petite fille qui...*(She's a little girl who...) in the descriptions of both. And though Elizabeth Alione certainly shows affection for her daughter, it is not overpowering love.

There is another, more detailed, exploration of a relationship between mother and daughter in the story of the beggar-woman told by Peter Morgan in *Le Vice-consul*. This has far more importance in the novel than the mother-daughter relationships I have discussed above. The beggar-woman, or as she is at that point, the girl (*la jeune fille*), is cast out from her parents' house because she is pregnant. The narrative flows without clear separation from third person narration, to free indirect speech, to phrases in the first person, apparently uttered by the beggar-woman herself (via Peter Morgan). The effect thus produced is one of a narrative which drops in and out of the beggar-woman's consciousness, until, having successfully given away her child, she leaves Vinh Long and goes mad, after which her story is narrated entirely in the third person. Other figures, the mother, the child, or the white woman, for example, are all seen through her eyes, and her feelings, in relation to both her

44 *Détruire, dit-elle*, pp 80–1.
45 ibid, p 82.

mother and her own daughter, are articulated by the narrative. Thus the reader is given a daughter's eye view of her mother and a mother's eye view of her daughter, although they are both constructed as being the product of Peter Morgan's imagination.

In relation to her mother, the beggar-woman is shown as having ambivalent, but very intense feelings. Indeed, all the emotion she evinces is in relation to her mother, although the latter has sent her off with nothing but a threat: 'If you come back...I'll put poison in your rice to kill you.'[46] The daughter's main problem at the outset is, 'how not to go back?'[47] She feels too young to be separated and, despite her enforced physical separation, through free indirect speech the text shows her imagined conversations with her mother:

> Perhaps one day I'll tell you about the explosions from the quarries and the crows, for I'll see you again, I'm young enough to see you again, and why not, since we're both alive, you and I? Who else would I tell, who else would listen to me and be interested that I now care more for absent food than for you?[48]

When her child is about to be born, it is again of her mother that the beggar-woman thinks, to her mother that she wishes to give her child:

> She goes off, she goes off to look for a place to do it in, a hole, for someone who will take it when it comes and separate it completely, she looks for her tired mother who drove her out. On absolutely no grounds can you come back. She did not know, that woman, she did not know everything, a thousand miles of mountains, this morning, would not stop me from reaching you, you innocent, in your stupefaction you will forget to kill me, wretched woman, cause of everything, I will hold out the child to you and you will take it, I will throw it towards you and myself will run away forever. With the half-light of dusk some things must finish and others begin. It is her mother, her mother then, who will bring about this birth.[49]

The words 'a thousand miles of mountains...wouldn't stop me from reaching you' here is reminiscent of the way in which Luce Barragues' sexual desire for Tiène is expressed in *La Vie transquille*. The same power and the same determination is there in both cases. All the beggar-woman's desire is constructed as being in relation to her mother except when she is so hungry that she temporarily forgets

46 *Le Vice-consul*, p 10.
47 ibid, p 9.
48 ibid, p 20.
49 ibid, p 25.

her in favour of food. After a hallucination, in which she sees her own mother and siblings in another family, she renounces her plan to return, no longer sure to whom she would be returning: 'Why was it precisely her mother that she saw? Precisely her brothers and sisters? What was the difference now between these and those?'[50] 'Her way, she is sure, is the definitive abandonment of her mother',[51] but she does not forget her mother. After her own daughter has been born and successfully given to the white woman, she thinks again of her mother, who remains the only addressee of her thoughts, now that the baby is gone; Her mother is the beggar-woman's only guarantor of her own sanity as a separate, thinking subject: 'To see that woman, the most wicked woman she has ever known, without that what is there to become? Who?'[52] The beggar-woman still sees her mother as all-powerful, 'the origin, the cause of everything bad, her crooked destiny, her pure love'.[53] However, return is now impossible, 'she will never find the path again', and undesirable, 'she no longer wants to find it again'.[54] The separation is complete. Yet, directionless now, the beggar-woman sinks into madness, without any evidence of active desires of any sort on her part beyond that invested in the word 'Battambang': 'She will say nothing other than this word in which she is locked away, her shut up house'.[55] She has not found a substitute, or substitutes, for her mother, objects in relation to which she can be a subject of desire and build an identity, so the separation reduces her to imbecility.

Like other women figures in Duras's work, but with a different object' the beggar-women's desire in relation to her mother is masochistic. 'Her mother, thin, angry', who, 'all at once, blasts her memory',[56] appears in her dream, 'with a cudgel in her hand'.[57] After the beggar-woman has given away her child, her fantasy of return is indicated thus: 'to go back to her mother, to go back to play, to go back to the North to say hello and laugh with the others, to be beaten by her and to die under the blows.[58] The only revenge she imagines for her mother's treatment of her is to forget her, even temporarily: 'She will go back to tell her, tell this ignorant woman who drove her out: I've forgotten you.'[59] Any other form of remonstrance is completely out of

50   ibid, p 28.
51   ibid.
52   ibid, p 67.
53   ibid.
54   ibid, p 65.
55   ibid, p 62.
56   ibid, p 64.
57   ibid, p 10.
58   ibid, p 67.
59   ibid, pp 20–1.

the question. The mother is all-powerful origin, not only of 'every-thing bad', but of love as well. It is the mother who 'calls to distribute hot rice'[60] to the children who have run off after she has beaten them, and when the beggar-woman receives 'a rice cake placed before her', in the market place where she thinks she has seen her mother, the gift reinforces her belief in her mother's presence 'What hand could have given it to her, if not her mother's?'[61]

In contrast to her mother, the beggar-woman's daughter appar-ently occupies a negligible place in her affections. Before the birth, the ungendered baby is referred to as 'the rat',[62] which devours every-thing its mother eats and whose hunger starves her. Once the child is born and proves to be female, she becomes 'the siamese twin',[63] who must be separated from her mother because she cannot be fed. The narrative does not dwell on the period of a year or so in between the child's birth and the episode in which she is given to 'the white lady'. The effect is to create an impression of a kind of benign indifference on the part of the beggar-woman towards her baby, which changes to concern when it becomes apparent that the child will die, but which has nothing of the intensity of feeling that the beggar-woman shows towards her own mother, or that which Anne-Desbaresdes or Sara dis-play in relation to their sons. The beggar-woman is apparently relieved to be able to give away her daughter to someone who will look after her, but she shows no signs of distress at having to leave the child. Like her own mother, although with far less cruelty, she has done what must be done and rid herself of a daughter who can only be an encum-brance. In the beggar-woman's story, as in other work by Duras, the narrative is little concerned with the mother's feelings of love, or of anything else, in regard to her daughter, although in other areas, great stress is laid on the mother's emotions in relation to another figure.

Un barrage contre le Pacifique portrays the relations of a mother to both a son and daughter, crystallising in one novel the contrast perceptible between the two when different works by Duras are compared. The relations between members of the family are shown primarily through the daughter's eyes using free indirect speech. What is thus produced is a portrayal of Suzanne as witness to the passion of Joseph and their mother for each other. Between Suzanne and her mother there is a certain sympathy and understanding: '[their mother] thought she knew Suzanne better than Joseph',[64] but Suzanne is the butt of her beatings, the addressee of her rantings

60 ibid, p 65.
61 ibid, p 27.
62 ibid, p 19.
63 ibid, p 51.
64 *Un barrage contre le Pacifique*, p 98.

and the child who must be married off, if necessary to M. Jo and even, when marriage to M. Jo has proved impossible, to 'young Agosti'. Joseph, on the other hand, the more mysterious, of the two, has a certain authority over their mother. He stops her from beating Suzanne – eventually – and he is largely responsible for alienating M. Jo, whom their mother, in spite of her scruples, does not wish to discourage. When Joseph leaves for the first time, their mother is distraught: 'This absence drove her to despair and made her take to her bed and sleep all day as she had done after the collapse of the dykes.'[65] When he finally leaves with Lina, forever as the mother and daughter think, she has an attack of her illness, takes to her bed and finally dies. The departure of her son, although inevitable, is a terrible blow to her, one which she has long been trying to ward off. She says: 'There was nothing for him to do here anymore. No matter how I searched, nothing.'[66]

After Joseph's departure, although Suzanne is still with her, their mother has nothing to live for and tells her daughter that it would have been better if Joseph had killed her straight out: 'He should have filled me full of buckshot before he went, since he's so good at it...'[67] On Joseph's side, although he leaves with Lina knowing it will make his mother suffer, 'Nevertheless, he loved her. He even thought, he said, that he would never love another woman as much as he loved her. That no woman would ever make him forget her.'[68]

Suzanne is the one to whom each recounts their feelings about the other. Her own feelings about her mother are not recounted, other than in the scene which follows the mother's death, when Suzanne is distraught.:

> She died soon after Agosti's return. Suzanne lay pressed against her and for hours she also wanted to die. She wanted it desperately and neither Agosti, nor the still so recent memory of the pleasure she had had with him could stop her from returning one last time to the unruly, tragic intemperance of childhood.[69]

Even in the account of their grief, however, the description of Joseph's reaction – as witnessed by Suzanne – seems more violent and intense:

> He was slumped on the bed, on their mother's body. She had not once seen him cry since they were very small. From time to time he

65 ibid, p 181.
66 ibid, p 304.
67 ibid, p 305.
68 ibid, p 284.
69 ibid, p 359.

raised his head and looked at their mother with terrifying tender-
ness. He called to her. He kissed her. But the closed eyes were filled
with a violet shadow, deep as water, the closed mouth was closed
on a vertiginous silence.[70]

Joseph's distress is portrayed as more active than Suzanne's.
Rather than simply wishing to die, he tries to elicit a response from
his mother, to reactivate their relationship. It is the end of that
relationship that Suzanne witnesses. In describing her reaction, the
narrative places her in relation to a lover, Agosti, and shows how
grief at her mother's death obliterates him from her mind as she
temporarily reverts from her separated self to the 'unruly, tragic
intemperance of childhood'. In the account of Joseph's reaction,
however, there is no mention of a relationship other than that with
his mother. Physical separation, his desire for Lina, nothing has
affected the primordial attachment of mother and son, nor does any
other figure intrude into the passage to suggest that anyone else
could be as important to him, as Agosti appears in the passage
concerning Suzanne.

Similar to the portrayal of family relations in *Un barrage contre le
Pacifique* is that of *Des journées entières dans les arbres*. Again, in this
latter text, a woman figure in the position of a daughter witnesses
the end of the relationship between mother and son, or at least the
impossibility of their being in the same place. Like Suzanne in *Un
barrage contre le Pacifique*, Marcelle perceives the intensity of the
feelings of each for the other, a relationship from which she is excluded and further distanced than was Suzanne by virtue of the fact
that she is not the mother's daughter. The relationship between the
mother and Jacques is complicated by the fact that Jacques is a
grown man, so that things that his mother loved in him when he was
a child, such as his refusal to go to school, his spending 'whole days
in the trees', have turned him into a gambler with a job in a night-
club, who mistreats his girlfriend. It is his inability to conform that
the mother loves – her other children, who all have 'good' jobs and
have done well for themselves do not interest her – but at the same
time, she regrets his waywardness. Jacques is aware of her regret
and finds it unbearable: '"I still had that witness to my cowardly
life," he thought, "she must die, she must."'[71] However, the night
before his mother's departure, he still behaves like a child:

He threw away his cigarette and collapsed on to the bed at his
mother's feet, his arms over his head.

70　ibid.
71　*Des journées entières dans les arbres*, p 68.

'I can't work. I...don't want to work.'
His mother was still smiling.
'My little boy'.[72]

Like *Un barrage contre le Pacifique*, *Des journées entières dans les arbres* tells the story of a son's separation from his mother and, here again, it is only the mother's death that can bring about that separation. The mother does not want to let go of her son, even now he is a grown man. Marcelle on the other hand, motherless, is looking for a replacement for the one she never had: she explains, 'I like them all, you see [...] The bad ones as much as the good ones, it's a vice, you know. Even this one, for example, I can't imagine that one day I could get fed up with her'.[73] Marcelle wants to adopt the mother, whilst Jacques wants to separate himself from her. Neither are successful.

Finally, with the publication of *L'Amant*, the portrayal of family relations in *Un barrage contre le Pacifique* and *Des journées entières dans les arbres* are given ostensibly autobiographical references. Here, Duras portrays the ambiguous love between mother and daughter. In a manner reminiscent of the beggar-woman, she calls her mother, 'that trash, my mother, my love'.[74] She portrays her mother as more interested in her sons than her daughter: 'The head-master says to her, "your daughter, Madame, is top in French". My mother says nothing, nothing, she's not pleased because it's not her sons who are top in French'.[75] Here too, the mother has a particularly intense and fraught relationship with the older brother, who remains, in spite of his faults, her favourite. 'She asked that this one should be buried with her. I can't remember now in which place, in which cemetery, I know it's in the Loire. They are both together in the grave. Just the two of them. It's as it should be. It is an image of intolerable splendour.'[76]

The overall pattern that emerges in Duras's portrayal of mother-hood shows mothers as having intense and exclusive relationships with their sons and comparatively lacking interest in their daughters. In early texts portraying the mothers of older sons, this relationship is presented as a problem for both mother and son insofar as the son desires his separation from the mother, whilst remaining profoundly attached to her. The separation is a painful process. In later novels, where the son is a small child, the emphasis is the mother's love in all

72   ibid, p 95.
73   ibid, p 25.
74   *L'Amant*, p 31.
75   ibid.
76   ibid, p 164.

its incredulity and intensity. In relation to daughters, such incredulity and intensity are absent, being replaced by concern, affection and sometimes feelings of hostility. Otherwise, as in those novels in which Anne-Marie Stretter appears, the narrative makes little of the relationship between mother and daughter beyond stating the daughter's existence. The only relation between mother and daughter with the intensity of feeling Duras portrays in mother-son relations is that of the beggar-woman to her mother. Here however, the intensity is mainly on the daughter's side, and the mother's feelings are not expressed, beyond her anger and her desire to send the pregnant daughter away.

Such differences in the portrayal of relationships between mothers and their children of either sex correspond in a very close way to Freud's description of such relations. According to Freud, the little girl's narcissism is dealt a severe blow by the discovery that there are such things as penises and that she does not have one. This leads, he says, to penis-envy and the three possibilities: loss of interest in sex; disavowal of the new knowledge; 'normal femininity'. However, the desire for the penis does not, says Freud, go away, even for the little girl embarked upon the latter course. For she now takes her father as love-object and 'the wish with which the little girl turns to her father is, no doubt, ultimately the wish for the penis, which her mother has refused her and which she now expects from her father. This wish, Freud says in his paper on 'Transformations of Instinct', 'becomes the wish for a man, and thus puts up with the man as an appendage to the penis'. However, returning to the paper on 'The psychology of women', Freud continues: 'The feminine situation is, however, only established when the wish for a penis is replaced by the wish for a child – the child taking the place of the penis in accordance with the old symbolic equation.'[78] But the sex of the child is, he says, all important: 'The only thing that brings a mother undiluted satisfaction is her relation to a son; it is quite the most complete relationship between human beings, and the one that is most free from ambivalence.'[79]

It is such unambivalent feelings of love specifically for the son that Duras portrays in her novels, in particular in those novels where the woman is the mother of a young son. I have suggested that the 'femininity' that Marini hears speaking through Duras's work is the voice which arises from the 'feminine' position, equated by Freud

---

77 Freud, 'On transformations of instinct as exemplified in anal erotism', in *Standard Edition*, Vol XVII, p 129.
78 Freud, 'The Psychology of Women', pp 164–5.
79 ibid, p 171.

with the ascendancy of the passive rather than the active sexual
drives and an acceptance of castration, by Lacan with being the
phallus. If this is so, then unambivalent love for the son coupled with
– in the cases of Sara or Anne Desbaresdes – sexual passivity or even
masochism in relation to men is just what one would expect it to
articulate. Duras seems once more to be faithfully reproducing the
structures defined by psychoanalytic orthodoxy here. Certainly, in
her work following *La Vie tranquille*, the only area in which the
woman figures' desire manifests itself clearly is in relation to their
sons. In this context it is also interesting to return to Grunberger's
view that the lack of narcissistic satisfaction that little girls receive
from their mothers leads them to narcissistic overcompensation in
adult life. For Duras's women figures certainly seem to suffer from
a lack of maternal appreciation in their youth, and to be highly
narcissistic adults.

THE MISSING FATHER

In terms of the lack of object-love for men and the passivity of their
sexual aims, coupled with intense love for sons and ambivalence
towards, or lack of interest in relation to, daughters, Duras's women
figures fit easily into the Freudian description of 'normal femininity'.
However, there is one aspect of the Freudian account which appears
to be missing, and that is the girl's love for her father. Fathers as
such figure but little in Duras's work, as indeed her own father, dead
in her infancy, hardly appears in her portrayal of her life in *L'Amant*.
Suzanne, Marcelle and the beggar-woman have all reached an age
by which, if they were really good Freudians, they would have
rejected their mothers and turned their desire towards their fathers,
or men. But this does not seem to have occurred. Marcelle has
neither father nor mother, but it is only the latter that she misses.
She says she loves Jacques ('alas!'[80]), but her desire for a mother
does not seem to have diminished. The beggar-woman has a father,
but thinks of him only once. Suzanne's father is dead and she never
thinks of him. If one uses a Lacanian framework, and sees the
paradigmatic transferral of the girl's desire from mother to father as
arising out of her perception of the mother's desire as being for the
phallus-bearing father, then Joseph, as object of the mother's desire
in *Un barrage contre le Pacifique*, could be seen as having assumed
the position of the father for Suzanne. And certainly, if Suzanne's
sexual desire has an object, it is her brother. However, the beggar-

80 *Des journées entières dans les arbres*, p 65.

woman, and to a lesser extent, Marcelle, seem to have retained a pre-oedipal attitude towards the mother.

Marini, in her extensive analysis of the story of the beggar-woman, sees it as a myth recounting the beggar-woman's rejection of the patriarchal mould into which her mother wants to place her, where women are objects of exchange between men, always culturally determined as the Other of men and unable to differentiate themselves as subjects in relation to each other. According to Marini, by becoming pregnant without being married, the beggar-woman has allowed her desire free rein, that is to say, it is not sanctioned by being directed towards the man whose property she is, i.e., a husband. She therefore cannot define herself in relation to her mother, says Marini, because the only possible positions available to her in a patriarchal culture are that of unseparated daughter, or that of identification with her mother by becoming a mother herself and the property of a husband, as opposed to the property of a father. The beggar-woman is in neither of these positions and so, says Marini, she has no way of separating herself from her mother and establishing herself as a woman who is different from her mother, defined in relation to another woman and not to a man. For the beggar-woman, says Marini, there is no new order: 'The myth remains powerful of the woman who is wretched and unhappy when she does not have the support of masculine speech, when she walks out alone, loses her way in the country of the feminine instead of passing from father to husband'.[81]

I think Marini has a point here. However, in the beggar-woman's daughter she sees new hope. The infant is separated from her mother, but given, not to a man, but to another woman. No men are involved in the passing of the child from one woman to the other and thus, according to Marini, a possibility is created for the girl to identify herself in relation to other women rather than men.

However, I feel it must be noted here that not only does the beggar-woman herself become mad and sterile, but her daughter is almost certain to die, which does not seem to me to augur well for the new order of the feminine in Duras's work. Nor should it be forgotten that the entire story is presented in the text as the imaginings of a man, Peter Morgan, although he is a most unobtrusive narrator. I find Marini's analysis of 'the myth of the beggar-woman' interesting in its exploration of the relations of desire between women, but it seems to me to fall into a trap set – quite unwittingly no doubt – by Duras's writing, which is that of equating an identification in the feminine position, as the Other of men, or as the phallus, with an essence.

81 Marini, op cit, p 200.

In almost all her work after *La Vie tranquille*, Duras portrays women as always the objects of men's looks, men's investigations and men's desire, and the reader is offered identification with a man or men in the masculine subject position from which to investigate the woman object. The narratee is constructed in a masculine position, since the woman figure investigated from this position is always constructed as Other. I am using 'masculine' here both in the sense of an identification in the position of desiring subject, having rather than being the phallus, and in the sense of 'of men', since women occupy such a position rarely, if at all, in Duras's work. I would suggest that it is this all-pervading masculine overview that takes the structural place of the 'missing father' in Duras's work, providing the context in which the desire of the women figures manifests itself. This masculine overview is not constructed as problematic in itself but it facilitates the construction of the desires of the women figures as problematic, which is also what happens in general in our culture. The thorny old question of 'what do women want?' again.

But this is not the only way of constructing women figures, as Duras herself proves in *La Vie tranquille*. The voice with which 'the feminine' speaks is not the voice of women; although it may indeed be the voice of Woman, the Other of Man the subject. No woman can completely identify with Woman in either (or both) of her two incarnations as object of men's desire and other. The different permutations of possible identifications for any human subject are infinite. Duras has, however, concentrated her (phallic) desire to create on reproducing and recharging images of Woman. Perhaps this is the result of a desire to reconcil the two polarities of masculine and feminine within her own psyche. However, I do not wish to speculate at length on Duras's motivations for her work, which are, I think, her own affair. What interests me here is the possible significance that this restaging of the meeting of two polarities might have; what does it do for the reader and how does it fit into the wider dynamics of the shifting meanings attached to the two sexes and relations between them?

CHAPTER 8
Order, Chaos and Subversive Details

Although Duras's novels are works of fiction, in both the structural place they give to women, and the way in which they portray 'what women want', they resemble the writings of theorists using the Lacanian theoretical framework to look at women's sexuality such as, in addition to Lacan himself, Montrelay, Marini, Irigaray, Lemoine-Luccioni, and many more. In the work of these writers, most of whom are women, women's desire, sexuality and relation to language are seen as difficult or impossible to define. Apart from Irigaray, the Lacanian women say little about their own way of writing, but one assumes they have adopted what is in their own terms the masculine position. Certainly they write about women as being different, as objects of investigation. Marini says that Duras writes from 'a place which is radically other, that of the feminine',[1] but does not gender her own place of departure. Iriagaray writes of the 'other language'[2] which has yet to emerge and which, according to Marini, can now only manifest itself as silence, whilst Lemoine-Luccioni, Montrelay and Lacan all see 'the feminine' as excluded from 'the nature of things which is the nature of words', although both women allow their sisters access to a masculine Symbolic order via secondary psychic formations, and only Lacan is adamant that Woman does not know what she is talking about.

With the exception of Irigaray, all these writers see women in the context of heterosexual relations as objects of the desire of the male subject, or else in relation to their mothers. It is not surprising that their work should be linked with that of Duras, since the underlying assumptions and range of concerns of the latter are similar. Certainly this is true in her writing following and including *Moderato cantabile*,

---

1   Marini, op cit, p 62.
2   Irigaray, *Ce sexe qui n'en est pas un*, p 77.

which is that which is most often discussed in the context of psycho-analysis. In these later novels Duras writes about 'beings of desire and fear'[3] portrayed as figures in the context of familial or (hetero) sexual relations, but other social relations between them are, if mentioned, not explored. Feminist claims for both Duras's writing and that of Lacanian psychoanalysis are that they acknowledge the existence of and explore (where possible) the regions of 'unrepresent-able' femininity, showing up masculinist domination for what it is: the suppression of difference and denial of the Other. The idea is that, whether or not 'femininity', or 'women's desire' is constructed through the workings of 'feminine drives' or as the result of the respective positions of women and men in relation to desire (positions which are at present inevitably fixed according to gender), women's desire has always been denied expression. The way to remedy this situation is then seen as being to demonstrate that such is the case so that women and men will realise a) that the feminine position exists and b) that women's desire as it springs from that position, which is the position of object of desire, has never been recognised. This, runs the argument, is what Duras's writing does:

> The spaces built into the very heart of the language-inheritance through Marguerite Duras's writing practice define the place in which a new signifier can arise. Out of this we can suggest the following hypothesis: the subject – whether it be masculine or feminine – is no longer born simply out of the binary play of a single signifier qualified by plus and minus, the phallus, but out of the space made by the play between two different signifiers.[4]

Venet in her article suggests similarly:

> M Duras's writing could be defined as feminine writing which is disconcerting because it does not conform to logical masculine discourse; ambiguous in that it inevitably has recourse to the masculine language of society to speak the feminine; and creative in that it says something else, beyond literal meaning...[5]

As I have indicated above, whilst I think that the view that women have a specific 'feminine' relation to language grounded in a psychic organisation produced by 'feminine drives' has a rather shaky theoretical basis, I do think it is valid to describe Duras's writing as giving a place to femininity, where this is defined as a position within a relation of (sexual) desire and not as an effect of

3 Blanchot, 'Détruire', p 141.
4 Marini, op cit, pp 47–8.
5 Venet, op cit, p 6.

fixed meanings attached to anatomical makeup. And as I have tried to show, some of the women she portrays in this position are constructed as the subjects of more or less unutterable, but nevertheless present, desires. But having said this, I cannot agree with the feminist argument that has been put forward in relation to Duras's work for it relies on the assumption that representations of woman-as-object-of-desire usually represent the woman as being without desire herself. However, I would argue that, on the contrary, it is basic to the construction of a woman as object of desire that she be seen also as subject of desire. The important factor which either facilitates or precludes her construction into the position of object of desire is the kind of desire of which she is seen as being the subject.

As I have discussed above in relation to fetishism, representations of women as objects of desire do also portray them as subjects of desire as well. Duras herself shows a clear understanding of this in her portrayal of herself as an object of desire in *L'Amant*: 'It wasn't a question of attracting desire. It was present in she who aroused it, or it did not exist.'[6] And the desire of 'she who aroused it' is principally narcissistic, constructing her always as an object for someone else: 'As I want to appear, so I appear. Beautiful too, if that's what people want me to be, or pretty; pretty, for example, for the family, for the family, no more, I can become everything that people want from me. And believe in it . . .'[7]

It is intrinsic to the portrayal of the adolescent in *L'Amant* that she should have this powerful narcissism, which manifests itself in the ability to make herself into an object of desire, principally for 'the man from Cholon'.

In representations of a woman as an object of desire, an element of her own sexual desire, either potential or already present, is always built in. Whether it is solely narcissistic, or produced in relation to other (male) subjects, inviting their desire (as Lemoine-Luccioni suggested), the focus is always on this sexual desire, whilst other areas in which the woman's desire might be produced are either excluded or given lesser importance. Generally speaking, representations of women as objects of desire do not show them immersed in their work or artistic creativity: women who are used to advertise cars are never shown driving them, but rather draped over them, narcissistically inviting the gaze of the spectator. The myth and mystery surrounding Marilyn Monroe constructs her not as the fine actress she clearly was, for whom making a film was work, but simply as a 'sexy' woman – vulnerable too, perhaps to reduce the

6 *L'Amant*, p 28.
7 ibid, p 26.

threat her powerful image might otherwise pose. Representations of women as objects of desire construct them as desiring to be desired – by men. Perhaps 'the enigma of Woman', the mysteriousness of the beautiful object, arises out of this narcissism – a part of the woman's desire is always directed towards herself.

The other area in which a woman's desire may traditionally be represented in a positive light is that of the family. However, this area and that of sexual desire are also traditionally mutually exclusive. A mother may be represented as a subject of sexual desire but not, without stigma, in front of the children. By the same token, representations portraying mothers as objects of desire, that is, as inviting the desire of men, are also usually condemnatory of the woman. Perhaps the roots of this mutual exclusivity lie in the child's distress at discovering the existence of the mother's desire as well as in the patriarchal Law which requires that a woman restrict her sexual relations to one man to guarantee his paternity. Whatever its motivations, it is certainly one which Duras's texts uphold.

Beyond the realms of the sexual or the familial, women's desire is often either simply not represented, or else shown as dependent on or subordinate to the two more conventionally recognised forms. Aspects of a woman's personality or behaviour at work are far more often attributed to the repression, sublimation, or deviation of her heterosexual 'sex-drive' than is the case with men, particularly if the woman in question seems more involved with her work than in sexual relationships or with children. In men such a balance is traditionally acceptable and is unlikely to lead to the same level of comment and speculation on their sexuality. Perhaps we owe a debt to psychoanalysis insofar as it indicates that the popular wisdom concerning women can also be extended to men, giving a primacy to the sexual in the psychic workings of individuals of both sexes.

Unfortunately, however, psychoanalytic theory has done little to extend the general recognition of women's desires as they arise in areas other than those of sexuality and the family. Indeed, concepts such as penis-envy or the masculinity complex may be used against a woman who seems too determined to overstep the boundaries traditionally confining her desires. Changes so far made in the ways women are represented, the inroads into areas traditionally reserved for men, such as representations of workers, thinkers, politicians, athletes and other sublimators, are due more to a gradual movement of which psychoanalysis is quite possibly symptomatic, but which it has not necessarily facilitated, that is, the changing position of woman in many societies, including our own.

Seen in this light, the construction of women's desire in Duras's work is quite similar to other, more obviously conventional representations of women. Almost all of Duras's women figures are either mothers or lovers or both and very few of them are portrayed in any other context. The exceptions, the eponymous heroine of *Madame Dodin*, or the servant of *Le Square*, disappear from the later work. And as objects of desire Duras's women are almost clichés: innocence and the awakening of (narcissistic) desire are crystallised in Valérie Andesmas and suggested in the portrayal of the childlike Alissa, perhaps also in Lol V. Stein, who has remained 'unhealthily young'. Certainly the latter has the mysterious quality which is a familiar attribute of the *femme fatale*, coupled with a determination to get what she wants, the exact nature of which is not clear, but which requires the participation of a lover. Anne-Marie Stretter is an example of the rich and gracious lady of leisure who fills her empty life with lovers and has the wisdom of her mature years, a beautiful and mysterious haven of intuitive understanding, whilst Tatiana Karl is the woman whose narcissism is lacking in self-sufficiency, whose sexual desire is too easily visible and comprehensible for her to be enigmatic, and who is portrayed as abject, an 'admirable whore'.

Almost clichés, but not. Duras's women do not have the banal familiarity of the cliché. The reader who accepts the place of the narratee will not be struck with the humdrum familiarity of Anne-Marie Stretter or Valérie. The secret of this lies largely in Duras's style, in the 'blanks' which compel the reader/narratee to participate in the telling of the story by interpreting what seems to be missing and by investing her/his own desire in the figures and in the text as a whole. What Duras has done, and often with consummate skill, is to hone down the scope of her texts so as to allow the maximum power to accrue to the image of the central woman figure. She has eschewed those aspects of realist novels which are productive of 'character', the likes, dislikes, habits, moods or particular ways of speaking of any given figure which differentiates her or him from another. Thus, she does away with all the manifestations of that figure's desires as they exceed the specifically sexual or familial, as well as the ways in which any figure's desires within sexual or family relations manifest themselves in particular and individual ways.

Novels of psychological realism tend to use such devices in an attempt to mirror reality, since the desires of extra-textual human beings are in evidence in all kinds of areas besides the sexual and the familial. Such details construct a particular figure as an individual, distinct in her/his specificity from other figures and from the narratee. However, since such novels also most often portray women in the context of either sexual or family relations, it is possible not to include such details of character without breaking down the basic structure around which many realist texts are built. The structural status of a character does not depend on her/his personal idiosyncrasies.

In Duras's later work the figures are whittled down to a point where they almost lose their capacity to appear as 'beings like us', their desire being constructed entirely in the context of the structural relations around which the text is built, usually a sexual relation. The reader is asked to adopt the position of the narratee and to concentrate all her/his attention on this structural relation, within which the woman is constructed as the object of desire whose own desires manifest themselves just enough in the required area – that of the sexual relation – for her to be produced as a desirable object, and not too much for her to lose her mystery and power. At least this is a balance which I think Duras strikes with the greatest success in the most acclaimed of her novels. There are exceptions, as always, to the format I have just outlined: the early novels of course, the structure of *Le Square*, the role of Maria in *Dix heures et demie du soir en été*, that of Claire Lannes in *L'Amante anglaise*, source of death rather than love, or that of Sabana in *Abahn Sabana David*, where again it is Thanatos rather than Eros who is at work. However, when women figures are portrayed as subjects of desire, Maria or the maid in *Le Square*, their desires are contained within the areas of sexual or family relations.

So Duras's novels give refined and crystallised versions of a particular way of representing women, which is widespread in our culture. This form is the one which constructs an individual image of a woman as a particular instance of Woman, source and object of (men's) desire. The reference points of Duras's work have been discussed by other critics, for example Marini, whose words I shall borrow here:

> [Marguerite Duras] starts, for example, with the stereotyped schemas of romantic, psychological or popular novels – the domain to which they try to restrict women, writers or readers –, stories all ultimately built to the same pattern – adultery, consuming passion, crimes of passion, family duties, elementary conflicts, whose basic givens, unfolding and resolutions are all known in advance.[8]

I think the most obvious intertextual links of Duras's work are those with 'romantic' fiction, which is, as Marini points out, precisely a domain traditionally reserved for women writers and readers. However, I part company with Marini after this, for according to her, 'It is all these models whose messages Marguerite Duras sub-

8　Marini, op cit, p 54.

verts by dislocating them',[9] whereas I would argue on the other hand that what Duras does is precisely the opposite. Rather than dislocate the model, she strips it down to the skeleton, a skeleton which will only permit the flesh to be laid on its bones in a specific way – by the narratee. It is her particular skill that she is then able to draw the reader to take up that position and to concentrate on the process of reconstruction of that which the text only suggests. This she does by her use of very clear, simple and yet evocative language, describing in many cases only the visible, with undisturbed authority and a complete concentration on the matter in hand: the story of desire and/or death. Not much happens in most of Duras's novels, most could be retold as very basic love stories. What gives them their particular quality is that the process of reconstruction is never completed. The crucial element which would make the reader's inference into certainty is constructed as beyond the scope of the text, an irretrievable 'blank. Duras is not inviting her readers to learn something, to understand 'what happened' and to think about it as they will; she is inviting them to feel something through an act of identification in the place of the narratee. She is inviting them to lend their own desires to flesh out her portrayal of the workings of desire between two (or more) figures.

Herein lies the immediacy and power of Duras's work, arising from the reader's participation in the text. However, I think it is misleading to suggest that by this process the text subverts the models to which it refers. For after and including *Moderato cantabile*, almost all Duras's novels demand that the reader/narratee draw on all the intertextual references to (for example) 'romantic' fiction at her/his disposal, whilst also banishing them from consciousness whilst reading. 'How,' asks Marini, 'can one read the work of Marguerite Duras without creating silence and emptiness at the threshhold of the reading room?'[10] My interpretation of this question would be that in order to get the most out of reading Duras, the reader must temporarily suspend all her/his own preoccupations and identifications which might get in the way of her/his adoption of the place of the narratee. S/he must draw unconsciously on the intertextual references of, say, 'romantic' fiction and other representations of women as objects of men's desire to carry her/him across the 'blanks'.

If *Moderato cantabile*, for example, permitted a reading where it was possible for the reader to 'understand' a precise meaning in what is related and the enigma of Anne's desire were solved, then s/he could compare it with other texts, other representations, in terms

9   ibid, p 55.
10 ibid.

of the meanings it produces and how it does so, as s/he was reading, or at least on reaching the end. But the end of *Moderato cantabile* leaves a 'blank'. S/he can of course, as I am doing here, think about the meaning(s) that the novel produces, but the text itself has an alibi in that the solution to its problem is beyond its scope and it can never be pinned down. Furthermore, to try to do so spoils the pleasure, and feels ungrateful, running contrary to the role of the reader/narratee. All the same, meanings are produced in, for example *Moderato cantabile* or *Le Vice-consul*, even if the reader is invited not to dwell on them too much and to concentrate on the pleasure of fascination involved in their production.

The effects of this are twofold. Firstly, by inferring unstated meanings which are not allowed to become fully conscious, the reader is led tacitly to reinforce them, at least while s/he is reading. This process can be seen at work elsewhere in the way in which jokes reinforce and reproduce certain traditional meanings, for example, the way in which in England the word 'Irish' is used to mean 'illogical' as well as 'coming from Ireland'. The projection of undesirable qualities on to the inhabitants of another place with which one's own home has close historical and linguistic links is common to many cultures and no doubt serves a function in the construction and perpetuation of a group identity. But the idea that Irish people are illogical is not expounded in serious theoretical works in England. Indeed, if it were it would no doubt have far less currency, for it is propagated highly effectively through jokes and unstated assumptions.

In order to laugh at the joke or to understand the story, the addressee must understand the idea that the Irish are illogical, s/he must assume it as a basic given and from that position can prepare for and understand the punch-line. The idea itself is not brought out and examined, but each time the link between 'Irish' and 'illogical' is made, and the pleasure at repetition of the old idea in a new configuration produces a laugh, or just a smile, it is reaffirmed, even though, if asked to discuss the matter seriously, none of the individuals participating in the joke-telling say that they really believe in the innate illogicality of the Irish. The idea remains unconscious and may be retrieved to surface in contexts other than that of ritual joke-telling if required. *The Sun* newspaper used the power of the unconscious assumption to strengthen meanings at a time when Mrs Thatcher and the rest of the EEC leaders appeared to be at odds, by featuring anti-French jokes, a tactic which aims to generate support for the 'British' (i.e., Mrs Thatcher's) position against 'the French', without necessitating a detailed exposition of the arguments, which might bore the paper's readers, confuse them, or even turn them against the position that the paper wished them to espouse.

In Duras's work unstated assumptions are similarly reinforced by the very necessity of their remaining unstated. In fact the reader's desire to 'understand' gives those meanings which have apparently been suppressed more credence because it is in the 'blanks' of the texts that the answers to the questions they ask apparently lie. The 'suppressed' meanings, the unstated assumptions may not be explicitly present in the text, but the reader will already have learnt to read and understand stories of sexual desire elsewhere for they are all around us and our own desires and ways of thinking about sex and love are formed in the context of these other representations. For the woman reader, Duras is restaging the old problem that women face of confrontation with representations of Woman as the signifier of the presence of (masculine) desire. She offers her readers the place of the male subject in reading her novels, from which to see women as more or less compelling manifestations of 'the absolute object of desire'.

In our culture all women have to find ways of identifying themselves in relation to archetypal images of Woman. Amongst feminists, responses vary. Some have rejected identification with her altogether, along with all her outward trappings of makeup, dresses etc., and others have not; some enjoy watching other women perform as an object of desire, others do not. But whatever our individual responses, the images are still there and they retain their power. We have to deal with them. I do not think Duras's later writing facilitates this process, although undoubtedly it harnesses the power of images of Woman, the power of the archetypal feminine as our culture defines it. For the reader/narratee is held by a kind of fascination, a hinting at veiled knowledge, but cannot move from that fascination through to understanding and on from there. The demands of the text are absolute.

The effect created is reminiscent of Lemoine-Luccioni's description of the fascination and mutual mirroring of mother and daughter, or the Imaginary fascination of Lacan's mirror phase, both of which need to be broken for the subject to move on. The reader cannot maintain a grip on her/his separate identity while reading and s/he who reads thinking 'Yes, but...' will miss both the pleasure and the point. So my dispute with claims that Duras's writing carries feminist meanings is on the grounds that it concentrates exclusively on and repeats traditional images of women as manifestations of Woman the Other and does not allow for interaction and difference between women. Some feminists might take the view that any representation of a woman as powerful has implicitly feminist effects, no matter what form that power takes. However, this is not a view I share, since I think that finding a way of relating to the power of

Woman the Other actually gives individual women a lot of trouble.

However, the fact that women, whether feminists or not, have found Duras's work fascinating and have felt touched by it seems to me to have implications for feminism. It is clearly not sufficient to decide that certain ways of representing women are 'male-defined' (even in the case of Duras's work, where almost all women are seen through implicitly or explicitly masculine eyes) and to reject them on those grounds. They appeal to women too and will not cease to do so because some feminists find them restricting. I cannot see what purposes will be served by those of us who enjoy her work denying ourselves the pleasure on grounds of ideological purity.

On the other hand, I do not think that we should try to justify that pleasure by upholding the power of the Woman-as-phallus as the means to women's liberation. It is quite possibly as old as patriarchy itself and has not helped us a great deal yet. My own view is that the main problem with such representations is that they are culturally dominant. If other kinds of representations of women, in relation to each other and each other's desires, in different relations to men, were more frequent, the power that now accrues to women as incarnations of Woman might become more diffused through these other manifestations. After all, men must also identify themselves in relation to archetypal Man – and they don't all find it so easy, but they seem to have more variations to play with. So I would argue for equality of diversity, rather than greater restriction, in the ways that women are portrayed, a diversity which already exists in a rather embryonic form, although not, it should be said, within the work of Duras.

It is not just in their representations of women that Duras's novels reinforce traditional and familiar meanings. *Moderato cantabile* for example restages the myth of the free-flowing sexuality of the working-class man, which releases the frustrated middle-class woman's pent-up desires, where her repressed husband has failed. My own thoughts turn to D H Lawrence and Wilhelm Reich as earlier purveyors of this myth of the working man's uninhibited sexual potency, but it is sufficiently widespread for examples not to be needed. In another area of myth, *Le Vice-consul* offers an image of India as the great ungraspable country of starving millions, seen from the rather unsettled viewpoint of the ruling whites. E M Forster produced a fine example of this particular way of representing India in *A Passage to India* (complete with a woman with an unutterable secret), but the undifferentiated starving of the 'Third World' looks out at us daily from charity posters and television programmes and the exotic decadence and cultural poverty of colonial rulers as viewed by their compatriots in Europe is also familiar enough. *Le*

Vice-consul constructs India as the great unknowable Other and Indians as individuals do not figure at all, unless it be as examples of suffering humanity – *les lépreux*. Ninette Bailey encapsulates the view of India and the Indians as it is produced in *Le Vice-consul* in her article in *La Chouette* no 6. Speaking of the vice-consul's act of smashing mirrors and shooting lepers she says: '...the sound of gunshots, the smashing of broken mirrors and cries, that is, another form of language, language returned to a primitive state and thus meeting the primitive needs of the Indian masses: hunger.'[11]

Bailey's formulation is, I think, very apt in relation to *Le Vice-consul*. The novel portrays, in some detail, a few white figures who are disturbed, even horrified beyond the bounds of sanity by an un-differentiated, inarticulate mass, presented as products of the white figures' imagination and represented by the beggar-woman and her 'primitive needs'. Nothing here contradicts the kind of assumptions common amongst peoples of imperialist nations that the conquered nation is at a lower stage of civilisation than their own and that, rather than living in a society run on complex rules and reflecting distinct and ancient cultures, its people have remained at the level of 'primitive needs'. There are, of course, many other representations of India circulating in Europe. India the land of spirituality, of riches, of natural beauty, of bizarre customs. None of these is really in evidence in *Le Vice-consul* and none of them intrudes into the myth of India the Incomprehensible which the novel upholds and which is the way India must be constructed by the reader in order to make sense of the text, whatever s/he may or may not think about the country otherwise.

This brings me to the second effect of the importance given to the actual process of inference in Duras's novels as opposed to any pos-sible 'message' or meanings produced in them. The later novels construct representations in terms of a binary system of presence or absence of meaning, where apparently expressive and transparent language is opposed to silence or 'oblivion'. However, these texts do not allow for the simultaneous presence of conflicting meanings. The meanings offered to the reader have been very carefully constructed so as to be as uncontradictory as possible. This effect is perceptible both at the level of the language of the novels and also at the level of the political or ideological meanings they produce.

To look at the language first, the binary effect of presence and absence of meaning is fostered by the bare style Duras uses, without rhetorical devices, which allows the illusion of one-to-one correspon-

11 Ninette Bailey, 'Une écriture de la subversion: Lecture narratologique du *Vice-consul* de Marguerite Duras', in *La Chouette* no 6, p 52.

dence of the word with its referent to go unimpeded, producing as nearly as possible the illusion of fixed and unitary meaning. Any specific 'subjectivity' of the narrator disappears into what appears to be a narration of the visible, of things present, from a point of view which is that of *l'objectif.*[12] Even in sections where, as in *Le Ravissement de Lol V. Stein*, the narrator is also a figure in the novel who 'invents' what is described, or, as in *Le Vice-consul*, the narration apparently enters into the thoughts of one of the figures, the language still maintains its apparent uncontradictory 'clarity'. This produces for the reader an effect of certain knowledge perforated with 'blanks', the latter being not points of conflict in the discourse, but rather absences of meaning. That the reader draws on inter-textual references to make sense of the text is not acknowledged by the text itself, other than at points of obvious reference to other works by Duras. This form of reference within the context of Duras's work, coupled with the bare but highly literary style and the sparsely described and clearly fictitious location of the closed 'durassian universe' tends to have the effect of lifting her writing out of its inter-textual context. The reader does not think about other texts or images whilst reading. The result is that Duras's texts set up oppositions: between that which can be described and understood, usually constructed as that which is visible, and that which cannot; and between meaningful language, which fixes and describes, and the 'blanks', which appear as instances of the inarticulable and unknowable.

On the ideological level, an analogous opposition is discernible. This is between the social status quo as constructed in the novels and its rejection in favour of the absence of any social structure. No other possibilities are offered. The 'transparent' language Duras uses appears to describe simply what is, but does so in a manner which implicitly denies the specificity of its own ideological context and connotations. This is not to deny that Duras's work is critical on an ideological level. It is, but from a position which, by producing one order of things as the only thinkable order, can oppose to it only the end of all order.

This opposition can be seen for example in the dinner-party scene in *Moderato cantabile*, which is clearly critical of the manner in which the meal takes place:

> The salmon passes from one to the other following a ritual which nothing disturbs, unless it be the hidden fear of each that so much perfection might suddenly be broken or stained with a too obvious

---

12 *L'objectif* can be translated either as 'the camera lens' or 'objectivity'.

absurdity. Outside, in the gardens, the magnolias are developing their funereal flowering in the black night of emerging spring.[13]

This paragraph taxes with absurdity the ritual of eating the salmon, that is to say, it refuses to accept the rules of the dinner-party as a framework for understanding what is happening, but rather steps outside them, opposing the artifice of the ceremony of the passing of the salmon with, not only nature in the form of the magnolias and the 'emerging spring', but also with death and 'the black night'. The order of a bourgeois dinner is criticised and its ceremony denied its significatory function, reduced to the absurd. But this is not ostensibly from the point of view of some different order or orders of things, a different set of meanings, but in the name of a refusal of ritual or order and a 'return' to a 'natural' world of death and unutterable desire.

The opening paragraphs of Chapter VII, of which the above is one, establish a hierarchy of 'truth' or 'authenticity'. The world of the dinner-party is produced as one of ritual, of invented rules or conventions in terms of which the ritual has meaning, and of fear of the breaking-down of those rules. The reader is given a certain amount of interpretation or explanation of events, implying that s/he might not instantly understand the meaning of the proceedings and also undercutting any effect of self-evidence that the ritual might have. In contrast, the descriptions of the world of flowers, desire and death give no interpretations. The reader is required to interpret un-aided, to recall the meanings which have accrued to the magnolia flower, to be aware of all the connotations of these descriptions. In this way the dinner-party is portrayed as a constructed ritual, produc-tive of 'artificial' meaning, liable to collapse into absurdity, whilst the description of the world outside, which carries no interpretations, no acknowledgement of the existence of a framework or frameworks in the context of which it has meaning, enables its meanings to appear 'natural', beyond the grasp of language.

The symbolic resonances of the natural world, magnolia flower, night, the wind and spring, acquire this appearance of 'naturalness' and of being more 'real' because the reader is required to infer them without being told how to, aided by a vast number of inter- and intra-textual references which must remain, for the most part, unconscious. The effect produced is thus one of an immediacy of understanding without words. The reader, if s/he is to enjoy the fascination exerted by the text, must take up the position of the narratee and read as if

13 *Moderato cantabile* pp 91–2.

the resonances of meanings attached to the description of the magnolia flowers are both coming from her/his own psyche and are at the same time universal, the point where the pre- or extra-linguisitic fundamentals of human existence meet her/his specific individuality, via the specific experiences of Anne Desbaresdes and Chauvin. S/he may, however, as I do, wish to investigate the 'invisible' conventions which give meaning to Duras's magnolia flowers, which are no more or less 'artificial' or constructed than those governing a dinner-party. For here, as throughout most of her work, Duras's narrative style renders the conventions on which it rests as unobtrusive as possible, and is selective in what it interprets. Both are necessary in order to create the effect of an objective style interrupted by 'blanks', of order undermined.

The opposition of 'artificial' oppressive order and a kind of primaeval, inarticulate chaos which breaks into and appears to undermine that order can be identified in all of Duras's work, but particularly in the later novels. Bailey discusses this oppositional structure as it operates in *Le vice-consul*'s portrayal of colonial society. She points to many different instances of opposition in the text, which she links to an opposition of whites and 'natives' which 'underlies the entire text'.[14] As in *Moderato cantabile*, there is an opposition between an unstable structure of social meanings and an inarticulate chaos upon which that structure has been erected, with the white figures representing those who have a place in the world of meaning and the Indians and the beggar-woman being those who remain in chaos. Bailey makes this point in her study of a passage from *Le Vice-consul* which describes Anne-Marie Stretter, Michael Richard and Charles Rossett driving to the Prince of Wales hotel through the paddy fields:

> So present together for the one and only time, apart from the Indian servants, are Whites on the one hand, who have left the protective enclosure of the Residency, and natives on the other. In the rest of the novel the 'suffering hordes of Calcutta' only exist within the discourse of the text, evoked in the indistinctness of a common, inarticulate voice: 'Again Calcutta cries out softly' (p 158) – 'Muffled howlings again, along by the Ganges' (p 154). 'Here, although it is still anonymous and dumb, the crowd can be counted, is countless moreover, next to the three Whites'.[15]

In *Le Vice-consul*, the white figures, who have names and other attributes, stand in marked contrast to the 'native crowd'. Or per-

14   Bailey, 'Discours social: Lecture socio-critique du *Vice-consul* de M Duras', in *Literature and Society – studies in Nineteenth and Twentieth Century French Literature*, presented to R J North, C A Burns ed, Birmingham University, 1980, p 5.

15   ibid, p 4.

haps I should say it is the 'native crowd' which stands in marked contrast, as irredeemably Other, to the white figures from whose point of view the text is narrated. Theirs are the eyes through which the reader is invited to look upon the 'suffering of India'. Nevertheless, as in *Moderato cantabile* the text constructs the same somewhat paradoxical hierarchy, which makes of the 'blank' which is India the ultimate reality which the whites (*les Blancs*) try to make sense of in their artificial way. Thus they, attempt to recreate structures of meaning which were possible in Europe (although liable to be overthrown, as suggested by the vice-consul's 'joyful happiness at Montfort') and erect them on the vast and shifting foundations of the enigmatic East, which stands, in the novel, for Reality in all its excess. Bailey makes a similar point in her analysis:

> The car drives though a fluvial landscape: 'black junks advancing through the waterways, between the paddy-fields with their black water. Here and there there are patches newly sown, brilliant, soft green spaces, painted silk' (ibid). This time there is a contrast between the elements that make up the landscape, the double black of black junks and black water, which connote, as is right, the native, whilst the occasional touches of colour, green connoting the home country of the Whites, are rendered unreal by the substance of cloth and the optical illusion of painting: '*painted silk*'. There is an opposition to be read here: the black reality of the native context, the brilliant unreality of the notations linked to the Whites.[16]

One might wish to argue that Bailey is making assumptions in her analysis that the 'black' of junks and water must connote 'native', whilst the bright splashes of colour like painted silk connote Europe. However, I think that such an opposition of 'black reality' and 'brillant unreality' is most certainly encouraged in *Le Vice-consul* by the opposition of 'artificial' European civilisation and the countless millions of unheard Indians with their needs which may be portrayed as 'primitive', but which are also implicitly all the more 'real' for all that. Elsewhere, Bailey reiterates the point:

> . . . insignificant words of the guests at the embassy, repetitive and stereotyped, the lies of the vice-consul's interminable speeches at the Circle. Talking to say nothing: to these empty words the text opposes the dumbness of the beggar-woman, the silences of the ambassador's wife, but above all the cry. A whole range of sound is associated with the vice-consul: detonations, the smashing of

16 ibid.

broken mirrors, cries. An inarticulate language, which the text valorizes above that which is articulate language *par excellence*, literary discourse.[17]

Whilst I would be unwilling to confer the name 'language' upon bangs and crashes which, although they no doubt signify something, do so less by reference to each other, as linguistic elements do, than by reference to the action which produced them, I agree with Bailey's basic thesis that *Le Vice-consul*, presenting the reader with a choice between 'empty words' and 'silence', suggests that the latter is preferable, more 'real'. However, Bailey and other writers have seen this opposition in Duras's work as a subversion of dominant ideological positions, and this is a view I cannot share, for reasons similar to those I have discussed in relation to claims that Duras's work is feminist.

For *Le Vice-consul*, or any other of Duras's novels, can only be seen as subverting language, representations of society, or anything else if one accepts the binary vision they propose, which opposes language/rules/meanings to silence/screams/chaos. Duras's texts portray figures who have apparently stepped out of any specific position within different social relations, leaving them only the general categories of woman/object and man/subject in which to place themselves. All the variations of discourse which mark differences of position in such relations, and which produce meanings which may be at variance with one another, are reduced to the most simple literary language. In the novels following *Moderato cantabile*, all Duras's figures speak a very literary French, be they workers, Laotian beggars, rich and idle housewives or murderers. The differences that might therefore be perceptible between them via the language they use are thus removed, as are the social contexts of those who do not fit into the category of the rich. As the literary French they speak is also the language traditionally used in narration, it does not appear marked with the specificity of its usage when used in a literary work as Duras has done, but becomes apparently transparent; at least in the kind of unselfconscious reading which her work requires of the reader/narratee.

Nevertheless, this literary style has connotations of social class – the educated bourgeoisie – into which all the figures, no matter what their declared social status, are thus spirited. (This implicit social positioning may facilitate the reader's willingness to believe in their lack of concern with the details and problems of everyday life, concerns traditionally associated with the poor, although no doubt the rich suffer from them as well.) Such undifferentiated style allows

17 ibid, p 52.

the construction of the figures as undifferentiated human beings, stripped of the differences societies construct. Their speech does not mask them as different from each other. Instead the emphasis is on its constant failure to express the fundamentals of love and death, which are perceived as present in screams and in silence. Bailey has pointed to this lack of differentiation in *Le Vice-consul*, where she finds not only a 'form of writing that does away with demarcations by use of the pronoun *'on'* ('one')',[18] but also an abolition of difference via the collapse of language: 'So it is through the cry, in the absence of articulate language, that the indifferenciation of human beings is postulated.'[19]

So Duras's novels offer a vision of the world in which certain human beings – almost always white, Gentile men – construct artificial meaning upon a fundamental chaos to which women, children, Indians, Jews and some white Gentile men have access. Duras's concern is not with the conflict between the different constructions which might be produced from different positions, but with the relation of particular, and in Western Europe ideologically dominant constructions to their absence or collapse. I do not think that this really undermines those ideologically dominant constructions. Indeed, if anything it shores them up, since the texts rely, in order to be able to produce the effect of 'blanks', upon implacability and lack of contradiction. This lack of contradiction can be seen both in the way that the workings of the world are portrayed in the texts and in the language which is used to portray them.

In the schema proposed by Duras, meanings and their absence are like yin and yang, or two sides of the same coin. The irony of the 'subversion' operated by the 'blanks' in Duras's work is that it relies on the reader's ability to draw on, understand and accept, at least for the duration of her/his reading, precisely those ideological elements it is supposed to be subverting: traditional representations of heterosexual desire, of decadent white colonials faced with the seething black masses, or of the grandeur and ceremony of a bourgeois dinner in contrast to the animality of the working man. No alternative visions are offered to counter these representations, which we are asked to use to fuel our journey through Duras's novels. No ripples suggestive of a different way of seeing or of understanding the vision come to trouble the smooth surface of the images she produces for us, unless, that is, we the readers make them ourselves, in which case the texts become impossible to read with the same pleasure of fascination. The only option Duras offers to escape the confines of the social and linguis-

18 ibid, p 50.
19 ibid, p 52.

tic structures which she presents as being so fixed is that of 'capital destruction', through (sexual) desire, death or madness.

This fits very well with the views expressed by Duras in 1974 on effective political action, which she saw in terms of refusal.

> But the people who are denouncing a whole load of things are calling for political action, when the first thing to do should be to refuse to do things. They should be telling people first of all, before all the programmes: 'Don't pay your telephone bill, go shoplifting, don't buy any more cars, don't vote, don't pay your tax.' There'd have to be millions of us doing it.[20]

There are obvious problems with such a strategy. Duras is ignoring two basic points here. The first is that shops, cars and taxes are bound together in intricate variations of social structures rather than being simply aspects of the same monolith which can be rejected in its entirety. The second is that we human beings are characterised by our construction, wherever we are, of complex social structures – of meanings. The axiom 'nature abhors a vacuum' applies also to the human psyche. We cannot just do away with Meaning, but we can change meanings and the structures in which they are produced.

The difference between Meaning, seen as a structured process of production, and meanings, which are what is produced in the workings of the process, is a crucial one. Duras sees the process as the problem. Her answer is to posit the end of Meaning as the way forward: 'Let the world run to rack and ruin, to rack and ruin, that's the only politics possible.[21]

Because she presents a vision of the world in which language can only tell lies, the truth of human existence being inarticulate, she does not explore the different ways in which different people use the same language. Because she presents language as a maker of 'artificial' order, or as a babble, she does not investigate the details of the contradictions, conflicts and excesses of meaning which it can produce and which themselves generate new meanings, and by apparently lifting the utterances of her figures out of the specificity of social context (beyond the literary), she also suppresses the political dimension of language itself.

In her concentration on Meaning rather than specific meanings and the relations between them, Duras's approach resembles that of psychoanalysis as I discussed it in Chapter III above, and in this sense, her work has particular similarities with that of Lacan, who also deals in general psychic structures and does not go in for lengthy

---

20 *Les Parleuses*, p 108.
21 *Le Camion*, Paris, Gallimard, 1977, p 74.

discussion of individual manifestations of his general laws. Freud fills his pages with examples, which not only prove his point about, for example, the general rules governing the workings of the unconscious, but also testify to the differences of meanings and positions in relation to those meanings which are unconsciously produced, and their specificity to the individual and context in which they occur. Lacan's writings on the other hand are mainly presented as extracts from a monolithic, all-embracing theory, which claims to account for every manifestation of desire, every production of meaning, within the general structure it elaborates, without concerning itself with the investigation of individual cases, the few exceptions being most often allusions to Freud's patients.

I think it is reasonable, although perhaps a little ironic, to say that both Lacan and Duras are producers of monoliths: the former attempts to encompass the structure of the human psyche, whilst the latter constructs a vision in which all ordering processes are part of the same restrictive structuring of primordial chaos. Both are concerned with the opposition of the monolithic structure they have constructed and the absence or lack upon which it is built and both seem to deny the possibility of real change and the importance of history by denying the production of difference and by refusing to look at detail. Thus both reinforce dominant representations, especially those of relations between the sexes. Lacan's 'Woman' is an abstraction, a particular position in a theory of relations of desire which owes, I suspect, as much to conventional representations of heterosexual relations as it does to analyses of individual men and women that Lacan may have undertaken. In the same way, Duras's 'ravaged beings' are the result of a refinement of novelistic conventions concerning the creation of 'character' which, by eschewing any 'irrelevant' detail, produces figures who are only a little more than points in a narrative structure. Perhaps the symbiotic relationship of their writings is symptomatic of this similarity.

Duras's writing has been called subversive because it shows up women's silence, constructing it as more 'true' or 'real' than the meaning produced in language, perforating and disturbing the dominating chatter of men. However, dominant meanings and representations that women (and/or men) might wish to change cannot just simply be absolished, others must be produced to combat, and eventually to supercede them. Indeed, they already exist. As I have discussed above, the kind of representation of woman-as-object that Duras produces are distillations of a particular aspect of the way in which women are generally represented in Western cultures. But there are other types of representation which could be drawn on. Even the most traditionally portrayed wives, girlfriends and mothers are often provided with quirks of character to make them 'individuals', different from other women as well as just examples of Woman the object of desire, and which allow them to be also, albeit in a small way, portrayed as subjects of desire.

These are the very details that Duras eschews and yet I think it is precisely by looking at and concentrating upon those details of women's difference from one another in terms of our desires and actions that we can escape from the constraints of being always either seen as manifestations of Womanhood or honorary men. The dominant picture within society at the moment is one in which men, the subjects, the unmarked sex, are always primarily examples of Womanhood. If this division is to change and become more balanced, no doubt the manhood of men, the fact that they are not just human beings, but specifically male human beings, will require more emphasis, so that women can gain a greater measure of individuality. Dominant representations of subject and object positions in the context of heterosexual relations will have to be disturbed. But of course, there are other representations, even now, and it should be stressed that those positions have never been immutably fixed.

In this light, then, I would not hold up Duras's work as a landmark in the journey towards the end of women's oppression. However, there is one important aspect I have ignored thus far in my analysis of the feminist implications of her work, and that is the impact of Duras herself as a writer. She is now widely acknowledged to be one of France's great contemporary writers, particularly since she was awarded the Goncourt prize in 1984 for *L'Amant*. For however far her work may, in itself, reinforce traditional representations and divisions of the sexes, the fact that it is a woman's work also affects the way that women are regarded generally. Duras is an immensely skillful and highly individual writer, and, though her own portrayal of herself in *L'Amant* is chiefly as an object of men's desire, it is as an innovative and powerful writer and film-marker that she has deservedly found wide acclaim. When her readers contemplate Anne-Marie Stretter, or Lol V. Stein, those obscure objects of desire, they will also remember that these fictional figures have been fashioned from the desires of an impressively authoritative subject, who makes words do just what she wants them to do: a very particular woman, Marguerite Duras.

BIBLIOGRAPHY

I WORKS BY MARGUERITE DURAS

Novels and récits[1]

Les Impudents, Paris, Plon, 1943.
La Vie Tranquille, Paris, Gallimard, 1944.
Un Barrage contre le Pacifique, Paris, Gallimard, 1950.
    Translated as *The Sea Wall* by Herma Briffault, New York, Farrar, Straus &
    Giroux and London, Faber & Faber, 1986.
Le Marin de Gibraltar, Paris, Gallimard, 1952.
    Translated as *The Sailor from Gibraltar* by Barbara Bray, New York, Pantheon,
    and London, Calder, 1966
Les Petits Cheveaux de Tarquinia, Paris, Gallimard, 1953.
    Translated as *The Little Horses of Tarquinia* by Peter DuBurgh, London, Calder
    1960.
Des journées entières dans les arbres, including: *Le Boa, Madame Dodin, Des Journées
    entières dans les arbres, Les Chantiers*, Paris, Gallimard, 1954.
    Translated as *Whole Days in the Trees* by Anita Barrows, New York, Riverrun,
    and London, Calder, 1984.
Le Square, Paris, Gallimard, 1955.
    Translated as *The Square* by S P Rivers, London, Calder.
    Also in: *Three Novels*, London, Calder, 1977 and in *Four Novels*, translated by
    Richard Seaver et al, New York, Grove, 1965.
Moderato Cantabile, Paris, Minuit, 1958.
    Translated as *Moderato Cantabile* by Richard Seaver, New York, Grove and
    London, Calder, 1966.
Dix heures et demie du soir en été, Paris, Gallimard, 1960.
    Translated as *Ten-thirty on a Summer Night* in *Four Novels*, New York, Grove,
    1965, and in *Three Novels*, London, Calder, 1977.

---

1   The distinction between novels and *récits* is one made in many bibliographies, including
that published by Minuit. It has not been formally established by Duras herself to my
knowledge, some of her texts bear the designation *roman* on the title page, but *récit* is never
used in such a way. However, I have used the two terms as the distinction seems to me to be
a valid one.

L'Après-midi de Monsieur Andesmas, Paris, Gallimard, 1962.
> Translated as *Afternoon of Monsieur Andesmas* with *Rivers and Forests* by A Borchardt & Barbara Bray, London, Calder, 1965. Also in *Four Novels*, New York, Grove, 1965 and in *Three Novels*, London, Calder, 1977.

Le Ravissement de Lol V. Stein, Paris, Gallimard, 1964.
> Translated as *The Ravishing of Lol V. Stein* by Richard Seaver, New York, Pantheon, 1986.

Le Vice-consul, Paris, Gallimard, 1965.

L'Amante Anglaise, Paris, Gallimard, 1967.
> Translated as *L'Amante Anglaise* with *Suzanna Andler* and *La Musica* by B Bray, London, Calder, 1975.

Détruire, dit-elle, Paris, Minuit, 1969.
> Translated as *Destroy, she said* by Barbara Bray, New York, Grove, 1986.

Abahn Sabana David, Paris, Gallimard, 1970.

L'Amour, Paris, Gallimard, 1971.

L'Homme Assis dans le Couloir, Paris, Minuit, 1980.

Agatha, Paris, Minuit, 1981.

L'Homme Atlantique, Paris, Minuit, 1982.

La Maladie de la Mort, Paris, Minuit, 1982.
> Translated as *The Malady of Death* by Barbara Bray, New York, Grove, 1986.

L'Amant, Paris, Minuit, 1984.
> Translated as *The Lover* by Barbara Bray, London, Collins and New York, Pantheon, 1985.

La Douleur, Paris, Minuit, 1985.
> Translated as *La Douleur* by Barbara Bray, London, Collins, 1986.

Plays

Les Viaducs de la Seine-et-Oise, Paris, Gallimard, 1959.

Théâtre I: Les Eaux et Forêts, Le Square, La Musica, Paris, Gallimard, 1965.

L'Amante Anglaise, Paris, Cahiers du Théâtre National Populaire, 1968.

Théâtre II: Suzanna Andler, Des journées entières dans les arbres, Yes, Peut-être, Le Shaga, Un homme est venu me voir, Paris, Gallimard, 1968.

L'Eden Cinéma, Paris, Mercure de France, 1977.

Théâtre III: La Bête dans la Jungle, after Henry James, adapted by James Lord and M Duras, *Les Papiers d'Aspern*, after Henry James, adapted by M Duras and Robert Antelme, *La Danse de la Mort*, after August Strindberg, adapted by M Duras, Paris, Gallimard, 1984.

Films and Screenplays

Hiroshima Mon Amour (screenplay), Paris, Gallimard, 1960.
> Translated as *Hiroshima Mon Amour* by Richard Seaver, New York, Grove, 1961.

Une Aussi Longue Absence (screenplay), in collaboration with Gérard Jarlot, Paris, Gallimard, 1961.

Détruire, dit-elle (film), 1969.

Jaune le Soleil (film), 1971.

Nathalie Granger (film), 1972.

India Song (screenplay), Paris, Gallimard, 1973.
> Translated as *India Song* by Barbara Bray, New York, Grove, 1976.

La Femme du Gange (film), 1973.

Nathalie Granger, followed by *La Femme du Gange* (screenplays), Paris, Gallimard, 1973.

India Song (film), 1975.
Baxter, Vera Baxter (film), 1976.
Son Nom de Venise dans Calcutta Désert (film), 1976.
Des Journées Entières dans les Arbres (film), 1976.
Le Camion (film), 1977.
Le Camion (screenplay), followed by *Entretien avec Michelle Porte*, Paris, Minuit, 1977.
Le Navire Night (film), 1978.
Césarée (film), 1979.
Les Mains Négatives (film), 1979.
Aurélia Steiner, dit Aurélia Melbourne (film), 1979.
Aurélia Steiner, dit Aurélia Vancouver (film), 1979.
Le Navire Night, Césarée, Les Mains Négatives, Aurélia Steiner, dit Aurélia Melbourne, Aurélia Steiner, dit Aurélia Vancouver (screenplays), Paris, Mercure de France, 1979.
Vera Baxter ou les Plages de l'Atlantique (screenplay), Paris, Albatros, 1980.

Miscellaneous

Les Parleuses with Xavière Gauthier, Paris, Minuit, 1974.
    Translated as *Woman to Woman* by Katerine Jensen, University of Nebraska Press.
'Ce que parler ne veut pas dire', interview with M Duras in *Les Nouvelles Littéraires*, Paris, 15/4/1974.
Les Lieux de Marguerite Duras with Michelle Porte, Paris, Minuit, 1977.
Marguerite Duras: Articles by M Duras, Jacques Lacan, Maurice Blanchot, Dionys Mascolo, Xavière Gautier, Benoit Jacquot, Pierre Fedida, Viviane Forrester ..., Paris, Albatros, Ça Cinéma series, 1979.
L'Eté 80, Paris, Minuit, 1980.
Les Yeux Verts, special issue of *Cahiers du Cinéma*, Paris, Edition de l'Etoile, 1980.
Outside, Paris, Albin Michel, 1981.
    Translated as *Outside* by Arthur Goldhammer, Boston, Beacon Press, 1986.

II CRITICAL WORK ON MARGUERITE DURAS

Books

Marcelle Marini, *Territoires du féminin avec Marguerite Duras*, Paris, Minuit, 1977.
Henri Micciollo, *Lire aujourd'hui Moderato Cantabile*, Paris, Hachette, 1978/9.
Madeleine Renouard and Ninette Bailey (eds), *La Chouette* no 6 (special issue on Duras), French Department, Birkbeck College, University of London, September 1981.

Articles

Ninette Bailey, 'Discours social: Lecture socio-critique du *Vice-Consul* de Marguerite Duras', in *Literature and Society – Studies in Nineteenth and Twentieth Century French Literature*, presented to R J North, C A Burns (ed), Birmingham University, 1980.
Susan Cohen, 'Phantasm and Narration in Marguerite Duras' *The Ravishing of Lol V. Stein*' in *The Psychoanalytic Study of Literature*, Joseph Reppen and Maurice Charney (eds), Hillsdale, New Jersey, The Analytic Press, 1985.

Bruno De Florence, 'About *India Song* and Marguerite Duras', in *Undercut* no 2, London, London Film-Makers' Co-op, August 1981.

Michele Montrelay, 'Sur le Ravissement de Lol V. Stein, in *L'Ombre et le Nom*, Paris, Minuit, 1977.

Elizabeth Lyon, 'The Cinema of Lol V. Stein', in *Camera Obscura* no 6, Berkeley, Camera Obscura Inc, Fall 1980.

Trista Selous, 'Evidence of Struggle – Problems with *India Song*' in *Undercut* nos 3/4, London, London Film-Makers' Co-op, March 1982.

III FEMINIST THEORY AND LITERARY CRITICISM

Parveen Adams, 'Representation and sexuality' in *m/f* no 1, London, 1978.

Parveen Adams and Jeff Minson, 'The "subject" of feminism', in *m/f* no. 2, 1978.

Simone de Beauvoir, *Le Deuxième Sexe*, Paris, Gallimard, Idées series, 1949.
Translated as *The Second Sex* by H M Parshley, London, Cape, 1953.

Maria Black and Rosalind Coward, 'Linguistic, social and sexual relations: a review of Dale Spender's *Man Made Language*' in *Screen Education* no 39, London, Society for Education in Film and Television, Summer 1981.

Elizabeth Cowie, 'Woman as Sign', in *m/f* no 1, 1978.

Interview with Hélène Cixous, conducted by Christine Makward, translated by Ann Liddle and Beatrice Cameron, in *Sub-stance* no 13, Madison, University of Winconsin Press, 1976.

Anne-Marie Dardigna, *Les Chateaux d'Eros ou l'Infortune du Sexe des Femmes*, Paris, Maspero, 1970.

Beatrice Didier, *L'Ecriture-Femme*, Paris, PUF, 1981.

Jane Gallop, *Feminism and Psychoanalysis*, London, Macmillan, 1982.

Luce Irigaray, *Speculum*, Paris, Minuit, 1974.
Translated as *Speculum of the Other Woman* by Gillian C Gill, New York, Cornell University Press 1985.

Luce Irigaray, *Ce Sexe qui n'en est pas Un*, Paris, Minuit, 1977.
Translated as *This Sex which is not One* by Catherine Porter and Carolyn Burke, New York, Cornell University Press, 1985.

Interview with L Irigaray, in *Ideology and Consciousness* no 1, London, May 1977.

Mary Jacobus (ed), *Women Writing and Writing about Women*, London, Croom Helm, 1979.

E Ann Kaplan (ed), *Women in Film Noir*, London, British Film Institute, 1978.

Sarah Kofman, *L'Enigme de la Femme dans les Textes de Freud*, Paris, Galilée, 1980.

Elaine Marks & Isabelle de Courtivron (eds) *New French Feminisms*, University of Massachusetts Press, 1980 and Brighton, The Harvester Press, 1981.

Juliet Mitchell, *Psychoanalysis and Feminism*, London, Penguin. 1974.

Ellen Moers, *Literary Women*, London, The Women's Press, 1978.

Michèle Montrelay, 'Inquiry into Femininity' taken from *L'Ombre et le Nom*, translated by Parveen Adams, *m/f* no 1, 1978.

Laura Mulvey, 'You don't know what's happening, do you Mr Jones?' in *Spare Rib* no 8, London, February 1973.

Laura Mulvey, 'Visual pleasure and narrative cinema' in *Screen* Vol 16 no 3, London, Society for Education in Film and Television, Autummn 1975.

Dale Spender, *Man Made Language*, London, Routledge and Kegan Paul, 1980.

Virginia Woolf, *Virginia Woolf Women and Writing*, London, The Women's Press, 1979.

Tel Quel no 74: 'Recherches Féminines', with articles by Julia Kristeva, Michèle Mattelart, Martine Leibovici, Jacqueline Risset, Chantal Thomas, Viviane Forrester, Sophie Podolski, Anne-Marie Houdebine, Christine Maurice, Elizabeth Rasy, Paris, Winter 1977.

IV **OTHER THEORETICAL AND CRITICAL WORKS**

Roland Barthes, *Le Degré Zéro de l'Ecriture*, Paris, Le Seuil, 1953 and 1972.
  Translated as *Writing degree zero* by Annette Lavers & Colin Smith, London, Cape, 1967.
Roland Barthes, *Mythologies*, Paris, Le Seuil, Points Series, 1957.
  A selection of essays translated as *Mythologies* by Annette Lavers, London, Cape, 1972.
Rosalind Coward and John Ellis, *Language and Materialism*, London, Routledge and Kegan Paul, 1977.
Terry Eagleton, *Criticism and Ideology*, London, Verso Editions, 1978.
Sigmund Freud, *The Standard Edition of the Complete Psychological Works of Sigmund Freud*, Vols VII (1953), XVII (1955), XIX (1961) and XXI (1961), London, The Hogarth Press and the Institute of Psycho-Analysis and New York, Basic Books Inc.
Sigmund Freud, *New Introductory Lectures on Psycho-Analysis*, London, The Hogarth Press and the Institute of Psycho-Analysis and New York, Norton.
Michel Foucault, *Histoire de la Sexualité* Vol I: *La Volonté de Savoir*, Paris, Gallimard, 1976.
  Translated as *History of Sexuality Volume 1* by R Hurley, London, Allen Lane, 1979.
Stephen Heath, 'Difference', in *Screen* Vol 19 no 3, Autumn 1978.
Stephen Heath, *The Sexual Fix*, London, Macmillan, 1982.
Karen Honrey, *Feminine Psychology*, New York, W W Norton, 1967.
Ernest Jones, *The Life and Work of Sigmund Freud*, London, Chatto & Windus, 1953.
Melanie Klein, *Envy and Gratitude*, London, The Hogarth Press and the Institute of Psycho-Analysis, 1975.
Julia Kristeva, *Le Texte du Roman*, Berlin, Federal Republic of Germany, Mouton/de Gruyter, 1976.
Jacques Lacan, *Ecrits I*, Paris, Le Seuil, Points Series, 1966.
Jacques Lacan, *Ecrits II*, Paris, Le Seuil, Points Series, 1971.
  Translated in *Ecrits: A Selection* by A Sheridan, London, Tavistock and New York, Norton, 1977.
Jacques Lacan, *Les Quatre Concepts Fondamentaux de la Psychanalyse*, Paris, Le Seuil, 1973.
  Translated as *Four Fundamental Concepts of Psychoanalysis* by A Sheridan, London, Hogarth and New York, Norton, 1977.
Jacques Lacan, *Encore*, Paris, Le Seuil, 1975.
Jacques Lacan and the Ecole Freudienne, *Feminine Sexuality* Juliet Mitchell & Jacqueline Rose (eds), Jacqueline Rose trans., London, Macmillan, 1982.
Jacques Leenhardt, *Lecture Politique du Roman*, Paris, Minuit, 1973.
Eugénie Lemoine-Luccioni, *Partage des Femmes*, Paris, Le Seuil, 1976.
  Translated as *The Dividing of Women or Woman's Lot* by Marie-Laure Davenport & Marie-Christine Réguis, London, Free Association Books, 1987.

Jean Baker Miller (ed), *Psychoanalysis and Women*, London, Penguin, 1973.

Tzvetan Todorov, *Symbolisme et Interpretation*, Paris, Le Seuil, 1978.
Translated as *Symbolism and Interpretation* by C Porter, London, Routledge & Kegan Paul, 1983.

Marcia Westkott, *The Feminist Legacy of Karen Horney*, New Haven and London, Yale University Press, 1986.

Anthony Wilden, *System and Structure*, London, Tavistock, 1980.

INDEX

Adler, Alfred 32

Bailey, Ninette 243, 246–9
Barthes, Roland 91
Black, Maria and Coward, Rosalind
    14–16
Blanchot, Maurice 122–3, 126
'blanks' 9, 12, 18–19, 52, 59, 78, 87,
    97–139, 141, 144, 148–9, 152, 160,
    164–5, 184–5, 201, 204, 206, 210,
    215–17, 234, 239, 244, 246–52
Booth, Wayne C 94, 141

Camus, Albert 127, 145
Cixous, Hélène 4, 60–2, 64, 69

Dietrich, Marlene 197
Dolto, Françoise 47
Duras, Marguerite: works by
    (chronological order)
    La Vie tranquille 10, 153–4, 156–7,
        186–7, 203–4, 206, 213–14, 223,
        232
    Un barrage contre le Pacifique 11,
        87–97, 103–4, 109, 127–8, 131,
        138, 140, 149, 156–60, 163, 182,
        186, 205, 213–15, 225–8, 230
    Le Marin de Gibraltar 127, 140, 158,
        161–3, 170–1, 183, 186, 203–5,
        213
    Les Petits Chevaux de Tarquinia 11,
        159–61, 163, 168, 182, 186, 205,
        213–15, 218–20, 225, 230
    Des journées entières dans les arbres 149,
        155, 158, 163, 215, 227–8, 230
    Le Boa 154–5, 186–7

    Madam Dodin 149, 154–5, 157–8, 237
    Les Chantiers 155, 157–8, 161, 176,
        183, 187–8, 192
    Le Square 11, 149, 158, 163–4, 237–8
    Moderato cantabile 1, 11, 97–111, 113,
        127–32, 135, 137–9, 141, 144–5,
        149, 151, 153, 164–8, 170, 182–3,
        185, 188–9, 200–1, 206–8, 210,
        212, 217–23, 225, 230, 233,
        239–40, 242, 244–6, 248
    Dix heures et demie du soir en été 127,
        129, 150–8, 167–70, 183, 185,
        214–15, 220–2, 238
    Hiroshima mon amour 167, 214
    L'Après-midi de Monsieur
    Andesmas 129, 168–71, 183, 189–92,
        194, 196, 214, 237
    Le Ravissement de Lol V. Stein 16–17,
        76, 110–14, 117, 120, 129, 132–33,
        136, 140, 142–5, 150–1, 163,
        170–2, 175, 181–3, 190–2, 200,
        206, 208–10, 212, 214–15, 220–1,
        217, 244, 252
    Le Vice-consul 113–22, 124–5,
        130–2, 136, 142–3, 150, 172–5,
        178, 181–2, 191–2, 194–5,
        200–1, 209–10, 212, 220–5, 230,
        237, 240, 242–4, 246–9, 252
    L'Amante Anglaise 127, 129, 132, 150,
        174–6, 185, 213–14, 238
    Détruire, dit-elle 122–7, 130–1, 143,
        150–1, 153, 176–8, 181, 192, 216,
        222, 237
    Abahn Sabana David 178–9, 238
    L'Amour 125, 129, 131, 133–5,
        142–4, 150, 179–83, 185, 192,
        215–17

La Femme du Gange 142
Les Parleuses 18–19, 180
India Song 76, 125, 136, 142–3, 150, 195
Son nom de Venise dans Calcutta désert 143
Le Camion 178
Aurélia Steiner, dit Aurélia Melbourne 136
L'Homme assis dans le couloir 129, 209–10
Agatha 184, 205, 214
L'Homme Atlantique 184
La Maladie de la mort 129
L'Amant 10, 130, 142, 144–5, 149, 153–5, 176, 184, 192–5, 197–201, 213–16, 228, 230, 235, 252
La Douleur 130, 142, 158, 184
Monsieur X. dit ici Pierre Rabier 158
Albert des capitales 158
Ter le milicien 158

feminine language 3–7, 11–19, 52, 56–9, 78–9, 87, 137, 152, 202, 203
feminism 1–10, 12–18, 32–5, 53, 75–86, 196, 199–200, 202, 234, 241–2, 252
fetishism 9, 23, 86, 145–9, 184–98, 210–12, 235
Flaubert, Gustave 144
Forster, E M 242
Freud, Sigmund 4, 19–33, 39–40, 43–5, 47, 52–3, 59, 65, 70, 73, 79–85, 146, 210, 217, 229–30, 251

Gallop, Jane 73, 80–1
Gauthier, Xavière 18–19, 76, 87, 133, 180
gender 5, 7–9, 25, 29–33, 47, 65, 85–6, 200–1, 233–5
Grunberger, Béla 74–5, 230

Heath, Stephen 46, 80, 82–3, 185, 195
Hell, Henri 136
Horney, Karen 30–3, 60, 79

Irigaray, Luce 4–6, 17–18, 53–63, 65, 69, 71–80, 82, 137, 196, 198, 200, 233

Jones, Ernest 28–9, 33, 47, 52, 60
jouissance 5, 41–50, 58, 60, 64, 66, 71, 147–8, 211

Klein, Melanie 29–30, 47, 79
Kristeva, Julia 140

Lacan, Jacques 4–6, 8–9, 17, 33–48, 51–3, 54, 56–7, 63–5, 69–73, 76–85, 94, 132, 139, 141, 146–7, 185, 199, 230, 233, 241, 250–1
Lawrence, D H 242
Lemoine-Luccioni, Eugénie 65–70, 73–4, 76–7, 79, 198–9, 233–5, 241
Lévi-Strauss, Claude 54, 204
Lyon, Elizabeth 76

Marini, Marcelle 6, 11–19, 58, 126, 202–3, 231, 233, 238–9
Mistler, Jean 97–8, 139, 141
Mitchell, Juliet 21, 25–9, 33, 80–1
Montrelay, Michèle 4–5, 16–17, 47–55, 57, 60–6, 69, 74–7, 79, 137, 144, 172, 181, 198, 233
Mulvey, Laura 195–6, 211
Munroe, Marilyn 197, 235

narcissism 38–9, 67–9, 72, 75, 79, 86, 154–5, 170, 196, 199–201, 212, 216, 230, 235–6

Other (the) 36, 40–3, 48–9, 51, 57, 65, 67–72, 74, 79, 139–40, 148, 189, 198–200, 212, 231, 243

Poulet, Robert 144

Reich, Wilhelm 242
Rimbaud, Arthur 38
Robbe-Grillet, Alain 109

Saussure, Ferdinand de 40
Selous, Bernadette 139, 141
Showalter, Elaine 3
Spender, Dale 13–18, 196

Thatcher, Margaret 85, 198–9, 240
Todorov, Tzvetan 94
Tolstoy, Leo 90

Venet, Sylvie 12–16, 234

Wilden, Anthony 82–3